PRAISE FOR DYLAN HOWARD

"Dylan Howard is the rare combination of cutting-edge journalist, true crime commentator and relentless investigator. Howard passionately brings comprehensive and groundbreaking analysis to the most compelling mysteries of our time."

—Dr. Phil McGraw, host of TV's #1 daytime talk show, Dr. Phil

"Dylan Howard is one of the finest journalists writing today. His depth and breadth of experience are second to none; he follows every intricate angle of a story and exposes the truth. As a former detective, I know firsthand the skills that make an exceptional investigator, and Dylan has them in spades."

—Bo Dietl, former NYPD homicide detective with over 1,400 felony arrests

"A tabloid prodigy."

—Jeffrey Toobin, CNN and The New Yorker

"The king of Hollywood scoops."

—Adweek

"When Dylan Howard focuses his attention to investigating a case, you can be sure he will uncover sensational new information that we, as readers, viewers or listeners, will find astonishing."

—Dr. Drew Pinsky

"The go-to guy for authoritative showbiz news and analysis on cable and over-the-air television."

—Los Angeles Press Club

Aaron Hernandez's
KILLING FIELDS

Aaron Hernandez's
KILLING FIELDS

Exposing Untold Murders, Violence, Cover-Ups, and the NFL's Shocking Code of Silence

DYLAN HOWARD

Skyhorse Publishing

Skyhorse Publishing books may be purchased in bulk at special discounts for sales promotion, corporate gifts, fund-raising, or educational purposes. Special editions can also be created to specifications. For details, contact the Special Sales Department, Skyhorse Publishing, 307 West 36th Street, 11th Floor, New York, NY 10018 or info@skyhorsepublishing.com.

Skyhorse® and Skyhorse Publishing® are registered trademarks of Skyhorse Publishing, Inc.®, a Delaware corporation.

Visit our website at www.skyhorsepublishing.com.

10 9 8 7 6 5 4 3 2 1

Library of Congress Cataloging-in-Publication Data is available on file.

Jacket design by 5mediadesign
Jacket photos: Getty/AMI

Print ISBN: 978-1-5107-5497-3

Printed in the United States of America

This book provides a startling insight into the darkest corners of American sports, where nothing is quite like it seems.

To those, like Michelle, Don, Jarrett, and Bo, and others, who participated in our investigtion, and who believe the truth is out there and still worth searching for, I thank you.

To the brave new witnesses who stepped forward—in the hope of providing justice to innocent families—your role can never be underestimated.

TABLE OF CONTENTS

FOREWORD

"I just wanted to tell you this morning that I love you. You never have to question us. I will stop questioning you and us. I realized through our thing over the past few days how much I love you and how much I want you and us. Mainly how I want you [to] know what real love, real loyalty is, and to experience someone who is with you through all in life. We will have ups and downs. Times of some pain and suffering, but together we will make it right. I'm sorry for overreacting, but it's something I have to work on, because I'm used to being done dirty my whole life.

"I know I have my own issues as we all do, but you could always keep it real with me too. It will help me grow too. Just know I'm here for you to help you through all in life. I've got your back, your front, and your side, and you for eternity. I know I'm going to go through hell dealing with you in life, but I can't ever give up on you, because that's the type of love I have. Now you see why love is my weakness in life and how I go so hard for the ones I have love for. All your issues are and will always be my issues. We will try to avoid all with respect, but if your crazy mouth gets you into shit, I'll be there always, even though I'm going to want to beat your ass after, LOL. Never question me or hide anything. That's all I ask. I got you.

"I hope you have a great day, you will. Come to my door, ASAP. I miss you so much. You should be wide awake, knowing you sleep all fucking day, LOL. I just wish we were cellmates, so I could at least kiss you on the forehead and say I love you. Then let you sleep while I make sure you have your coffee ready when you wake up. (Spoiled bitch!) I wouldn't have it any other way. I truly love you that much. No words can describe it, nor will it ever, but I'm still stressing.

"You told me you didn't want to be on the block anymore. Did you really mean that? I mean, I've said way worse, so I understand, but still, it made me almost hang myself. I can't even imagine them separating us. I'll feel like I'm missing all of me. Fuck half of me. I love you that much. I just wanted you to begin this day knowing how loved you are and that you have someone through it all in life. Someone who will never not stand by you, not have your back, but only show you true love and true loyalty like you never experienced. I have you forever. I haven't told you in a little, but you are perfect. I know I'm blessed to have you. I will let you know that forever and no matter what we have to overcome, we all have to grow in life. It's a never-ending growth in life, but I'll be with you through all of it. True ride or die."

—Aaron Hernandez jailhouse letter to lover Kyle Kennedy

AUTHOR'S NOTE

"We can easily forgive a child who is afraid of the dark; the real tragedy of life is when men are afraid of the light."

—Plato

Shakespeare couldn't have written the twisted tragic tale of Aaron Hernandez.

A rise to fame that left in its wake destruction, revenge, scorned lovers, families divided, and murder... and for what? To keep a secret? Yet what could be deemed so dark that a famous athlete would risk everything—his family, his fortune, and his fame?

For the past two years, a team of investigators and I have conducted hundreds of hours of interviews with those who knew him the most, sought previously unreleased documents under Freedom of Information laws, uncovered and questioned new witnesses, obtained text messages and recordings of dozens of jailhouse phone calls, and visits between Aaron, his family, and his friends. At times, we faced pushback. At times, things stopped adding up. That was when we knew we had to dig deeper. Luckily for us, this was precisely what the law enabled us to do.

Many of the previous investigations into the life or Aaron Hernandez were hamstrung by the simple fact that Aaron was still alive. When an individual is still living, it can be virtually impossible to obtain files, visitation audio, sealed court documents, or any evidence related to their case. But when a person dies, this information can be made public.

This is what allowed us to relaunch an investigation into his life and death with the goal to uncovering the real truth.

Thus, following the death of Aaron, our team of law enforcement experts were able to get far more access into his personal life. Here, for the first time ever, we had information that ultimately led to credible leads and evidence, piecing together the puzzle he left behind.

We fought tirelessly with law enforcement to unseal documents and obtain clues that might have been overlooked—and we traveled to Florida, Massachusetts, North Carolina, Las Vegas, and Connecticut, leaving no stone unturned to uncover a grisly path of ghastly terror that Aaron left behind.

All to answer one lingering question. Why?

***

Aaron Hernandez was the superstar tight end for the storied New England Patriots—the most successful sports team of the past half century. He was blessed with a new $40 million NFL contract, lucrative endorsement deals, a beautiful fiancée, and a perfect young daughter.

He was, on the face of it, the living embodiment of the American Dream: the boy from a broken home on the wrong side of the tracks whose raw talent and sheer determination to succeed took him all the way to sporting superstardom and made him an idol to millions.

But even as the crowds chanted his name and the pundits tapped him for all-time greatness, Aaron was spinning out of control. Unbeknownst to almost everyone, the Patriots' Pro Bowl tight end was also a drug addict, a bully, a gangster, and a murderer … and as we have discovered, he was being torn apart by a terrible secret he would do anything to protect.

"I'd rather go to jail for fucking murder than have this get out," he told a stripper in the summer of 2013. Within weeks, he had done just that.

For the first time, this book will reveal just what it was he was referring to—and it was not, as everyone has previously assumed, his secret sexuality.

***

Aaron Hernandez's Killing Fields is not another retelling of the Aaron Hernandez story. It is a groundbreaking active investigation into each of the murders that Aaron has been linked to; and through dogged investigative reporting and detailed analysis from experts including forensic scientists and police officers, this book uncovers some startling new conclusions about every one of those homicides.

We also return to the scene of the only murder Aaron was convicted of and piece together the real motives that drove him to kill … a theory so explosive it will send shockwaves throughout the entire NFL establishment and sport itself. And we question just how culpable the NFL themselves might be for the tragedy of this brief, anarchic, tragically destructive life.

The story of Aaron Hernandez is a glimpse into the dark heart of the American sporting dream. It's about how the system not only facilitates horror—but perpetuates it. It's a story of power, corruption, and violence unprecedented in NFL history.

INTRODUCTION

Even in death, his presence was enormous.

At 27 years old, Aaron Hernandez was massive, bigger than life. Six-foot-two and 250 pounds—all of it muscle. It was a wonder to the prison guards who found his body that the bedsheet with which he'd hung himself had been strong enough to hold him.

On April 19, 2017, Aaron was discovered at approximately three in the morning in his cell within the general population unit at Souza-Baranowski Correctional Center, a maximum security prison in Lancaster, Massachusetts. Aaron had killed himself by carefully fashioning the sheets of his bed into a noose. One end, tied around the bars of the window above him. The other, placed around his own neck.

For a man known for impulsive, brash behavior, his preparation for what would be his final act had been comparatively careful and methodical. It showed forethought. It was—in essence—a kind of horrible ceremony.

Aaron wanted to die. First, he had jammed items from within his cell into the cell door. This was to prevent anyone from intervening and trying to save him in the event lost his nerve to hang himself. He had also squirted a soap or shampoo-like substance across the cell's floor—possibly to make it difficult for the guards to intercede; possibly to prevent himself from having second thoughts and searching for a footing.

Next, Aaron had written the words "John 3:16" on his forehead in ink. The meaning of this within a mind as crazed as Aaron's is anyone's guess. This Bible verse is probably the most quoted in all of Christianity. In most translations, it reads:

For God so loved the world, that he gave his only begotten Son, that whosoever believeth in him shall not perish, but have everlasting life.

Was Aaron seeking everlasting life? Was he seeking to convince himself that the next world awaited?

Either is possible.

However, there are other explanations that seem to line up better with what we know of the shamed NFL star.

Aaron may have scrawled these words defiantly, and with a specific audience in mind. Whoever found his body—and whoever described that body to others—would be forced to include this detail. Aaron was sending a message that he was giving up on this world. This world that had been a place of terror, horror, and paranoid anxiety for him. He had had enough, and he was letting everybody know it. He was going to live somewhere else.

But the adornment to his forehead was not the full extent of it.

Using his own blood, Aaron also decorated the walls of his cell with a strange pastiche of surreal imagery.

He attempted to draw a pyramid with an eye atop it. Many who saw it have compared it to the eye on the back of a dollar bill. Pregnant with symbolism and occult meaning, it is known as the "Eye of Providence" and was originally meant to symbolize the eye of God watching over humanity. Yet it has also been pointed out by conspiracy theorists that it has connections to Freemasonry, to religious cults, and secret societies. It was perhaps in this spirit that Aaron added his final flourish, writing the words "ILLUMINATI" in capital letters just beneath it. We do not know to what specific sect or conspiracy Aaron was referring to. Perhaps he could have simply been trying to give the impression that he felt the forces of the universe had aligned against him.

If this was a glimpse inside his mind at the time, it offered more questions than answers.

There are reliable reports that Aaron was not sober in his final moments—which included this period of artistic inspiration. After his body was discovered, his fellow inmates shared with authorities that they had observed Aaron smoking massive amounts of K2 in the hours leading up to his death. K2 is a powerful artificial drug meant to replicate the effects of marijuana. However, it is known to produce dangerous side effects not found in cannabis, including emotional detachment, paranoia, extreme anxiety, and agitation. In sum, K2's effects on the brain can be more significant than those of marijuana, making the drug more unpredictable and dangerous.

It is difficult to know what Aaron was thinking under the effects of this drug, if he was thinking at all.

Before his suicide, Aaron had prepared letters to the important people who still remained in his life. As was widely reported in the media at the time, he wrote a letter to his daughter, Avielle Jenkins-Hernandez, another to his fiancée, Shayanna Jenkins, and one to his lawyer, Jose Baez.

The note to Aaron's fiancée is strange and filled with pseudo-mystical references, many of them misused and nonsensical. (Aaron was not as skilled at communicating through the written word as he was at playing football. If he had been, he would have been another Shakespeare.) In his writing, Aaron speaks of an afterlife and again invokes the "JOHN 3:16" verse that he would wear on his forehead in the final moments of his life. He wishes his fiancée well.

The letter to his daughter is loving and brief. He tells her he will be waiting for her in heaven one day, and recommends several self-help books to her. (In a jailhouse taped call, he said of his daughter: "I miss one thing. My freedom, that's not what I miss. I miss one thing, and obviously my daughter. It was the same thing I missed when I was on the streets so it's not that big of a deal.")

Finally, the note to his lawyer Jose Baez is surreally collegial—as though Baez were a fellow gangster, or perhaps a drinking buddy. A bro. A teammate. Aaron acknowledges all the work his lawyer has performed on his behalf, then threatens to attack him—supernaturally, from beyond the grave?—if he misbehaves in the years ahead. Aaron ends by requesting Baez contact Aaron's favorite rappers to send his love to them.

However, as this book will reveal, there is now new evidence that Aaron penned a fourth letter that was intentionally suppressed and obfuscated by that lawyer, Jose Baez. As this volume will explore, this fourth letter has the potential to blow apart what the public believes it knows of Aaron Hernandez, his mental state at the time of his suicide, and his motivations for doing what he did. As it happens, this mysterious, hidden fourth letter turns out to be the true "final chapter" in the story of who Aaron Hernandez *really* was.

But back to the night in question. . .

***

With his cell decorated with appropriate nods to the mystical, his forehead adorned with a Bible verse, and his letters to loved ones carefully laid aside, Aaron experienced his final waking moments. He readied the makeshift noose. He slipped it around his neck. He propelled himself forward, possibly off of the top of his bed. And he ended his life.

Aaron was not considered to be at risk of suicide. Although he was not a model inmate—and had been disciplined for a variety of offenses while incarcerated, which according to Massachusetts State Police records obtained by this author included possession of tobacco, twice disrupting the unit in which he lived behind bars, possession of contraband, fighting, and the possession, manufacture, or introduction of a gun, firearm, weapon, sharpened instrument, knife, or poison component thereof—it was never suspected that he might take his own life. Yet as we have come to learn, he was not being regularly checked by guards on the night of his suicide, and there was no camera trained on his cell.

From the outside, even though he had been sentenced to life in prison without the possibility of parole, his life was not hopeless. There were still ups in addition to the downs. He had been exonerated for his alleged role in a double murder only five days before—even though he lied to beat the rap, as we will uncover. He had a loving family. He still had legions of admirers who—even considering the perversity that came with extolling a convicted murderer—celebrated his work on the field and hailed him as an integral part of one of the greatest football teams of all time.

But other things were in that cell with Aaron.

Things that made it impossible for him to live another day longer.

Foremost, there was the knowledge that he had let down everyone who'd ever meant something to him. He'd squandered a $40 million payday and a dazzling career as one of the greatest tight ends in the history of the NFL. He had let down his team, his teammates, and his city. He had also let down his family. (Aaron's brother, Jonathan Hernandez, wrote a book that characterized his final interactions with Aaron as filled with urgings from Aaron to embrace life, to stay on the straight and narrow, and to appreciate all the positive things surrounding him. Looking back now, it's disturbingly clear that these admonitions to his brother stemmed from his own failings. They were the things that Aaron had not been able to do himself.)

But these were only the demons that were known at the time.

There is powerful new proof that Aaron was also a conflicted soul who had never grappled with the truth of his own sexuality. He was bisexual, had numerous encounters with men, and may have even contracted HIV. And though he had been an effective shapeshifter his entire live—moving seamlessly between a life of thuggery and violence, to that of a star athlete on the field, to a private life of gay romance and drug indulgence—he had eventually been forced to kill in order to keep these twisted double lives separate. That was what had put him in jail for life. And the plan had not even worked. His secrets had leaked out anyway.

For those who looked on from the media and elsewhere, the cellblock suicide of Aaron was just as flummoxing and strange as his life had been. It went against the grain. It didn't make sense. The narrative was not supposed to go like this.

The NFL was celebrated as a machine for creating opportunity. Within its folds, players from troubled homes could find kinship and fellowship. Players who had grown up in privation, poverty, and insecurity could achieve wealth and stability. And anyone was welcome. Your race, religion, color, or creed didn't matter. If you could throw or catch or tackle better than the rest, you were in.

But this is the story the NFL *likes* to tell. . .

Aaron's story should have ended in redemption; a man like he was supposed to be able to leave his rough beginnings behind.

He may have been born into rough circumstances, sure, and had to run a gauntlet of drugs and violence each day. . . but now that's all over. Now he buys his mom a house in the suburbs. Now he makes public speaking appearances at high schools about the importance of *resisting* drugs and gangs. He starts a charity and begins mentoring youth from the community. He adjusts to a life of safety and status.

That's how the story is *supposed* to go.

You're supposed to leave the street behind. You're supposed to trade petty concerns over street beefs and money owed to drug dealers for easier, better preoccupations. You memorize the new offense. You learn how to comport yourself appropriately at a postgame press conference. You adapt to the sudden lifestyle of privilege.

Who wouldn't want to make that trade?

The answer is Aaron Hernandez.

***

Aaron was intent on writing his own story. Once inside the NFL, he chose to run *back into* the gauntlet. To use the wealth, clout, and power that came with being a celebrated NFL player to augment his gangster lifestyle. To be a thug. To supercharge it.

Instead of leaving one world for another, it is now clear that Aaron chose to keep a residence in both. He became a wealthy, beloved NFL player, yes. People bought him drinks in restaurants and invited him to parties. He smiled in television commercials and endorsed products.

But he was still a gangster—inside and outside of the huddle. He was still someone who solved problems with violence. (While most of Aaron's teammates were able to put up a barrier between their lives on the field and their private lives—doing extreme violence to the opposing team, but turning it off when they walked back into the locker room—for Aaron, it was all one thing. All the same song. All the same game.) Aaron used his NFL connections to take his criminal life to new levels that were as exciting as they were insane. He drove better cars. Scored better drugs. Hired more expensive strippers. And fought to protect his secret, other life all the more fiercely—from teammates, family, friends, and even his fiancée, Shayanna.

Doing so, he became a man of multiple worlds.

While other NFL rookies were leaving their former, rougher selves behind, Aaron was fighting to maintain all his identities. And understanding why is the key to this whole story.

One explanation is that he simply did not know it was possible to change.

Aaron has been characterized as famously aloof from the other players on his college and pro teams. He did not like to socialize with teammates, preferring to hang with his own crew. So, Aaron may have been blind to the examples all around him of players who had made good and changed for the better now that they were in the big game.

But that blindness may have also been intentional. You can't be made to see what you don't *want* to see, even if it is right in front of you.

Aaron chose to serve multiple masters because, that way, he could have everything he wanted. He chose to remain connected to a criminal element, and to live a criminal lifestyle. He chose to identify outwardly as solidly heterosexual with a soon-to-be-wife, but maintained a rich and secret sex life with other men. He chose to be the smiling, "All-American" football player on billboards and in commercials, yet when the cameras clicked off and the stadium lights dimmed, he engaged in behaviors that no product or brand would stand behind, and which no sane parent would want a child to emulate.

Aaron did it because he could.

Since high school, maintaining double lives had always worked for him. He dared to believe it would continue to work on the biggest stage in all of professional sports.

And, for a while, it did.

But then it fell apart and destroyed him. By the end of his life, Aaron was a man living in paranoia and terror. He worried his many criminal acts might finally catch up to him. Ruin his career. Send him to jail. Or even leave him looking down the barrel of someone else's gun.

It seemed not a question of if, but only when.

And even that is not adequate. Beyond the crime and violence, Aaron hid other aspects of who he truly was. He hid the truth of the love of his life. Of his true self. What he truly wanted.

The last one may be, in the end, unknowable.

It has been easy for observers in the media and other authors of books on this topic to look at his story and ask: "What did Aaron Hernandez want? What did he hope would happen? What was the end goal of all this madness?"

The disturbing truth is Aaron himself may not have known completely. As you will uncover in the chilling pages ahead, he was not known for long-term planning. He simply reacted.

Moment to moment, Aaron did whatever—in his view—needed to be done. That might mean catching a touchdown pass, but it might also mean using violence to solve a problem. It might mean using the clout of football stardom to get out of a criminal charge. And, in extreme cases, it might mean straight-up murdering someone whose existence presented a risk to exposing his many secrets.

Aaron wanted to live without consequence. To live a life of total freedom, in which he was beholden to no authority—whether it be a coach, another gangster, or the justice system itself. To do whatever he wanted, whenever he wanted.

An impossible task, surely. But Aaron was known for doing the impossible. For being special. For working magic.

***

As a star tight end at the University of Florida, he had set records for the most catches by any player at his position. In 2010, when he started playing for the Patriots, he was the youngest player in the entire league. Yet that didn't stop him from setting a team tight end record for catches in his first season.

Aaron could always do what needed to be done.

Until, suddenly, he couldn't.

By the time of his arrest, Aaron had become like a master secret agent, seamlessly balancing a strange collection of multiple personas. The star NFL player on one of the league's most beloved teams. The doting father engaged to a woman with whom he had pledged to spend the rest of his life. The gangster who had never really left the hardscrabble New England streets behind. The drug user and thug who thrived on chaos and violence. And the closeted bisexual with a private life that ran contrary to his public and private personas.

How many men died in that cell when Aaron took his own life?

By any fair estimation, it was more than one.

The sheer energy Aaron had to expend in order to keep these multiple lives afloat at the same time is staggering. A man of record-setting football talents, he proved equally capable of remarkable feats of deception—and yet there was another, hideous way that Aaron was "above and beyond" his peers.

After he was dead, Aaron's brain was studied and found to be riddled with the most advanced case of chronic traumatic encephalopathy (or CTE) ever discovered in a man only 27 years of age.

We know the symptoms of CTE, and they are almost a description of Aaron himself—as if, by the end, he *was* the disease.

Uncontrollable mood swings. Violence. Homicide and suicide. Poor judgment. And giving the feeling to those surrounding you that you have multiple personalities, or are multiple people.

CTE does not explain everything about Aaron, surely. As we learned, according to those who knew him, these personality traits had been with him since his earliest days, well before his brain could have begun to feel the concussive effects of helmet-to-helmet hits.

To truly understand this man who would throw away a life of opportunity in a frenzy of violent madness, we must examine the raw, hidden core of his existence. It may be confusing and incomprehensible at first glance, but looking more closely and it makes a horrible kind of sense.

To some, Aaron is the story of institutions—family, communities, the university system, the NFL—that failed, at every turn, to fix the problems brewing inside this young man. Each saw his horrible, gaping need, and each was too terrified to address it. So they simply passed him off to the next link in the chain. They kicked the can down the road.

But these institutions cannot be blamed entirely.

Aaron was the kind of record-setting football talent that comes along once in a generation. He was also an unimaginable concoction of pathologies set one atop the other. His perversions were as staggering as his appetites. His self-interest and lack of remorse were matched only by his chronic instability and need for violence.

Seldom is a man of such strange and conflicting derangements given so much power, and given the power to ruin his own life so completely.

Outwardly, Aaron was a football legend, but he carried deep, dark secrets into prison and to the grave. What were his motivations for murder? What was the catalyst?

This book is an attempt to answer these questions more completely than has ever been attempted before. It is the product of years spent unpacking his life, firsthand exclusive interviews with those who had access to his most secret moments, and the review of thousands of police and court documents connected to his story. All of it puts together a picture of how one of the NFL's most talented stars could become a cold-blooded killer—and ask the very valid question if he was one of America's worst serial killers.

By the time Aaron killed himself, he had evolved into something else. Something that legions of Patriots fans who'd once adored him would now find unrecognizable. He was a drug addict, a gang member, a violent bully, and a murderer. More than that, he was a man who had never not been leading a secret, double life.

Consider what we have uncovered here—the sheer magnitude of the demons within the man—and perhaps you will conclude, as we have, that his story could have ended no other way.

CHAPTER 1

Mom: "I mean Dad kept us all, if you knew, Dad kept us all grounded."
Aaron: "I know."
Mom: "He really did."
Aaron: "Exactly, he let things go but he didn't let it get out of control."
Mom: "Exactly."

—Aaron Hernandez, jailhouse recording

Aaron Hernandez was big, but his father was bigger.

In their hometown of Bristol, Connecticut, Aaron's father, Dennis, was known informally around the neighborhood as "The King"—which spoke both to his physical presence and his position of trust he held in the local community.

Dennis was handsome and a natural-born athlete. (Those first familiar with his son Aaron would probably agree that Dennis looked very similar to his son, albeit with a mustache and a 1970s Afro.) Dennis would play football in high school and then briefly at the University of Connecticut, but would never make it to the pros. For most of his adult life, he worked as a janitor. Still, he was regarded as someone who was doing relatively well for himself. He had survived his own rough-and-tumble upbringing and, after several brushes with the law, seemed to have "gone straight." In the neighborhood where he lived, Dennis was known as one of the honest, upstanding presences that mothers might hope their own sons would emulate.

In addition to Aaron, Dennis had an older son, Jonathan, three years Aaron's senior. Both Aaron and Jonathan would attend Bristol Central High School, the same school their father had attended.

Until his untimely death at the age of just 49 during a routine hernia surgery, Dennis was a powerful presence in the lives of both boys. He encouraged them to excel in sports, and to be leaders on the field. But unfortunately, there was a darker side to it. When shouted encouragement was not enough, Dennis also often sought to motivate his sons ... with his fists.

Dennis beat his sons, but the boys must have noticed how their father was careful only to do this when the family was out of public view. From an early age, Dennis Hernandez would provide Aaron's first tastes of violence—and also of deception.

Growing up, Aaron and Jonathan were regularly punched by their father, and on a variety of pretexts. Aaron and Jonathan shared the same bedroom in the family house, which made access to both of them easier. Dennis's mind-set seemed to be that if he was beating one, he might as well beat the other.

Whenever Dennis felt that his sons lacked proper motivation in any area of their lives, he applied his fists. Failures on the sports field were regularly met with a punch when the boys returned home. And just to add a perverse bit of unpredictability, sometimes they were beaten for no clear reason at all; maybe Dennis had a bad day or too much to drink. He didn't need a reason to take it out on his sons, and he made that clear. They could be beaten whenever he felt like it.

And while Dennis Hernandez freely used violence to express himself with his sons, in the eyes of all who saw the family in public, Dennis was nothing more than an occasionally stern disciplinarian. At high school football games, Dennis shouted to his sons from the stands. Sometimes he might raise his voice angrily, but that was usually the extent of it. (If any violence was to be meted out due to lackluster performance, it would always wait until they were back at the house.)

It is no great leap to guess that Aaron modeled himself after his father, and that this behavior showed that violence could be acceptable ... as long as it was concealed.

As Aaron would observe, Dennis Hernandez was the kind of man who always seemed to be secretly up to something. As a younger man, he had run with a rough crew, but had a knack for avoiding consequences. He was once questioned in connection to a murder and burglary involving one of his running buddies, but was never arrested or changed. In 1992, while Aaron was little more than a toddler, he was charged with trying to buy cocaine. In between, there were always small brushes with the law that amounted to nothing.

Dennis's romantic life was usually a mess; he and Aaron's mother, Terri, divorced and then remarried amid much drama. (The couple filed for bankruptcy when Aaron was nine years old, revealing massive, secret debts.) There were always rumors of other women, and of Dennis cheating when Terri wasn't around.

Though Dennis didn't strike his sons at football games, the coaching staff was not always so lucky. In one well-documented instance, displeased with play-calling, Dennis punched one of Aaron's coaches in the face, breaking the man's glasses. (The police were called, and Dennis was ordered to simply compensate the coach.)

In the end, the only thing that gradually put a stop to Dennis's unruly ways was Father Time. As he grew older, he became less physical with those around him, including his sons. Aaron and Jonathan growing into towering sportsmen themselves also certainly had something to do with it.

Dennis knew what it took to succeed in a world where physicality determined much. And it was clear that—despite his ability to lash out in violence—he loved his boys and wanted them to thrive in that world. He was not wealthy, but Dennis tried to provide the tools that would allow them to grow into strong young men. He built a gym in his basement, and made sure his sons always had access to a pool and a basketball court. To boot, the family lived far enough out that Aaron and Jonathan could always take to the woods whenever they felt like exploring.

Dennis also strove to provide motivation. In the summers, he would regularly rouse his sons early in the morning and encourage them to spend their days in physical activity. Sometimes he made them run drills like a coach. This probably blurred together worlds that might have remained distinct for most youngsters. For the Hernandez boys, coaches were like dads, and dads were like coaches. Getting ahead in the world—and getting respect—meant succeeding at physical things. (For Dennis, there was no other world, and there was no other way. Not really.) And in this world, these father/coach figures sometimes bent or broke the rules. They seemed to live by their own code, and could do what they wanted. And this too—Aaron doubtless observed—was part of being a man, of being powerful.

Running drills alongside his brother in the summer heat, growing further into manhood with each step, it was all one thing to young Aaron Hernandez. All the same.

These sweaty, exhausting roads eventually led to high school. And high school was the place where Aaron truly began to feel his powers. For a young man who had grown up with his father's fists an omnipresent threat—and with his father's double life as a model to emulate—Aaron was about to put everything he'd learned into practice.

CHAPTER 2

"The thing that used to get me mad and not like being around you is you make assumptions about me, you truly don't even know me."

—AARON HERNANDEZ, JAILHOUSE RECORDING

The day he showed up to his first day of high school, Aaron Hernandez was already enormous; nearly reaching his full NFL height by the time he was a freshman. He towered above most of his teammates at 6-foot-2, weighing more than 200 pounds, and was tremendously muscular. From his first fall practice, Aaron seemed destined to become a star on the football field.

But high school was also a place where the young Aaron would begin to learn the advantages of deception. Modeling his father, he experimented with being one man in public and another in private. It was surprisingly easy to do, he found, and took to it like a fish to water.

Aaron was also handsome and popular. He was one of the kids everybody knew and liked—teachers and students both. By his junior year, he was setting Connecticut state records for pass receptions. Everyone saw big things in his future. He was the big man on campus.

He was perfecting the "All-American" persona, and it seemed to come to him with ease.

But then there was the other life—the secret one that Aaron had grown and cultivated just as diligently as he had grown his football skills.

Out of view of adults (and all but a few close friends), Aaron became a very different young man.

He was profoundly addicted to marijuana. He had begun using the drug occasionally as a freshman, but soon he found himself ramping up his indulgence, and it quickly became close to constant. He never let up—even for big tests or big games. He smoked almost any time he was unobserved.

There is room to wonder if Aaron's ability to play record-breaking football while stoned may have given him additional confidence to cultivate a double life. Clearly, he was able to play while high. Drugs did not impact him negatively, like his coaches and trainers insisted they would. This probably made Aaron feel special and untouchable. As if the rules did not apply to him. It *proved* he could maintain a foot in both worlds with no one the wiser. And if he could get away with this. . . what else could he get away with?

As it turned out, drug use was only the tip of the very large and very secretive iceberg.

In a working-class community where homophobia ran rampant, Aaron was also able to use his skills of deception to conceal his burgeoning bisexuality.

While he openly dated girls throughout high school, Aaron also maintained an active sex life with men—with none other than the quarterback of the high school football team, Dennis SanSoucie, who was also the head coach's son. Both knew that were their relationship to be discovered, it would mean being ostracized by their friends, beatings at the hands of their fathers, and maybe even an end to their football dreams.

But Dennis and Aaron were good at keeping secrets.

The two had been chums since middle school, when their fooling around had first begun. They were also marijuana-smoking pals who never missed a chance to light up.

Dennis came out as a gay individual in his twenties, and in exclusive interviews for this book and companion television documentary, describes his relationship with Aaron. Dennis's first-hand knowledge provides a remarkable and yet unrevealed perspective on Aaron's life during this period.

Dennis recounts that their earliest days together involved an immediate connection that was allowed to grow over time:

Me and Aaron clicked very quickly. We were playing football together. We were probably one and two; the two best players on the team. We liked to clown around, and we had a good time. It carried on into school and afterschool activities also. Growing up, in middle school, we weren't too close. About 10 to 15 minutes away. Then I had moved closer to the high school my sophomore year, which put us about five minutes away from each other.

Growing up so close together—not to mention playing on the same football teams—gave Dennis an insider's view of the explosive personality of Dennis Hernandez, Aaron's father. Dennis recounts how strain created by Aaron's paternal influence almost drove their dads apart.

The first year of tackle football, which is called Mighty Mites, my father was the head coach. Mr. Hernandez, Aaron's father, was going to be an assistant coach on the team. Due to some disputes with my father and his father, Aaron didn't make weight to play in Mighty Mites so he went up to the next level, Junior Pee Wee, and then Aaron's father wasn't coaching with my dad. That became a big rift.

I was young, so I don't really know all the ins and outs. His father didn't really agree with my father's coaching philosophy. I had told my dad one day that while hanging out with a friend Mr. Hernandez had come by. The guy's name was Marty Somner. We were hanging out where he worked. It was a RadioShack shop and he was going over different plays and things like that, and he didn't like the way my father was going to run the team. When I went home that day, I told my dad about it and he didn't really like what Mr. Hernandez had to say. He gave him a call and told him that he wasn't welcome to coach on the team.

Dennis told us, however, that the hatchet was buried once the two reached high school and their ability to make remarkable accomplishments on the field became apparent.

He continues:

Actually, the one cool thing that I look back on is the parents; my parents, his parents were always still cool with us having a friendship. They didn't let that get in the way of me and Aaron. Eventually, that burden was buried when I was playing quarterback my junior year. I can honestly say, Mr. Hernandez and my father, Tim SanSoucie, had no more issues. That hatchet was buried and Mr. Hernandez was happy that I was throwing his son touchdown passes.

Football kept Aaron grounded, and created opportunities for him. And creating opportunity seemed to be what he was all about. Dennis also recalled that Aaron seemed like an earnest student who was driven to do all he could to succeed—both on and off the football field.

> Aaron was a student that wanted to stay after class and do his homework before he went to his next class. He'd do anything to get ahead of the game. He was a guy who was really trying to better himself to get out of high school and into college.

It was also around this same time that a romantic relationship between the two boys blossomed into something more than just "fooling around." Both boys understood the need to conceal what they were doing. As Dennis recounts, their initial trysts usually took place in the house of a mutual friend:

> I didn't go over to their [the Hernandez's'] house very often. There was once or twice that I went over and me and Aaron hung in the basement. Played some video games and just did what friends do. We did engage in sexual activity at his house, the two times that I believe I was there. Due to the rift between the parents, we'd hang out once and a while, but it wasn't usually at each other's house. It was at a mutual third person's house. [Our sexuality] was something that me and Aaron were both naturally born with. We couldn't help it. Once we had connected, it was something that naturally happened. We weren't ashamed of it within ourselves, but I think we were in complete denial. We definitely didn't want anyone to know our secret. We were scared

that that secret was going to come out. I think what we both feared the most was our parents. Our fathers.

The secret sexual relationship between the two boys would continue for the rest of their time in high school. They were never discovered.

To this day, Dennis sees their relationship in high school as a sort of extension of the other things they did together. They spent time together in class. They were the first- and second-best football players on the same team. (Aaron was also skilled at basketball, and Dennis believes Aaron could have gone pro at that as well if football didn't work out.) Dennis and Aaron were also sometimes lovers. Yet Dennis doesn't feel it's accurate to attach anything more formal or specific to what they were (or weren't):

Google my name [today, in 2019] and it says "high school lover" or "high school boyfriend." [But really] I was just a friend of Aaron's. We had a brotherhood. I was his football buddy, and this [sex] was activity we engaged in because we wanted to engage in it, but it wasn't anything that we wanted to share with anyone else.

At first glance, the relationship between Aaron and Dennis seems like a tale of normal, healthy sexual exploration between two youngsters (kept quiet only because it took place in a less enlightened time). Unfortunately, there is evidence that a taboo gay relationship on the side may not have been all thrills and excitement for Aaron. This is because his sexuality was haunted by even more troubling demons. . . and he may have been trying to deal with them via his explorations with Dennis.

Though explicit details have never been provided, Aaron's brother, Jonathan, lawyers who have worked for Aaron, and other sources from the community have all confirmed that Aaron was sexually molested as a child. For the moment—at the time of this writing—none of these sources has been willing to confirm more than this on the record.

We can confirm that starting at the age of six, Aaron was forced to perform oral sex on an older male. This abuse continued for several years.

What is startlingly clear from the statements regarding the abuse is that being molested, sexually abused, and/or raped had a profound effect on Aaron, as it would anyone.

Like so many victims, the abuse suffered by Aaron clouded his sense of what might constitute "normal" and "healthy" sexuality. Distinctions that are clear and obvious to most people became fuzzy for him. Because the abuse occurred when Aaron was still growing into adulthood and finding his place as a sexual being, these forced encounters corrupted his sexual barometer, and his way of viewing sex and relationship was forever changed. Though we currently know few details about the molestation, it was kept secret until after Aaron's death—yet a fact confirmed from his own mouth to other inmates inside jail. Again, we have the theme of sex and concealment as a necessary part of Aaron's life.

Further compounding the molestation's impact on the young man's psyche could have been his father's role. Did Aaron worry about his father finding out about the molestation? If the molestation was at the hands of another man, for example, did Aaron fear his father would think he was gay?

The nature of these questions forever changed during Aaron's junior year in high school, when his father unexpectedly passed away. Throughout his life, nobody had meant more to Aaron than his father. There's no doubt that his incredible physical abilities had been there from the start, but it was his father who'd added the crucial element of discipline to the mix—both on and off the field. Later, in hundreds of hours of jailhouse recordings between Aaron and visitors, obtained for this book, he would use the word *grounded* when speaking of his father. The man had kept him "grounded," and at the same time pushed him to be all that he could be. He also depended on his father to help him steer clear of potential missteps. (An insider, who wished to remain anonymous, confirmed that when he started high school, Aaron told his father that instead of playing football, he was considering becoming a cheerleader. Dennis helped Aaron to see that the reward structure would be very different for these two activities.)

Yet at just 49, that mentorship would end. An infection from a routine hernia surgery ended the life of Dennis Hernandez. (As a testimony to the stature he still held in the community, it was said that the funeral of Dennis Hernandez was one of the largest and most attended in the history of Bristol, Connecticut.)

He spoke little about it, but we know that his father's unexpected passing must have been devastating for Aaron. Later in life, he would tell his mother that he wished his father had been there when he was in college, to counsel him through difficult moments. But would this counsel have made a difference in who Aaron became? We will never know.

Though clearly shaken by his father's death, there is no evidence that it lessened Aaron's proclivity for the forbidden. If anything, something in him may have been more fully unleashed by his father's passing. Aaron continued his clandestine relationships while continuing to use marijuana heavily. He also, at this point, began occasionally running with a new crowd of friends . . . a much rougher one.

It was not hard for Aaron to meet people who were engaged in criminal activity and affiliated with gangs. He began "dipping his toe" into this world simply by becoming closer with the dealers who sold him weed—hanging out and getting buddy-buddy long after the sale had been made. This then led to spending time with other customers of the dealer who were almost always older and often involved in crime. Local dropouts and toughs. Gang members known to the local narcotics detectives. Guys with records. According to many individuals we spoke to, it is during this later high school period that Aaron would begin to forge ties with the Bloods street gang organization. These ties would follow him until the end of his life.

We don't know what Aaron's mother and his brother thought of him hanging out with this new crowd (or if they even knew about it). However, there's no evidence that they tried to stop him from socializing with this rougher group of characters. As far as his immediate family was concerned, it seemed Aaron would be allowed to do what he wanted to do.

For his part, Aaron seemed to distance himself from them—seeing his father's passing as a sign that their family was irredeemably distorted. By his own characterizations, his own mother became cruel. As Aaron would later tell of this period in a recorded jailhouse phone call:

> Obviously my family—I don't know—went from being the best family
> in the world, to no family at all. . . So, like, your family is always happy

and together, and I always wanted my family to be like that. So then I would try and be nice to my mom, like "Oh well, even though she ripped me to shreds my entire life [I'll try]." And then when I needed her most, that's when she ripped me to shreds over and over. And then I was always trying to be nice to her and I had no respect for her so it never worked out.

Yet perhaps in this call, Aaron was too tactful to mention the other major event in his life that took place at the same time as his father's passing. After his father's death, it immediately emerged that his mother had been having an affair with the husband of another family member. Aaron's mother would eventually move in with her new man, and the two would soon marry. Not surprisingly, Aaron never really recovered from this. To the young man, the whole affair felt like a deep betrayal. His own mother had not been loyal to his father—and now his whole world was turning upside down.

On the outside, Aaron remained a local "golden boy." Nobody noticed that the support and discipline Aaron had once received from his parents were now coming from a street gang. Even so, accomplishments on the field continued and sports reporters began to speculate about where he might attend college. It was clear from his record-setting performances that the competition to recruit Aaron was going to be fierce. But what is most striking considering what we know now is how completely he maintained the exterior illusion of being a positive, happy-go-lucky kid.

In television interviews with local media covering high school football, he is kind, humble, and always has a smile on his face. He goofs around and jokes with his teammates. He is outgoing and extroverted, but without being overbearing or controlling. And—as so many local sports reporters remember—this personality stayed the same when the cameras were turned off, too. This mirth and positivity seemed genuine.

From all outward appearances, young Aaron Hernandez was the real thing.

CHAPTER 3

"Football just kept me grounded for six months out of the year, you know what I'm saying?"

—AARON HERNANDEZ, JAILHOUSE RECORDING

Colleges and universities were looking for someone who was that *real thing.* They found it in Aaron, and came circling like vultures.

As a local hero, Aaron had—of course—been recruited heavily by the University of Connecticut. Early in his high school career, it looked as though he was likely to end up a Husky.

There are reports that, as a sophomore in high school, Aaron had informally told UConn's football coach, Randy Edsall, that he would commit to attending. In addition, Aaron's brother, Jonathan, was already playing there as both a quarterback and wide receiver. Playing on the same team as his brother—even if it would only be for a year—had to be tempting. And to cap it off, his father had briefly played football for UConn. The family connection to the school and its football team could hardly have been stronger. (In fact, growing up, the family dog had been named "UConn.") This would complete the dynasty.

Yet something convinced Aaron to go bigger. Although UConn was a Division I school and nothing to smirk at, something told Aaron he ought to shoot for a school with a greater chance of winning a national championship. Something told him he should be part of a college football program with a better likelihood of landing him in the NFL.

And that "something" was University of Florida coach Urban Meyer.

Like Aaron, Meyer was something of a young phenom himself. He had played football himself at the University of Cincinnati, and soon after graduating took a coaching position at Ohio State. He had then bounced around for a few years as an assistant coach at Illinois State, Colorado State, and Notre Dame. Exposure to each of these programs had taught the young coach a thing or two about what was needed to create a successful football program—both on and off the field.

By the time he was giving his first head coaching job in 2001 at Bowling Green, the young coach was firing on all cylinders. He took a team that had finished 2–9 the year before, and led them to an 8–3 season. The next year he showed the turn-around was not a fluke by going 9–3. From there, more serious opportunities began to open up. Meyer moved to the University of Utah, where he had two exemplary years. In his first season with the Utes he ended with a 10–2 record and was named National Coach of the Year by the *Sporting News*. The following season, he took Utah to a 12–0 season. The Utes finished the year ranked fourth in the final AP poll, and many felt that they ought to have been named national champions.

At this point, Meyer was one of the most sought-after coaches in the land, and troubled programs all across the nation were scrambling to hire him to perform the kind of turnarounds he'd managed at Bowling Green and Utah. After much wooing, the honor finally went to the University of Florida, which signed him to a contract worth about $2 million annually. Meyer knew, however, that the task awaiting him in the Sunshine State would be unlike anything he'd done before. Bowling Green and Utah had been football programs with no major issues—that is, aside from terrible records on the field. They had no discipline problems, no scandals. The University of Florida, on the other hand, was known as a rough bunch, and the football team was often perceived as being out of control. Meyer would not only have to win games, but would have to manage a whole other kind of student-athlete.

It took Meyer just two seasons to win a national championship. In 2006, the Gators won the BCS title with a win over Ohio State. Meyer was lauded and offered a contract extension which upped his salary to about $3.25 million per year. Yet while he had taken his team to the pinnacle of success on the field, he had not adjusted the culture of his team. During Meyer's six-year tenure at Florida, 31 different players would be arrested—some of them multiple times—and many suspect that several others were privately reprimanded for bad behavior (but not arrested).

When Aaron arrived at the University of Florida in early 2007, he must have thought he'd come to the right place.

Aaron was looking for a college environment that would include everything he'd enjoyed about his high school experience.

He wanted to be the center of attention.

He wanted to win games and move closer to his dream of playing in the NFL.

But perhaps most importantly of all, Aaron wanted to continue living a double life—a special life where the rules and social conventions that bound others simply didn't apply to him.

And it looked like all that was going to be possible at Florida.

The school was obsessed with sports, and constantly gripped with championship fever. It was powerful and contagious, and seemed to have infected everybody. Not only were the football players winners, but the school's basketball team had just won a national championship, too.

The entire campus was crazy about UF athletics.

But Aaron may have also found the University of Florida so appealing because of Meyer's special way of recruiting prospective player.

His coaching philosophy was to draft freshmen players as young as possible, so he could mold them during their formative years. Unlike some coaches, Meyer didn't want 19- or 20-year-old freshmen (even though they'd be older and bigger). Even 18-year-olds were not optimal for him. He wanted students who still ought to have been playing high school ball. Accordingly, Aaron was just 17 years old when he showed up for his first classes at the University of Florida. And he didn't matriculate in the fall, like most students do. He showed up in January.

How was this possible?

The answer is that Meyer was able to convince Aaron's high school to graduate him early. (Meyer was something of an expert at this. No fewer than eight incoming freshmen on Aaron's team would be arriving via early graduation in 2007.) This meant that Aaron would skip his scheduled spring graduation with all of his friends. It was something that disrupted the traditional high school experience, but also made Aaron feel special and wanted … which he certainly was.

Meyer did not normally recruit in Connecticut. If he even looked at prospects in that state, he sent assistants to assess them. But when it came to Aaron, he'd traveled there personally.

Meyer understood the powerful impact that Aaron could have on the Florida program. He wanted Aaron, and wanted him badly.

When he traveled up to Connecticut, Meyer brought along assistant coaches with personal connections to the state. He hoped that their shared backgrounds would make them feel familiar and home-like to Aaron.

Meyer and his team were also not shy about invoking the NFL. They said flat-out that they believed Aaron had the potential to play at the game's highest level … however, that would only happen if he listened to them, trusted them, and took the enormous leap of faith that meant moving halfway across the country. This was seduction at its highest level, one source would tell me.

But did Meyer have any inkling of the secrets and demons that plagued Aaron behind the scenes? Was he able to detect any hint of the young man's troubled inner life when they spoke face-to-face?

As a coach famous for intuitively knowing his players inside and out, it is hard to imagine he failed to see that Aaron was a troubled young man. But then again, Aaron was already a master of disguise—an amateur kind of Frank William Abagnale Jr., the former con man, check forger, and impostor played by Leonardo DiCaprio in the movie *Catch Me If You Can*. A master at compartmentalizing and keeping his secret life secret. Maybe Aaron fooled Meyer, and maybe Meyer saw though the front Aaron was putting up. We'll probably never know for certain. Whatever the case, we *do* know that Meyer saw something he wanted.

And so he began an all-out assault.

In the weeks after their initial meeting in Connecticut, he flew Aaron down to take a tour of the university. For Aaron, who had hardly been out of the state of Connecticut, it must have seemed a whirlwind. He was introduced to prominent members of the football team. He met with coaches. He went to local exhibition games. And his tour guide for the visit was none other than the school's star quarterback, Tim Tebow.

And it worked.

Meyer had cast a spell, and Aaron was under its power.

He did need to fly home and "think about it." Before he even got on the plane to head back to Connecticut, Aaron made his intentions clear and public by recording a videotaped message saying that he was going to be playing for the Gators next year.

Meyer is known to be a famously effective recruiter with incredible powers of persuasion. But he could still not have *forced* Aaron to make this decision. And it tells us something about Aaron's own bravery and desire that he was willing to make such a leap.

In recording this message, Aaron showed that he was willing to break with his own family's tradition, and to disappoint the community he'd grown up in. He was willing to break the heart of his own brother, who dreamed of them playing on the same team. And, if the reports are true, he was willing to break a promise made to UConn's coach. Aaron was willing to do all this in order to get what he wanted. This speaks to his willingness to take risks, and to undergo pain and suffering in order to achieve a goal. In this case, the pain would be mental instead of physical. He would have to look his own brother in the eyes and tell him the dream of playing on the same college team together was not going to happen. (Perhaps this is why Aaron found it easier to say when looking into a video camera.)

Yet, by the time he returned to Connecticut, Aaron found that most people were still on his side. Even if they were disappointed by his choice, they understood why he'd made it. This was, after all, the University of Florida.

Even Jonathan supported his brother's choice. He knew what Aaron was capable of, and he was not going to stand in the way of Aaron playing for a championship team and chasing his dream of playing in the NFL. So, when the gears began to turn—and arrangements began to be made to expedite a move down to Florida—Jonathan was ultimately supportive. He'd once had the same kind of dreams. He understood.

Dennis SanSoucie also supported the choice—if only because it would involve leaving for greener pastures. As he remembers:

I think it was a bold move, but I think it was the best move somebody could make. I was so proud of him. Like, you're gonna go take it down south and get out of this bubble of Connecticut? How great is that?

Yet Dennis also saw the potential for trouble in a scenario that would involve Aaron proceeding to the unruly University of Florida without the guiding hand of a paternal figure.

Once Aaron's father had died, he definitely changed. He had more of a darker side to him, and I think a lot of that had to do with [him thinking], *Well, hey, I already know I'm going to a DI school to play football. I'm six-foot-two, 230 in high school. Yeah, I'm kind of in control of myself. I'm already kind of better than everybody else.* So that'd get to your head really quick, if you don't have a father to put you in place.

Dennis understood that Jonathan had had their father's guiding hand when he'd begun his own DI football career. Aaron would be facing that transition alone. Not only that, but he would be making the move to the top program in the country. To the national champions. The pressure on Aaron must have been enormous.

In addition to the physical distance from his hometown, and the pressure to perform at a premier college football program at just 17—legally, still a child—Aaron also faced other staggering challenges. Though it was made clear to him that his school was indeed willing to pull the strings that were necessary for him to get his diploma early, there was no way he was truly ready for college-level academic work. Though he had at various times made his high school's honor role, his SAT scores were not good. He especially struggled at reading and writing. His score on the verbal section of the SAT was below the minimum to even be considered by the University of Florida.

Aaron knew this, but the school assured him everything would be fine. All would be taken care of. They would give him special "remedial" classes, free of charge, in the subjects where he struggled. He would be given the benefit of the doubt when it came to grading his coursework.

On one level, this side of the offer may have made Florida's appeal even more enticing. Aaron was seduced by bending and breaking the rules, and here was a major university recruiting him by offering to bend their own rules just for him. Even in these initial negotiations, the University of Florida was sending a very clear signal: If you come here, you will not be treated like everyone else. You will be held to a different standard. *You, Aaron Hernandez, will be special.*

In this way, they sent a clear message to their fledgling star that their campus—even though it was 1,100 miles away—was going to feel a lot like home.

Yet there was danger in this as well. As a young teen, Aaron had systems in place in his life to keep his accountable. To keep things structured. Not only would college be much less regimented than high school had been, but the school itself was strongly hinting that Aaron could expect indulgences when he didn't quite deliver off the field.

Few journalists have researched this period in Aaron's life more than Boston-based investigative reporter Michele McPhee. In print, on TV, and on the radio, she has exhaustively reported on the trials and tribulations of Aaron Hernandez, and is intimately familiar with his headspace during this transition. In an interview for this project, McPhee shares a decidedly grimmer characterization of Aaron's journey to Florida:

> His father dies, and he gets recruited to go to the University of Florida to play football. He can't really read. His dad just died—but who cares?—because he was gonna make money [for the school]. He was gonna bring people to the games. He was gonna be an NFL standout. Urban Meyer was a legendary coach, and we know how integrity is not on the top of Urban Meyer's list when he's recruiting these young players, nor is their behavior, on or off the field, a priority for him because what he cares about is winning games, and what he didn't care about is whether or not somebody was a psychopath, running around the streets, while playing for the University of Florida.

To their credit, the University of Florida was as good as their word when it came to Aaron's academic help. He was given special additional classes at a local community college, and Aaron's professors graded generously. (The university maintained a relationship with the community college expressly for the purpose of serving football players who lacked the academics to pass college-level classes.) Though his writing was terrible, he always managed to come up with a passing grade.

But this was not the only special indulgence Aaron would need during his first days on campus. In retrospect, others wished they had been more demanding. Aaron's high school principal, Dennis Siegmann, has said he regrets allowing him to graduate six months early so he could go to University of Florida. "If I had to do it over again I would have fought tooth and nail not to let that kid graduate at mid-year," he would say in an interview after Aaron's death.

"It's all hindsight. We never got to see the full growth of Aaron Hernandez at high school—and would that have changed anything?"

Looking at the records from his first semester at the university, it's clear that Aaron began having brushes with the law pretty much from the get-go. He received two traffic tickets from local cops. (How many other violations did the police "look the other way" for because of his status as a football player? We do not know the specifics of that information, but eyewitness accounts suggest it happened often.) Aaron also drank in bars, regularly, even though he was not yet 18, much less the legal drinking age of 21.

But there was one particular shocking night of brutality that is nothing short of being so scandalous it leaves one asking how Aaron was able to get away with such antics for so long—illuminating the depths and scale of conspiracy to hide the truth.

Near the end of his first semester, Aaron was drinking in a bar (illegally) with Tim Tebow and some other friends. At the end of the night, a dispute arose, and Aaron punched an employee of the bar in the side of the head. (The police report, obtained by this author, details how the fight concerned Aaron's bar tab—and his unwillingness to pay it—but the exact circumstances leading up to the blow are not really known. According to many accounts, someone sent over shots to Aaron that he had not ordered—but happily consumed—and then later in the night was furious to receive a bill for them.) Whatever the true cause, the punch was no simple knock to the head. Because of Aaron's immense strength, the bar employee suffered a ruptured eardrum. It was a serious injury, and technically meant Aaron could be charged with a felony. Such a charge would put his continued ability to play college ball in jeopardy.

But at that moment, just as true consequences for his actions threatened to descend upon him, agents of the university descended instead. In a figurative and literal way, they surrounded and protected him. To Aaron, it must have seemed like angels coming down from high above.

Reports show that the police responded to the call about the punch at 1:17 a.m. Almost instantaneously, officials at the university were contacted, and they began concealing the true extent of what had happened. The cover-up ensued.

Many who have analyzed Aaron's tragic tale believe that this is the precise moment when the University of Florida should have allowed the young student athlete to learn a hard lesson. They should have confronted Aaron about his bad behavior and lawlessness. And most certainly, they should have allowed him to suffer the negative consequences of his actions.

However, as is all too common, they did none of this.

In addition to maintaining strong relationships with local law enforcement, the University had their own special "fixer" for such situations. He was a lawyer and a graduate of the university. His name was Huntley Johnson, and he'd made it clear he could be called upon, day or night, when such an issue arose. Though his relationship with the university was "officially unofficial," there was the sense that there was nothing he wouldn't do for the Gator football program.

This was not a simple case of damage mitigation.

Such relationships were (and are) not uncommon at major football schools.

Right before he passed away in 2017, Frank Deford, perhaps the nation's greatest living sportswriter, shared that he had once conducted a confidential interview with the president of one of the nation's Big Ten schools. In the interview, Deford related that the unnamed university president had said that when you're placed in charge of a major American university, you learn that there are three groups to manage—students, employees, and alumni—and each of these groups want different things. Namely: your students want sex, your employees want parking, and your alumni want football. So your life becomes managing sex, parking, and football.

Because of its importance to alums, universities are keen to make maintenance of the football program a central priority. Men like Huntley Johnson are willing to make themselves available to do special favors (and keep football programs strong), because it's what everyone wants. Everyone who make alumni donations, that is. For universities to continue to exist, they need to know what their alumni want, and give it to them to the best of their ability. To be clear, alumni at the University of Florida were not unusual or aberrant in this regard—football is a universal priority at schools across the United States.

The University of Florida's alumni did not clamor for the school's academic rankings to increase. For the graduation rate to climb. Or for new and better facilities or dorms.

No.

They clamored for football wins. And now that they'd had a taste of an honest-to-goodness national championship—and boy did they like the way it tasted—they wanted to maintain a successful football program like nothing they'd wanted before.

So when Aaron misbehaved, Huntley Johnson descended. The administration and coaching staff descended. The university's power in all its forms descended. And these things fell over Aaron like a warm, protective blanket. It was like he'd just pull the pin on a grenade, and before he knew what had happened, these powerful forces had thrown themselves between him and the blast.

Not only were these forces quick; they were also effective.

No formal charges were filed against Aaron, and the incident was kept out of general public knowledge for many years (long enough that he was years removed from the school). People around town might have heard that the freshman had punched a guy in a bar fight, but it was dismissed as undergraduate hijinks. A tussle. Horseplay.

Was the bar employee offered a large financial settlement by the university? Almost certainly, one would predict.

Was Aaron chewed out by the coaching staff for this misbehavior? Almost certainly, one would predict.

But what changed afterwards? Almost nothing.

However strongly his coaches and teammates might have confronted Aaron about his behavior that night, the combined actions of the school and the local community sent a different signal. "This is another confirmation that you will receive special treatment. You will get away with things others can't. When your bad behavior is discovered, the most powerful forces in the area will collude to make the issue go away."

The incident was just the first in a pattern of denial and cover-up—performed on Aaron's behalf—that would come to define the rest of his life.

No angry words from a coach or administrator could speak more powerfully than this. The cover-up spoke more loudly than any opprobrium from a coach ever could. Aaron was accustomed to being disciplined for his failings by his father's fists. Could a hollering, scowling football coach really hope to reach him? By this point, Aaron had evolved a mental armor that was very strong.

After his bracing by coach Meyer, Aaron would have been quickly returned back to the world of his teammates. They might have heard about the punch, but in his conversations with them, he would learn that the way he had been treated was not unusual.

The police might have wanted assault charges against Aaron, but with the victim no longer willing to press charges, there was little they could do to seek justice. Aaron was, essentially, going to "get away with it"—and the cops knew it.

During his time at the University of Florida, football players were arrested at a rate of about six per year. (These arrests would have to involve incidents too egregious for an officer on the scene to "look the other way.") In each case, the same angels descended to cover the player and minimize the impact. While a few were charged with various (often reduced) violations, most would suffer no real consequences.

Former NFL player Dereck Faulkner, who played for the Philadelphia Eagles in 2007 and college football for the Hampton Pirates, has seen firsthand how college towns collude to protect athletes in these sorts of situations.

In an exclusive interview, he shared his view on Aaron, and his thoughts on how they system worked to his advantage.

When you hear about any act of violence by anyone, and definitely on the college level as a student athlete, with Aaron, it's startling, and it's definitely something that's alarming because parents don't send their kids off to college to commit forms of acts of violence, nor do they want acts of violence against their own while in school. And definitely in a college town like Gainesville, where everything's pretty much contained.

In a college town, how it looks is you have your football team. Everyone knows each other. The bar owners, the restaurant owners, everyone knows everyone in the town—and the football players, they would be known. Aaron was known around. He's a star athlete, just like Tim Tebow or anyone else. So in a place like that, you don't really look to hear of that type of activity happening because everyone knows each other, it would be simple. If it was a disagreement, it gets handled and guys go about their way.

And in college towns, guys—the football team or the winning team—gets treated like royalty anyway. So it's definitely—it's disturbing to hear about that type of activity, but not uncommon.

But to actually block law enforcement and cooperate with them to cover this up, to me, it's reprehensible. To look at this particular incident and say here was an opportunity for people to step forward and say this is really sad, but we're going to have to throw him under the bus. He's going to have to be held culpable for his actions. And they didn't. And now that you look at the ramifications all these years later, it really goes back to that incident. And there's a sense that people want them to be held responsible for what happened.

I mean, it's really—it's that moment when you have the decision to do the right thing or not. And when you look at it this way ... do you know what I'm saying?

For the University of Florida, their decision to cover for Aaron was probably seen as "protecting their investment." The players themselves earned no official salary or pay, but were like rare pieces of gold that an expert prospector had spent end-less effort trying to find. And that gold prospector cost an arm and a leg.

At the time of the bar incident, Meyer's total contract was for $14 million over seven years—but that wasn't the total price tag by any measure. Some of his senior assistant coaches on his staff could make well into six figures. Then there were the other assistants, the strength trainers, and everyone else who worked for the program. Beyond Meyer's salary, there was a staggering investment to protect.

Nationally, it was a period of extreme inflation in college football costs. Salaries seemed to increase exponentially every few years but, for top programs like the University of Florida with games that were televised, revenues were also exponen-tial. If Meyer and his staff were the ones who could bring championships and renown—which, as it turned out, they were—then it would be worth the cost to the university.

And when Meyer began winning championships, the school was not about to question his methods. (They just wanted to keep this championship-winning train headed down the track.) Recruiting players young and assembling an army to cover their bad behavior seemed to be Meyer's calling card. The year before coming to Gainesville, the University had only one early enrollee on its football team. In his final year with the school, it had eleven. (And when Meyer left Florida for Ohio State University, there is evidence that he used the same tactics there. The number of high school players enrolling early at Ohio State rose steadily under Meyer, the number increasing nearly each year.)

On the field, it won championships.

Off the field, it brought more kids to college who weren't ready to do college-level work, and weren't mentally prepared for the stress of young adulthood.

Nationally, NCAA football can be said to be a success when it comes to gradu-ation rates. Perhaps because of the support and extra attention they receive, about 90 percent of America's college football players graduate within six years. That number, for *all* college and university students across all four-year institutions, is only about 60 percent.

What was the number in Meyer's early enrollment program at the University of Florida? Only 45 percent. Literally half of the national rate for football players.

Aaron walked into a program where the *majority* of early arrivals, like him, would not graduate. However, he also walked into a program that was crowning national champions and sending kids to the NFL—left and right.

Doing it Meyer's way involved risk, but it was the kind of risk that Aaron (and others) wanted to take.

As the handling of the bar fight and its aftermath made clear to Aaron, as long as he remained an asset to the school he could expect lots of help and special treatment. His sins would be swept under the rug and kept quiet; only a select few would every know what he had done.

Seen now, in the context of all that was to follow, this incident was just the first in a pattern of denial, cover-up, and consequence-free behavior that would define Aaron's life.

And that was just how he liked it.

CHAPTER 4

Mom: "You chose to go to Florida a year before that."
Aaron: "I understand that but I also was in a rush to get out of here, it
felt like we were close before I went away. I couldn't wait to get away."
Mom: "Oh I know. I know you were right."
Aaron: "I started a whole new life."
Mom: "But I wanted to be there for you."

—AARON HERNANDEZ, JAILHOUSE RECORDING

After the infamous bar incident, Aaron seemed to cool it for a while. He still partied, but limited himself to safe spaces. Instead of going out to bars, he attended parties thrown by other football players (and friends of the football program). These were places where he could drink alcohol—and continued to smoke *massive* amounts of marijuana—in relative peace. Weeks passed, and Aaron stayed off the negative radar. There were no further accounts of bad behavior—at least not in the public eye.

Meyer and the other coaches at UF might have dared to hope Aaron had been scared straight. Yet a shocking incident occurred on September 29, 2007, that led them to reevaluate everything.

On the day in question, a dark cloud had been cast over the city of Gainesville. After starting the season 4–0, the Gators had their first loss of the season, a 20–17 defeat at the hands of rival Auburn. The crowds of football fans that hit the business district and bars after the game were surly and angry; almost everyone was in a bad mood.

Late that evening, Aaron went with some friends to a Gainesville nightclub called Venue. In his retinue was fellow early enrollee Mike Pouncey (currently a center for the Los Angeles Chargers and whose twin brother Maurkice, now a center for the Pittsburgh Steelers, was a teammate at Florida).

Venue was a place frequented by members of the football team. More specifically, it was a place where they went to blow off steam. Arguments and fights were a regular occurrence—and those happened on the days that the Gators had *won*. People got knocked around. The cops got called. It was that kind of place.

Aaron and Pouncey arrived at the club to find a prominent university alum partying down. It was Reggie Nelson, who had recently been drafted by the Jacksonville Jaguars. Another NFLer, Chris Harris, was also present.

Sometime during the evening, a Gainesville local named Randall Cason entered the club. Shortly after, a beef broke out between the local and the football players. There were accusations that someone's gold neck chain had been stolen. (By some accounts, Cason had attempted to steal the chain from the neck of Mike Pouncey. Reggie Nelson is said to have stepped in and attempted to stop the scuffle over the chain, and it appears he was largely successful.) Most of the young men that had been involved in the incident were asked to leave the club. All of them, including Aaron, did so.

The men walked to the parking lot, got into their cars, and drove away.

Then, a few short minutes later, a gangland-style shooting occurred.

Cason had ridden away from the club in the back seat of a friend's car. He was with two other men. (The friends had been at Venue and may have also been involved in the scuffle.)

As they rode, Cason would later report that he thought the car was being tailed. Suddenly, a volley of shots rang out.

Cason would later tell the police that he saw Reggie Nelson and Aaron Hernandez approach the car from the sidewalk. Aaron shoved a handgun through the car's open window and started pulling the trigger. Blast after blast after blast. In the same moment, Cason stated that someone from the car that had been tailing them threw lit firecrackers out into the street, as if to conceal the handgun blasts.

Then, according to Cason, Aaron sprinted away into the night.

The incident left the driver shot in the head, and the second passenger shot in the arm. Only Cason—ironically, likely the intended target—was unscathed.

The driver, Corey Smith, was grievously wounded but not killed.

In an exclusive interview for this book, Smith's mother, Sandra Hines, explains the tragedy of the attempted killing.

> My son, Corey Smith, at the time was going to school to get his license to become an electrician. He was a single father raising two kids, his daughter and his son. His life was just good at the moment. That night, him and Justin, who was the other guy that was with him at the time... They decided they would go to the club... My son and Justin, they were being followed. They got to the corner of 13th at the red light. When they got there, someone walked up to the car. At approximately 4 a.m., I got a phone call telling me to get to the hospital as soon as I could. My son was shot. I'm thinking, "He's dead." And I began to pray. So as I arrived at the emergency room, the doctor came out. I asked him what happened. He told me my son was shot in the head. He made it through one surgery. He had another one to go, but he might not ever walk, talk again.

Later that morning, after the shooting, when the police would ask Cason to describe the shooter, he was adamant that he didn't need to describe the person in terms of age, race, height, or weight. He just told them he knew who it had been: Aaron Hernandez.

The police, however, eyed both Cason and his story carefully. The local police knew him as a low-level criminal who had been associated with gang activity. (In the aftermath, police would confirm that Cason had an illegal gun on his person at the time of the shooting. It was a .40 caliber pistol with the serial numbers filed off.) And as the police reached out to other witnesses, another issue arose. Other people who had witnessed the shooting from various positions on the street described the shooter as an African American man, about two inches shorter than Aaron.

"As they were waiting for the light to change, the Hawaiian football player and Reggie Nelson walked up to their car on the right side," according to the police report, which cited what Cason told detectives. "Then without saying a work [sic], the Hawaiian pointed a small handgun in the front right window and fired five quick shots. Cason saw Smith slump over with blood coming out of the back of the head, at which time the Hawaiian and Nelson took off running towards McDonald's."

Nelson was also brought in and interviewed by police. Obtained through a new FOIA request, his interrogation was made public for the first time in the course of researching this book. Nelson's interview is informative not only for what Nelson himself reveals, but also for what the police clearly do—or do not—know.

Early in the interrogation, Detective Sentrip of the Gainesville Police Department frames the situation for Reggie.

It was probably about 2:30 in the morning, so the clubs had let out. Okay? I guess a lot of people were going home. There was a lot, a lot of cars. A lot, a lot of people standing around at the gas station, over there at the place next door. They've got a deli and Holiday Inn, so there's people all over the place.

Anyway, best we know so far is that somebody got shot last night, okay? I don't know what your involvement was. If you were anything more than just . . . had no idea about what happened all the way. The one thing I do know is, you're not the person who did it. I can tell you that much. See what I mean?

So, we know you didn't do it. Okay? I can be honest with you right now. Reggie, you have...obviously, the sky's the limit for your future. All right? We're not trying to do anything to your career or anything like that. We're not trying to call Jaguars. We're not trying to call the newspapers and do all that other stuff okay. The sky's the limit, but I need to have honest.

I'm telling you right now, I know you didn't do it. Okay? I don't think you planned it. I don't this was a plan or anything like this. I want to try to tell you, you're not a suspect at this time. Okay? From what I have in my head right now, you're not a suspect in the crime. You're a witness, I think. Okay? But I need to know 100 percent, just lay it out there.

What happens is, if in the future that it comes back that you lied right now then all bets are off and I can't tell you what's going to happen.

Sentrip adds that: "We're interviewing the Pouncey twins right now. So they're talking about whatever happened last night."

Sentrip then shows Nelson a photo.

Sentrip: I also have a picture of a guy I want to show you too. His name is Randall. Do you know who Randall is?
Nelson: Uh-huh [negative].

Sentrip: Okay, we'll show you a picture.
Nelson: All right.

Sentrip: Just to see, you might know him by a different name. That might be his first name and you might know him by a different name. But I'm going to show you a picture here in a second, and see if you know this guy. Because he's somehow involved too, and we already talked to him. So we're trying to put all the stories together. The good news is, nobody's dead, so that's good news. Do you know that guy right there?
Nelson: Yeah. That's the one I was talking to last night.

Sentrip: What do you know him by?
Nelson: I don't know him by nothing.

Sentrip: You don't know him by name, you just know him by face?

Nelson: I just know him by face.

Later in the interrogation, Sentrip makes clear that the police are very curious about who the Pouncey twins may have been with—and Nelson eventually gives them the ID they are hoping for.

Sentrip: Who were they with, who were the Pouncey twins with?

Nelson: The Pouncey twins? They was with him and his brother, Jamar Hornsby, and-

Sentrip: We call him the other Cornelius Ingram, because they have the same number. And on TV they always say Cornelius Ingram, but that how-

Nelson: It ain't him.

Sentrip: ...yeah, it's Jamar Hornsby. The other Hornsby, yeah.

Nelson: There was another little Freshman, he was light skinned.

Sentrip: So is Jamar, is he a Freshman too?

Nelson: Yeah, no, he a Sophomore.

Sentrip: Okay. And then you said a tight end.

Nelson: Yeah, he was light skinned. He was with the Pouncey twins. I didn't know his name, I can't think of his name.

Sentrip: You'd recognize a picture of him?

Nelson: Yeah, I would know a picture of him.

Sentrip: I think somebody said his name was-

Nelson: He was light skinned, like he was mixed.

Sentrip: Right. What did they say his name was?

Nelson: But yeah, he was there.

Sentrip: Aaron?

Nelson: Yeah. That's it, I think that's his name. It might be Aaron. I would make sure-

Sentrip: How tall...Tall dude though, right?

Nelson: He about the size of the twins.

Sentrip: The same height as them? But not the weight.

Nelson: Not the weight.

Sentrip: Not many guys are the same weight as those boys.

Nelson: Nah.

Sentrip: All right. Let me go see if somebody knows who that boy's name is, and then I'll bring a picture.

Nelson: All right.

Sentrip: Okay? I think somebody right know. I'll be right back.

Nelson: All right.

Sentrip: They must have got this one off the website.

Nelson: Yeah, that's him.

Sentrip: Old high school picture. All right, yeah, his name is Aaron.

Nelson: Yeah. That's the last one with all of them at the club.

Nelson would also go on to confirm the events that had happened inside the club.

> **Sentrip:** So one of the Pouncey twins said that Randall snatched the chain.
> **Nelson:** Yeah, snatched his chain. And he was jumping around like, "Ha! I snatched your chain." And then that was the last thing that I heard from them, until I got outside. And then when we got outside after the club—
>
> **Sentrip:** Wait a second. Did he tell you that outside or inside, about snatching the chain?
> **Nelson:** No. Pouncey...Aaron told me that somebody snatched the twin's chain, and then they had went outside.
>
> **Sentrip:** So Aaron told you inside?
> **Nelson:** Yeah, Aaron told me inside. And then, I seen one of the twins, and he told me that somebody had snatched his chain. So after the club, we had went outside, we was in the parking lot, sitting there. And then after that, we was sitting there the I seen the twins. I was like, "Who snatched your chain?" Like, "The dude, Randall, in the gray tank top," snatched his chain.

Gainesville PD next reached out to Meyer's office and requested a photo of Aaron. It was sent over, and the police used it in a photo lineup. Cason picked out the photo of Aaron as the gunman. Even so, the police remained skeptical of his story.

While this was happening, familiar faces sprang into action on the university side. Aaron was taken to see Huntley Johnson for an unofficial legal consultation.

(What precisely the two men discussed is not known.) Shortly thereafter, the police department asked Aaron to come in and give a statement about the night in question.

He had been identified by victims, and it was clear the police were angling to file charges.

Aaron went to the police station directly from Huntley Johnson's office. He was placed into an interrogation room alone. . . where he promptly fell asleep.

The police thought this was odd. Preparing to be interrogated by law enforcement regarding alleged involvement in a murder would be a high-stress situation for most—if not all—people. Though there were many different reactions to it, falling asleep wasn't normally one of them.

A man might fall asleep in an interrogation room because he was so exhausted from the previous night that he literally could not keep himself awake. He might also allow himself to drift off if he did not understand the situation or its potential consequences. If he foolishly failed to grasp the seriousness of the matter.

And, yes, if a man knew he were guilty and doomed to be convicted, he might fall asleep out of sheer hopelessness, and because he has accepted the situation.

But if he were Aaron, there might be another possibility, too. Namely, that Aaron was gaming the system. He had been brought in to talk to cops before. He knew how it worked, and he wanted to throw them off. Make himself unreadable. Remind them that because of his position on the football team, they had better have amazing evidence.

Perhaps Aaron already knew that they didn't.

When officers finally roused him, read him his rights, and tried to begin the interrogation procedure, Aaron was uncooperative. He said he would not answer questions without an attorney present, and then clammed up.

In this moment, the officers were suddenly aware that they were not dealing with a wet-behind-the-ears college kid. This imposing young man was a seasoned pro—and/or he had pros from the university advising him.

In the days that passed, the police case for Aaron's involvement seemed to fall apart further when Cason was confronted with the fact that all of the other eye-witnesses on the scene had described a different-looking man. Cason was unable to account for this discrepancy. The police privately conjectured that Cason might be naming Aaron in order to get revenge for the beef over the stolen necklace.

In the end, Aaron never said anything further to the police. Not even in the presence of a lawyer. Two days after the shooting, Gainesville police lieutenant Keith Kameg was quoted in the *Orlando Sentinel* as saying neither Aaron nor Nelson were suspects. Police also said publicly that they briefly interviewed Aaron about the shooting—a now known lie, at least according to the police report, which explicitly stated Aaron declined to speak.

Then—finally—Cason changed his story. He said that he had *not* seen the shooter clearly, but simply *assumed* it had been Aaron.

And just like that, Aaron was off the hook—again.

Not surprisingly, Sandra Hines remains infuriated to this day:

> Aaron Hernandez... They were able to get a good lawyer. Nobody else, we couldn't find a lawyer. Nobody would help us. Nobody would, not even if we had money to pay them. We were told, like I said, it was him. It was Aaron. Then, all of a sudden it wasn't Aaron. All of a sudden, all the good leads that [they] were getting, gone. They let the football players get away with so much and sweep it under the rug, let them get away with it and go on like nothing's happened, you know.

Though the matter was settled in the eyes of the police, to this day, much mystery still remains in regard to this event.

What attitude did Aaron have about the shooting? If he had not himself committed it, then how did it make him feel, and why? (Certainly, he expressed no anger or indignation at being probed or questioned about a shooting he was not involved in.)

Because he had been beefing with Cason's crew at the club—and considering his attitudes about street violence generally—it's likely that Aaron personally felt that Cason and his friends had gotten what was coming to them. Had gotten justice—even if Aaron had not personally been the one to dispense it.

Whether it was a hatred for Cason and his friends, advice from the university, or simply adherence to the code of the streets, Aaron did not help the police with their investigation in any way. Though no longer suspected of being the shooter, he *had* been in the vicinity at the time of the shooting. Had he seen or heard anything helpful that would allow police to find the *real* shooter?

They would never know, as Aaron would never tell them.

Some years after the shooting, the *Orlando Sentinel* learned that a friend of Aaron's from Bristol had been in town visiting on the night of the shooting. It is still not known if he was with the group at Venue, or if he was even present on the night in question. The visitor's name has never been disclosed.

Aaron went back to playing football, attending class, and partying with his friends. He continued to smoke large amounts of marijuana, and did not conceal this from others on the football team.

Just as a mysterious cloak had descended on the night of the shooting, the air seemed to clear afterwards. Aaron remained a valuable asset for the Gators football program.

But already, the clock was ticking.

Coach Meyer had been correct regarding the massive physical presence Aaron would bring to the field. Yet the danger and lawlessness that stuck to Aaron like glue had followed him from Connecticut. By the end of his second year, there had been the barroom punch, the interrogation regarding the shooting, and many other, more minor infractions.

There had also been no "come to Jesus" moment. That is, Aaron had presented Meyer with no *believable* evidence of a conversion away from his criminal past.

To Meyer, having Aaron on the team would still appear to be a risk. Each day the young man stayed on campus was another day in which he might get into trouble. Aaron's trajectory was not promising.

A remarkably good football season did nothing to cool Aaron's appetite for partying, and his grades remained erratic. He made honor roll one semester, the next pulling very low grades and have to withdraw from classes that he was in danger of failing. Even an offseason Aaron was hard for Meyer to predict. Hard to know.

Yet, for a time, Meyer continued to gamble on the young man, because, on the field, his performance remained unquestionable.

Though high *during* most football games, Aaron went on to play exceptionally well during his junior season. He led the team in receptions, and was presented with the Mackey Award at the end of the season, an honor given to the best tight end in all of college football. The Gators also had an exemplary season, falling just short of a national championship (their only loss coming in the SEC champion-ship game against Alabama, who they had defeated in the same game the previ-ous season).

The end of the 2009 season was another turning point in Aaron's life. Like many football players in his shoes, he had a decision to make. Something to ask himself. Namely, was now the time to turn pro? He had been part of a champion-ship team as a sophomore and been named the best player at his position. He seemed to have done everything he'd set out to, and with a year to spare.

Both Aaron and Meyer were gambling men, and every gambler knows there's a time to put down the cards and walk away from the table.

From Meyer's perspective, Aaron definitely helped the Gators win games—but they had won games before him, and the coach knew they would win many after he was gone. At a program as strong as Florida, Aaron was far from the only card in the deck. And at the same time, Aaron also presented substantial danger to the program's reputation (and to members of the local community for that matter). Meyer had tried everything in his playbook to reform the tight end, yet nothing took. Aaron was unreformable. Several times, the coach had been forced to mus-ter all his resources in order to defuse serious problems that his star had created. Disaster had not struck—not really—but there had been plenty of near misses.

In the end, Meyer decided he'd had enough.

He gave Aaron an ultimatum: enter the NFL draft now, or be cut from the team.

We do not know precisely how Aaron reacted when given this news, but it is very unlikely that Meyer's words came as a surprise. Aaron had spent every favor in the favorbank with Meyer. He also knew that he had put the program's reputa-tion in danger several times.

He also knew that Meyer was generally a man of his word, not known to make idle threats. There was a real risk that the coach would actually cut him from the team if he did not leave.

In the end, it was probably no choice at all. There is no record that Aaron consulted anyone about it, or talked it over with friends or family. The NFL was going to be his next destination.

Like it or not.

CHAPTER 5

Aaron: "Football kept me away from a lot. You know what I'm saying, like half of the year I was just chillin'."
Mom: "Well you know what it came too fast and they still talk about you were the best tight end ever."
Aaron: "Yeah."
Mom: "Ever."

—AARON HERNANDEZ, JAILHOUSE RECORDING

At just 20 years old—the age when some redshirt freshmen are just starting their college football careers—Aaron Hernandez began the process of entering the NFL draft. Pro ball was new territory for the young man, and the fact that he was leaving without finishing his degree presented an array of challenges. However, the decision to leave school early for the NFL far from unheard of.

Dereck Faulkner—the former NFL player with the Philadelphia Eagles—was familiar with Aaron's situation and the kind of tactics used to bring him to the draft early. As he tells it:

> The NCAA *does* allow students to leave—to graduate early if they have the right credits and they've cleared the clearinghouse—NCAA clearinghouse. So they are allowed to leave, and it's completely legal. I think it gives a lot of universities the advantage to get a leg up, to get a guy into spring ball. He can get acclimated with the team and get acclimated with practicing and, obviously, getting some classes in. But I think in regards to Aaron, he did have a little bit of a past leaving high

school early, so it was more like, "Hey, let's move him to the new structured environment before something else may happen or wherever."
And it kind of gave him that opportunity to kind of start fresh
earlier.

And maybe for Aaron, they kind of compounded it in the sense of
like turning it strictly into a business early on. When you're an elite
athlete or elite football player, even dating back to the eighth grade,
you have scouts in schools watching you, offering you scholarships,
coming to your games, and sending you letters early on.

And as a high school athlete going early into college athletics, you
learn quickly that it is a business. And it's about performance. It's
about money. And you learn that early, and that may have been something that he got thrust into early on, which made it easier to go pro
when he did.

So, according to Faulkner, missing his senior year of college to turn pro may not
have seemed out of the ordinary for Aaron. Rather, it may have seemed an extension of the approach he'd been taking all along. Today, many NFL players are
granted early eligibility for the NFL draft. In 2018, 106 players were. And their
results make clear that many of them are fully prepared to make this transition.
But, surely, not all of them are.

The worlds of the NFL and NCAA Division I football are closely interconnected. *Very* closely interconnected.

Aaron knew that, when he left the University of Florida behind, he would not
be able to figuratively shed his skin like a snake and leave all his old sins behind
when he went pro. There was no chance to start fresh and new. Because of the
amount of attention he'd received from agents, scouts, and NFL coaches, there
would be no place to hide the kind of person he was. Prying eyes would look
under every rock. They would shine flashlights in all of his dark places. And—
perhaps most problematically for Aaron—where they could not find definitive
answers about the young tight end, they would rely on rumor and gossip. And
Aaron's situation gave them plenty to gossip about.

Like the other NFL hopefuls that year, Aaron attended the NFL Combine in

Indianapolis in early 2010. He was joined by several of his Florida teammates, including Tim Tebow. Unfortunately, directly prior to the combine, Aaron tore a muscle in his back, which eliminated his ability to show what he could do on the field. He made himself as available as he could for coaches and scouts, was weighed and measured every way a person could be, but was unable to take part in the workouts and drills that would demonstrate his physical prowess and capability.

Yet it was not his inability to participate in drills that had the scouts murmuring in concern.

Aaron's biggest problem was that there was no good reason that he should be seeking to forego his senior college season. (There were reasons, sure. . . just not *good* ones.) Aaron had been allowed by Coach Meyer to present the situation his own choice. To tell the combine the decision to turn pro after his junior year had been his own idea. But most of the pro scouts looking at Aaron had enough horse sense to realize this was not the case.

Aaron had done something. The question was, what?

The scouts knew about his rough upbringing and brushes with the law. Many NFL players came from similar backgrounds, however, and it is unlikely that juvenile hijinks and a bar fight or two in college would be enough for them to nix a strong prospect.

The possible role in a Gainesville shooting—and his being identified as the shooter by Randall Cason—were another matter. The scouts were probably ambivalent regarding whether or not Meyer would have the connections and power to paper over one of his players straight-up shooting people. However, the details of Aaron's presence at Venue nightclub on the evening of the shooting had some solid basis. In the best-case scenario, Aaron had poor choice in friends. While he might not commit shootings himself, he ran in a crew with proximity to those types of people.

Yet, remarkably, when the scouts took pen to paper and added up the pluses and minuses of drafting Aaron, it was something else entirely that put him on the bubble: his marijuana use.

It would be difficult for an NFL team to conceal it if a player used marijuana as regularly as Aaron was rumored to be using. It would be twice as difficult if the player liked to play while stoned, which Aaron did. The specter of drug testing was also more of a threat, at the time. No team wanted to invest both time and money in a player, only to bench him all season because he could never pass a drug test.

One NFL scout revealed his team's pre-draft file on Aaron, and one section stood out. It read. "Self-esteem is quite low; not well-adjusted emotionally, not happy, moods unpredictable, not stable, doesn't take much to set him off, but not an especially jumpy guy," the scout noted.

To his credit—or rather, to the credit of the team of agents representing him—Aaron chose to address the marijuana issue head-on.

Aaron (via his agents) wrote a remarkable letter and sent it to the New England Patriots, the team that he knew was considering drafting him. In the now famous (or infamous) letter—almost certainly *not* prepared with substantial input from the almost illiterate Aaron himself—an unusual plan is outlined that directly ties his compensation to his ability to pass drug tests.

Outlining a totally unique arrangement in the history of the NFL, it reads:

> I am writing in regards to some of the feedback I am receiving from my agents, Florida coaches, and other personnel. These sources have indicated that NFL teams have questions about my alleged use of marijuana. I personally answered these questions during the pre-draft process, but understand that NFL teams want to conduct thorough due diligence before making the significant financial investment inherent in a high draft pick. I have no issue with these questions being asked, but thought that it made the most sense to communicate with you directly regarding this issue so you would not have to rely upon second-hand information.
>
> Any information I volunteer to you about my past will be looked at with great skepticism as I am trying to get drafted as high as possible by an NFL team. As such, I thought that the best way to answer your questions and your concerns was to make a very simple proposition. If you draft me as a member of the New England Patriots, I will willfully submit to a bi-weekly drug test throughout my rookie season (8 drug tests during the 2010 regular season). In addition, I will tie any

guaranteed portion of my 2010 compensation to these drug tests and reimburse the team a pro-rata amount for any failed drug test. My agents have explained that a direct forfeiture provision in my contract along these lines would violate the CBA rules. However, I have instructed them to be creative in finding a contract structure that would work or in the worst-case scenario, I would donate the pro-rata portion of any guaranteed money to the team's choice of charities. My point is simple—if I fail a drug test, I do not deserve that portion of the money.

I realize that this offer is somewhat unorthodox, but it is also the only way I could think of to let you know how serious I am about reaching my potential in the NFL. My coaches have told you that nobody on our Florida team worked harder than me in terms of work-outs, practices or games. You have your own evaluation as to the type of impact I can have on your offense. The only X-factor, according to the reports I have heard, is concerns about my use of recreational drugs. To address that concern, I am literally putting my money where my mouth is and taking the financial risk away from the team and putting it directly on my back where it belongs.

In closing, I ask you to trust me when I say you have absolutely nothing to worry about when it comes to me and the use of recre-ational drugs. I have set very high goals for myself in the NFL and am focused 100% on achieving those goals. So, test me all you want during my rookie year...all of the results will be negative while I am having an overwhelmingly positive impact on the field.

Good luck with your preparations for the NFL Draft and feel free to contact me or my agency (Athletes First/David Dunn) with any questions.

Sincerely,

Aaron Hernandez
University of Florida

Strange as it was, the Patriots were willing to consider this letter because Aaron was no ordinary player. Yet they knew that the letter was only an attempt to pre-emptively mitigate the remarkable dangers and risks he would bring if he became a Patriot. Aaron had the kind of baggage that could terrify both a team's coaching staff and its public relations team.

Dereck Faulkner explains why the letter was necessary.

From his vantage point, it was the whole "Hernandez package"—not just the issue of marijuana use—that the letter was intended to address.

> In terms of the system—the draft system and what can make or break your draft stock. Yes, if you have off-the-field issues, marijuana issues, drug test issues, criminal history, anything that can kind of affect those things, yes, it will definitely drop your draft stock immediately. You'll become what they call a "high risk" for the organization. So a guy that's in the first round, it's a first-round pick that they're invest-ing—when I say they, the organization, the team—they're investing millions of dollars, you're not a high risk.
>
> For a guy that may have dropped to the fourth, fifth round like Aaron, he was considered a high risk. It's two different levels in regards to the draft: You either have your talent being evaluated or your off-the-field issues. And that also plays in the sense of what can obviously raise or drop your stock. For Aaron, he was a very, very high grade in regard to his talent. Talent was the first round. He was a great player. He was dominant. He was an All-American at Florida.
>
> As an All-American in college with a national championship team, he was pretty much slated to be a first-round pick. But with his off-the-field issues, I think that's ultimately what was his demise.

Writing a letter like this—laying it all on the line—meant taking a huge gamble. The only question was, would it pay off? Would the letter work? And on the day of the NFL draft, an answer emerged . . . sort of.

Yes, the letter *sort of* worked.

Aaron was indeed drafted by the New England Patriots, but not until the fourth round, and not until the final day of the draft. (He had had to sit and watch as seven of his teammates were drafted before him; three were taken in the first round.) He was the 113th overall pick of the draft. His signing bonus was a comparatively paltry $200,000. (Most fourth-round picks got a signing bonus of more than twice that. Yet, because of Aaron's behavior and self-admitted substance abuse problems, no one batted an eye at the Patriots' offering so little.)

Veteran New England sportscaster Joe Kayata is an expert on the Patriots organization. He suspects that, for the Patriots, it was a choice between drafting Aaron in the fourth round or not drafting him at all. This was because they saw the fourth round as a tactic for taming a nearly untamable maverick. With first-round leverage, the Patriots might not be able to present themselves as Aaron's best, last hope—which was what they wanted to do. Kayata explains how it works:

> They selected you. So they have the rights to you. They *could* trade. There's been situations like Eli Manning, and stuff like that, where he got selected by San Diego and he didn't want to play in San Diego, he wanted to play in New York. So, they worked out a deal and they traded him to the Giants. So, there's things that can happen, but the point is that you have a lot more negotiations and power when you're that number-one pick, or that first-round pick, compared to a fourth-round pick.
>
> And that's what the Patriots thrive on; they thrive on getting that maybe "diamond in the rough" or guys that maybe were former first-round draft picks, or who are really somewhere and struggling there, because of issues, and they bring them into their system.

As far as overall salary, Aaron would be earning about half a million dollars less than the top tight end rookies selected in that year's draft. In the eyes of many, this looked like a disappointment to Aaron. This was not how enterprising NFL careers were supposed to begin.

Dereck Faulkner, who had been there personally (and went undrafted), explains what it might have felt like for Aaron.

To be picked in the fourth round, I think it probably was a little bit of a shock to his ego. You know, you're immediately thinking, hey, the team looks at me as a fourth-round guy, not a first-round guy.

It's kind of like the pretty girl—the pretty girl syndrome. Like you're not the prettiest girl in the group anymore. So it most likely played a part. But he probably had to just get a grip and say, "Hey, I'm going. I've got a chance. I've got a chance to fulfill my dream and I've got a chance to ultimately help my family and make money."

So you look, and as an athlete, if I'm a guy and I know I'm big and strong and fast, but I'm still waiting to get picked, and five guys get picked in front of me and I'm looking around and I'm saying, "Hey, what about me?" And now your ego's going to be struck a little bit. You may have a little bit of a chip on your shoulder to say, "Why didn't I get picked first?" And ultimately, the biggest thing for an athlete that thinks about this is: "I just lost millions of dollars."

Though he might have "lost" millions of dollars compared to the tight ends picked ahead of him, privately, Aaron might have also felt like he had pulled it off.

Despite rampant drug use and out-of-control behavior, he was finally going to be living his NFL dream. It was happening, and it was real. Despite being too injured to even participate in the scouting combine, he had still been picked up by the most prominent franchise of them all. Moreover, he had done it as a kind of young prodigy; at 20, he was not only the youngest player on the Patriots. . . he was going to be the youngest player in the entire league.

Investigative reporter Michelle McPhee gives her take on this possible perspective, and the relief Aaron might have felt:

This guy finally has a chance to get out from under. He's gotten away with a shooting, allegedly. He's gotten away with an attack on a bouncer, allegedly. Who knows what's going on in his personal life. He still has a girlfriend and boyfriends at the time. And he gets picked up by the New England Patriots. He's a star! He's a mega-star! He's a good-looking kid. Girls love him! Everyone's happy! but this is not somebody who ever really fit in.

Aaron acted like a swaggering little boy every chance he got. He ran back to the street corner that he came from to hang around with the very lowlifes that he now had an opportunity to get away from. This is a guy who is not gonna get invited to Tom [Brady] and Giselle's [Bündchen] house for dinner. He was a guy who was very comfortable with jail life. Fit right in there. He was very comfortable with the gangbangers.

Even so, at this point he's to the NFL. He's in.

Whatever Aaron was feeling inside his own head, it was true that he finally had a foot in the door and the chance to prove what he could do.

But what *could* he do?

Nobody seemed to know. Some sportswriters at the time thought the Patriots had drafted a crude street thug whose many receptions on the field should have been credited to the exemplary QB throwing him the ball—Tim Tebow—and not Aaron himself. Many observers expected Aaron to sputter and fade. To accomplish little and be cut after a single season.

On the other hand, there were also well-credentialed, experienced football observers who thought the Patriots had made the best selection in the entire draft. This group saw the raw talent that Aaron possessed.

Kayata was one of many sports reporters looking carefully at the new tight end and wondering if the magic that had worked for the Patriots before—signing troubled players and developing them into stars—would work again in this case. It was also clear to Kayata that something was "up" with Aaron. The question was: *Would the Patriots be able to "fix" it?*

As Kayata, an award-winning sports anchor and reporter at NBC 10 in Boston, explains:

Aaron Hernandez was picked in the fourth round but, going into it, his talent level, he was a first- or second-round talent. Like this guy had it all. He just came off of a national championship at Florida. He was probably the top tight end in the country and, with all those tools and everything that he had, he was supposed to be the next big thing. He just had everything, but obviously he had off-the-field issues. He had character issues, and he had failed marijuana tests. So, that was a major red flag for any front office that wants to draft the guy. So he slipped and he slipped a ton, and Patriots are usually good at guys that slip because they can turn a diamond in the rough, or something like that, into the guy that they want.

Bill Belichick was a type of guy that would take on those guys, and you go all the way back. A lot of the guys had issues. Like a Corey Dillon, a Chad Ochocinco, most recently Josh Gordon who was out of football the last whatever years because of drug addiction, and he was basically banned from football for a number of years. And Bill is the type of guy that will take a chance on these guys because he believes in them and he believes that he can get them on the straight and narrow.

The Patriots, for their part, clearly knew that—like everybody else—they were going to have to wait and see just what they'd bought. Observers like Kayata understood that the Patriots were going to have hands full. Yet many were still optimistic.

Kayata adds:

> [Hernandez] was a guy that came in with, like, kind of a lot of baggage, but a lot of guys that come to the Patriots have a lot of baggage. There's a motto around here called "The Patriots Way" because people follow the Patriots' way of doing things. You have a lot of guys that come in with off-the field-issues—drug addiction, all types of issues. And they come in and somehow Bill Belichick and "The Patriots Way" is able to fix these guys and get them on the straight and narrow.

The selection of Aaron involved a quite literal handoff. He was being handed off from Florida coach Urban Meyer to famed Patriots coach Bill Belichick. Like Meyer, Belichick was one of the most accomplished and notorious coaches in football; his methods were controversial and often involved legal grey areas. But also like Meyer, Belichick got results—and delivered all that mattered. He won championships.

If Aaron had not attended a college program with such strict parameters—and ruled with such a strong hand—the naysayers might have been right about his chances in the NFL. He might never have been drafted at all. Pro teams looking at him might have decided there was too much risk of him immediately devolving into a drug-using street thug whose bad behavior would make him useless to the team.

But Meyer had proved it was possible—though obviously very difficult—to harness the raw muscular insanity of Aaron and use it to win football games. (And, also, to mitigate and cloak his actions off the field.)

Yet Meyer's experience with Aaron also showed that this might only be temporary. He was just too uncontrollable to handle for very long. Too wild. However you tried to rein him in, he would eventually burst out and become a problem.

In this way, the transfer of Aaron from Meyer to Belichick might have been less like a QB handing off a football and more like someone passing a hot potato (that was getting hotter by the moment and now threatened to become radioactive).

If anybody in the NFL was up for the task of harnessing Aaron's raw power at the professional level, it was Belichick.

As Dereck Faulkner opines:

> The New England Patriots [organization] was probably the best fit for Aaron because they're such a structured organization, and they're such a no-nonsense, football 24/7 type of pace. And for him, it's either you're going to abide and buy into our way of doing things, the New England Patriot way, or you'll be gone. And what he figured out probably early on was, all right, let me buy into what's happening here, and let me buy in so, ultimately, I can develop my career.
>
> The New England Patriots expect you to be professional on and off

the field to represent the shield, to represent the organization in the most positive light. They expect you to work hard on and off the field and ultimately be a professional. So I think New England, despite his having some issues, [felt] that they could help mold him into being the professional they wanted him to be.

Coach Belichick was a man known to dare where others did not. During his years in the NFL—both before and after Aaron—he would be accused of everything from recruiting irregularities to secretly videotaping the practice sessions of opposing teams to deflating footballs before a game to give his quarterback an edge.

And, vitally, Belichick was a sort of a "Teflon Don" like the gangster John Gotti. Charges had a way of never sticking to him. And when he *was* found guilty of having broken a rule, he was always able to negotiate the punishment down to a figurative slap on the wrist.

Belichick knew how to do dirty things and get away with them. In this way, many believed he might be the best-suited of all for dealing with Aaron.

The other thing Belichick had going for him was the degree to which the Patriots' fortunes mirrored those of the Florida Gators. Aaron would not be showing up to play with just any team. He would be playing for a premier program that had been winning championships. Like Florida, New England had the most (in)famous couch in the game (Belichick), and the dominant, golden-boy quarterback everybody loved to hate (Tom Brady). What's more, the fans did not need to be won over. There was no problem with ticket sales. The team's supporters were already drunk on the team's recent successes, and excited for more. This environment ought to have felt familiar.

In his early interactions with the Patriots, it was clear that the similarities were only going to take things so far. Aaron was still grumpy and standoffish. He did not get along well with his teammates. He took offense to small slights or gentle ribbings, interpreting them as signs of deep disrespect.

One reason for his gruffness—such as becoming obsessed with the street culture of "respect"—may have been because he was back home again, and falling back into his old ways.

But this was a crucial moment, a fork in the road for Aaron. The Patriots and head coach Bill Belichick's famed "Patriots Way" could give him stability and structure—and a chance to turn his life around. Maybe his last chance.

The physical move back to New England from Florida may have been one of the reasons why Aaron was never able to shed his tragic past. When most NFL players who grow up in rough circumstances hit the big time, they leave those circumstances when they move to a new town to play for a team. (They might come home to visit now and again, but for most of the year they are away and immersed in a new world. The connections to their younger days fade more and more with each passing year.)

Yet Aaron was in that small minority of players who found themselves playing in their home city. He had not been off at college long enough to sever the ties he had formed in Connecticut. Playing for the Patriots felt like coming home, and now he was poised to strengthen those ties with his home field, Gillette Stadium, the home of the Patriots, not a long drive from the community where Aaron grew up. It was practically in the same metro area.

Almost immediately after moving back, he began hanging out with a rough crew of felons, even putting some on his payroll. Chief among them was a local thug named Alexander Bradley whom Aaron hired to act as a sort of criminal fixer. Bradley could provide Aaron with an unending stream of guns and drugs. He was connected, and had the rap sheet to prove it. He had been arrested for dealing marijuana and cocaine, and also for physical violence. Because of Aaron's need to consume marijuana at a superhuman rate, the presence of someone like Bradley in his life was practically a necessity.

Bradley and Aaron found they had similar tastes, and the line between their professional and personal relationship was always blurry. They trusted one another. Bradley was known to often advance Aaron's large amounts of drugs on credit. (Aaron smoked a staggering four ounces a day, and would often need to buy more without having cash handy.) Aaron and Bradley spent many hours together playing video games and going to casinos. (As Bradley would later tell a jury, they were "best friends" by the start of 2012.)

Forging this connection with Bradley was one of the first big signs that Aaron was not going to use his NFL wealth and prestige to cut ties with his criminal connections, but rather augment them.

Yet it was not all weed and PlayStation for the rookie tight end. He took his work on the field seriously, learned the Patriots playbook almost immediately, and showed prowess on the field from day one. Despite his secret off-field immersion back into the criminal underworld, Aaron had a great first year in the NFL—especially considering his age. (In fact, Aaron led all rookie tight ends in yards for the season, despite only starting seven games.) It appeared that drafting him had been a shrewd move. Patriot fans were elated that Belichick had gambled on the wet-behind-the-ears college junior with the troubled history.

It is almost impossible to talk further about Aaron's performance on the field in 2011 without invoking Rob Gronkowski—or "Gronk" as he is known—in the same breath. Gronkowski was the Patriots' other starting tight end and, together, the two formed a powerful combination, catching passes and blocking like a pair of monsters.

Individually, they were arguably the best two tight ends playing in the NFL.

When they were combined, there was reason to believe they might be the best pair of tight ends in league history.

During his second year, the duo set new league records for touchdowns and receiving yards by any pair of tight ends ever. Though less quantifiable, when they acted as blockers, they absolutely terrorized opposing defensive linemen.

Aaron and Gronk became a famous pair. However, though they were always mentioned in connection to one another, they were not identical. Gronkowski was larger and more physical, weighing 20 pounds more than Aaron. Though he moved more slowly than Aaron, he could block even more effectively. Aaron might have been the literal gang banger in his personal life, but during games it was Gronkowski who struck fear into the hearts of those tasked with tackling or containing him.

Because Gronk created such a large, physical presence on the field, it often caused opposing defenses to focus on Aaron as a secondary concern. They did this at their own peril, because Aaron brought talents of his own. In addition to being smaller than Gronk, he was quicker—more deft and flexible. Where you could count on Gronk to try and run right through you, Aaron could juke you out of your shoes.

Sportscaster Joe Kayata puts it like this:

> [Hernandez] wasn't the biggest guy, but he was just so quick, so dynamic, and when you combined him with a guy like Rob Gronkowski they were a match made in heaven because they turned out to be the best tight end combo, I think, the NFL has ever seen. And they transformed the game because you had these two tight ends and Bill Belichick used it perfectly. And no other team has every used a two tight end set the way they did. And they kind of revolutionized football. And you had one guy that was Gronk, the big, tough, strong, blocking tight end. And then you had this guy Aaron Hernandez who was more like a wide receiver in a tight end position that was quick, fast, strong, and could catch.
>
> And initially people thought it was weird when they drafted two tight ends because what do you need two tight ends for? And then you see one type of tight end, and one's the other type. And then they kind of came together to form this unbelievable duo that the NFL had never seen.
>
> And both of them succeeded right away. It's like they were breaking records for tight end combos in that first season. I think Aaron had like five touchdowns his rookie year, and he was like this quick, fast dude. And he was just unbelievable on the field. Everybody saw star potential in both of them. Gronk is a future Hall of Famer. It's like when you think about it, it's like, wow!

Kayata's enthusiasm for the pair was typical.

Aaron's first NFL season culminated with he and Gronk making it to divisional round, where they lost to the New York Jets. In their second season, however, the pair took a trek to Super Bowl XLVI, where Aaron caught eight passes for 67 yards and made a 12-yard touchdown reception. Though the Patriots would lose, 21–17, to the New York Giants in a heartbreaker, the game turned out to be a great opportunity for Aaron to show off his powers on the biggest stage in the world. He had an epic game, leading the team in receiving yards while scoring one of their two touchdowns.

Fans who enjoyed the Coke-or-Pepsi debate over whether Gronkowski or Aaron was the superior tight end left the season with Aaron's Super Bowl performance etched into their retinas.

It seems that the Patriots liked what they saw as well. For it was not soon after Super Bowl XLVI when Aaron was rewarded with a seven-year contract worth $41 million, which included the largest signing bonus—$12.5 million—ever awarded to a tight end in the history of pro football.

The courtship was now over, and the Pats were ready to get walk down the aisle and get married. They were in it for the long haul. Whatever foibles Aaron brought to the table, this offer showed the organization had decided they could live with them.

During that second year in the NFL, Aaron's off-the-field behavior had been, mostly, contained. Only one police incident occurred during that season.

Aaron and a friend, Brandon Beam, had been pulled over late at night for driving erratically and going an astounding 65 mph *over* the posted speed limit. The vehicle belonged to Aaron, but Beam was driving. Though the pair had been drinking, the police officer on the scene let them go with just a ticket.

But that wasn't the end of it. When the pair arrived back at Aaron's house at around 3:30 in the morning, they started a screaming match and fistfight in the driveway so intense that multiple neighbors called 911. (Apparently, Aaron was furious with his friend for having put him in a situation where he was vulnerable to law enforcement. The pair could have both been arrested on the spot, and Aaron's SUV could have been taken. And if the police *had* found a pretext to give Aaron a drug test, who knows what would have happened.) Yet with the arrival of police on the scene, Aaron's anger seemed to fade and the fight ended.

In another incident, Aaron's brother Jonathan visited his brother in the seaside town and found him sitting alone on the roof of the townhouse holding a gun.

"I was like, oh my gosh, you know what's going on but there's so many things about that moment that are just so dark and sad," he has recalled.

"He still takes me in that moment from the expression and look on his face, I don't know how to explain it." Aaron was rubbing the gun on his chin.

Though they were certainly made aware of the situation, the Patriots couldn't have been too concerned about a driveway scuffle. A pair of young friends having a disagreement with fists was—through the lens of the NFL—certainly a forgivable sin.

This might have been the only event involving Aaron with the potential to make headlines in the sports pages, but it was not the only factor the Patriots had been wrestling with before making their big offer.

Coaches from high school through the NFL will tell you that there's more to winning than securing talented players and calling clever plays. (In short, there's a reason why champions in video game football don't go on to coaching *real* football.) Actual coaches have to manage numerous variables that are no less crucial when it comes to winning games. Players have to stay motivated. They have to believe in themselves. Their group needs to have an *esprit de corps*. Each player needs to feel valued and acknowledged. And personal conflicts between players need to be settled for the good of the team.

Though Aaron's performance on the field remained superlative—he and Gronk were setting all-time records, and had nearly won a Super Bowl—he still did not tick the right boxes when it came to his impact on the rest of the team.

Externally, Aaron seemed to have a good-natured rivalry with Gronkowski, but the two were not friends off the field—at all. They did not hang out or see one another at gatherings that were not mandatory. Aaron rarely said nice things about Gronkowski in interviews, and vice-versa.

When it came to the rest of the team, Aaron kept his distance with them too. It was very rare for him to befriend, or even to acknowledge other players on the Patriots. At the start of his rookie season, some of his teammates had thought he might simply be shy or slow to make friends. Now they knew he constantly radiated an impersonal coldness.

On the other side of the coin, Aaron was undeniably a hard worker. He usually took drills seriously—never leaving practices early and often staying late. (There are isolated accounts of Aaron not taking a particular practice seriously, and annoying star quarterback Tom Brady in the process, but they were few and far between.) Usually, Aaron maintained a strict focus, but it was always on himself. Always inwardly directed. Always on what *he* was going to be able to accomplish the following Sunday.

All this, the Patriots had *also* seen in Aaron's early years. Yet they were still willing to move forward with the marriage. To make a deal. To connect themselves—for better or worse—to this record-setting tight end for the next seven years.

It was a decision they were going to regret ... and much sooner than anyone expected.

CHAPTER 6

Aaron: "The thing that used to get me mad and not want to be around you was you make assumptions about me. You truly don't even know me. You truly don't know me."
Mom: "How can I know you when you never let me in?"
Aaron: "You don't know me, you barely knew me when I was a kid, like we weren't close for seven years. We talked maybe ten times a year, mom."

—AARON HERNANDEZ, JAILHOUSE RECORDING

After his $40 million contract was signed, Aaron Hernandez seemed to grow more confident. To change. To become a new man—at least in certain ways.

But as a theme that emerged throughout his career, this meant not progression, but regression. Where other pro athletes might have used a financial windfall to remake themselves as a legitimate member of society, Aaron wanted only to go back to the life of lawlessness and crudity that seemed to be his default setting.

In fact, he used this new money to buy a house in Plainville, Massachusetts. It was about 115 miles from Bristol, but you could take the highway the entire way.

Even the emergence of a regular, steady girlfriend—Shayanna Jenkins, whom he had first met in high school, who soon became pregnant with Aaron's child (a daughter they'd name Avielle)—did not motivate Aaron to find the straight and narrow path. Though they moved in together and eventually became engaged, Aaron did not treat Shayanna with the respect most fiancées would expect to enjoy. He repeatedly cheated on her and spent most nights away, hanging out with his friends instead of her and never explaining his mysterious whereabouts.

After signing his multimillion-dollar contract, Aaron's teammates noticed a change in his temperament, too. As the *Boston Globe* and other news outlets have reported, Aaron became increasingly mercurial and unpredictable around teammates. He could be aggressively masculine and bullying one moment, then surprisingly vulnerable the next. His teammates never knew which Aaron they were going to get. Some days he would be looking for a fight or an argument, while there were days he might want to have a deep personal conversation about his relationship with his mother.

There were also actions toward his teammates during this period that some believe may have had gay or bisexual overtones. For example, in the *Globe* interviews with his former teammates, Patriots players recall Aaron occasionally pulling out his penis and bringing up gay sex, or talking with a stereotypically "gay" lilt to his voice as a joke. It's clear from their own words that the other players didn't know how to interpret this. Was it a strange version of razzing and horseplay, or was Aaron making a veiled pass at them? Or was it something else entirely? (Some observers have suggested that Aaron may have been trying to "muddy the water" when it came to his own sexuality. He would conceal his secret life by acting like a gay stereotype, or blurring the line between what was sexual and what was locker room horseplay.)

However it was interpreted, this behavior was so disconcerting that Patriots players took to warning one another, so they wouldn't be shocked when it happened in front of them.

This detail is important because it shows the growing importance of Aaron within the organization. They would warn another about him *as opposed to* asking him to change his behavior. This was because Aaron now ranked with Gronk and Brady among the team's elite.

Aaron could be himself, and he knew it. Unfortunately for the less-accomplished Patriot players, this meant they had to deal with a man who often made them uncomfortable and confused.

Brandon Lloyd, former Patriots player and teammate of Aaron's, said Wes Welker once warned him of Aaron's "disturbing" sexual behavior in the locker room before they met.

He said in an interview. "I just want to warn you that he's going to talk about being bathed by his mother, he's going to have his genitalia out in front of you while you're sitting on your stool. He's gonna to have his towel and try to dry off in front of you while you're sitting at your locker. He's going to talk about gay sex. Just do your best to ignore it."

Lloyd added Aaron took normal locker room banter too far.

> We played grab ass, flipping towels, all the cheesy stuff that lands in movies. But the things that he was talking about was more graphic than us slapping each other on the ass laughing and giggling like what normally happens in a male locker room.

Lloyd also recalled how Aaron had mood swings where he would be "the most hyper-masculine aggressive individual in the room where he'd be ready to fight somebody in fits of rage, or he'd be the most sensitive person in the room talking about cuddling with his mother."

But he had never been big on hanging out off the field with teammates, but now, when he did show up, he was even stranger than he'd been before. The friends he brought along made the other Patriots feel uncomfortable. Pretty soon, they started leaving him off of the guest lists for events entirely.

And that was just fine with Aaron.

Increasingly, he no longer wanted to spend time with other Patriots or Boston sports celebrities. He even seemed to lose interest in his fiancée. During this period, night after night, Aaron went out only with his crew of criminal friends— Bradley chief among them.

That spring of 2012, Aaron lived as though his life were one never-ending bachelor party. He went to dance clubs and strip clubs, he spent money extravagantly, he drank and used drugs (and frequently drove his car while under their influence), he had secret sex liaisons with both men and women, and he surrounded himself with thugs, drug dealers—and even killers.

It was this last thing that set him apart from many of his teammates.

After all, Aaron was not the only NFL player who liked to party and get wild. But something in this new crew changed things. The vibe they gave off felt wrong to others whenever they came into contact with him and his crew.

NFL players are big and tough, and are used to being around other men who are big and tough. But these men around Aaron were big and tough and *actual killers*, and the other Patriots players seemed to be able to sense that a mile away.

This period might be the best example we have of how Aaron hoped to spend the rest of his days: A day job that generated a ton of money, and evenings filled with every vice imaginable. (And in the offseason, the requirements of the day job were quite limited.) Moreover, he was not having to expend a particularly large amount of effort to keep his second life secret—it seemed that nobody wanted to know.

Shayanna understood that her fiancée sometimes slept with other people, but as subsequent interviews with her have revealed, her attitude was as follows: "Just don't tell me about it. I don't want to know."

The Patriots organization never pressed him about what he did with his spare time (and any drug testing they *were* doing on Aaron seemed to never catch anything). As far as they were concerned, it was all good.

Likewise, his sponsors had no compunction about paying him to endorse products, despite his extravagant lifestyle.

And his teammates? They had removed themselves from his circle almost completely. He never saw them outside of "work."

Did this make Aaron sloppy? Did he conclude that he had become a master of living a double life?

It's possible. As the spring of 2012 drifted into early summer, Aaron must have felt as though he was unstoppable. Like he could truly do whatever he wanted.

Yet a change was coming that would begin to unravel everything that made this new lifestyle possible.

And it was only a few weeks away.

CHAPTER 7

"If I'm mad, I'm like everybody else. I'm like every other person that has turned their back on me."

—AARON HERNANDEZ, JAILHOUSE RECORDING

Any hopes Aaron Hernandez had of being able to keep his lifestyle under control were shattered in July of 2012—a shocking incident that is still being investigated and explored by authorities. It would change the life of the star tight end forever, threaten his beloved secret life, and—according to many—would signal the start of the machinations that would lead to his eventual downfall.

During this period, Aaron had fully fallen off the wagon—if he was ever truly on it in the first place. His life was about partying, drinking, using drugs, and—above all—feeling invincible because of his status as a star football player.

July 15 was a hot Sunday night, and Aaron was a powder keg looking to go off. He and Bradley had spent most of that day smoking weed together at Bradley's house, and had eventually found themselves at a nightclub called the Cure Lounge.

Aaron was strapped—carrying a .357 Magnum that Bradley had procured for him. However, near as the experts examining this case can tell, Aaron had not gone out that evening with the intention of causing violence to anyone in particular. But, as always, he remained ready to dish it out of he felt the occasion called for it.

And soon, by his reckoning, it did.

The pair had driven to Cure in Aaron's SUV. When they arrived at the nightclub, the bouncer crew insisted Aaron remove his baseball cap before entering. This reportedly put him in a sour mood, but he complied.

After midnight—with the nightclub still busy and loud—Aaron was accidentally bumped by a man named Daniel de Abreu.

De Abreu was a 29-year-old immigrant from Cape Verde, a small island nation off the coast of Africa. He was at Cure that night with four other Cape Verdean friends. He had recently relocated to the area, and had been in the United States for less than a year. He did not know many people in the community, and probably knew no one other than his immediate group of friends at Cure. (He was in America temporarily, hoping to earn some money—though so far he had found only low-paying custodial jobs.)

There's no evidence that Aaron knew or had ever seen him before that night. Nonetheless, the two men bumped, a drink was spilled, and Aaron became enraged.

According to witnesses, Aaron angrily confronted de Abreu. The Cape Verdean did not respond in kind, and seemed to want to de-escalate the situation. However, it was also clear that de Abreu did not recognize Aaron as an NFL superstar. This reportedly enraged the New England star further. Only the intercession of Bradley—who jumped between the two men—prevented Aaron from making it physical.

Moments later, Bradley convinced Aaron to step outside. They left Cure, walked down the street, and entered a different nightclub called Caprice.

De Abreu and his friends stayed inside Cure.

Both groups would remain in their respective nightclubs until the end of the night. Closing time, as both Cure and Caprice closed at 2:00 a.m. sharp.

Back out on the street, Aaron and Bradley took a stroll and smoked more marijuana. Several witnesses later reported seeing them. They probably looked like many other young men who were milling around nearby, hoping to meet women who were also exiting the clubs.

Then—at approximately 2:10 in the morning—they got back into Aaron's SUV.

A few minutes after that, Aaron and Bradley pulled up next to a car containing de Abreu and his friends; most of the men were on their phones and not paying close attention to their surroundings. But what happened next would shock onlookers.

Witnesses in nearby cars say they heard raised voices, that a racial slur was shouted, and that shots began to ring out. When it was all over, de Abreu and one of his friends, Safiro Furtado, were dead.

Five shots were fired at point-blank range—the slain men never stood a chance.

The other men jumped from the car and ran for help. Furtado had died instantaneously. De Abreu, according to witnesses, lived for up to two minutes after the shooting. He tried to speak but was not understood by those first on the scene.

His last moments were likely agony.

According to Bradley, after the shooting, he and Aaron drove to the home of a girlfriend of Bradley's. Once there, they tried to calm their nerves and looked online for any news about the shooting. Much to their relief, they found few specifics and nothing that appeared to link them to the crime.

Aaron often went to clubs like Cure, and his being in the general vicinity of the shooting would not, by itself, be suspicious. Several witnesses were questioned by police in the days that followed. None of those witnesses identified Aaron Hernandez of the New England Patriots. (Their descriptions of the shooter were, instead, incredibly vague. Most of them could have been describing Aaron, or a hundred other young men out on the streets that night.)

In the weeks that followed, police eventually revealed that they did not have any leads or suspects.

Nobody was arrested for the crime.

Now, however, we can see a pattern emerging. The manager of the bar in Gainesville, punched so hard his eardrum is ruptured, for daring to ask Aaron to pay his tab. No action is taken. In September that same year, Corey Smith is shot in the head, supposedly for disrespecting Aaron or his buddies. Aaron is identified by a witness but, again, the charges disappear. And now, a couple of guys who are said to have spilled a drink on Aaron in a club in Boston wind up dead. Aaron's car is seen at the scene, and police reportedly identify him on security camera footage.

And guess what?

Nothing happens.

Even though Aaron and Bradley seemed to have escaped the dragnet, a bad feeling settled over the rest of their summer. That fall, it got worse.

Aaron began his third season in the NFL, but his play was middling at best. He was plagued by injuries, and often sat on the sidelines. Fans and analysts alike began to doubt whether he really was a $40 million man. Perhaps the Patriots had bought a lemon.

As sportscaster Joe Kayata puts it:

> That year he didn't play a ton of games; he was out a lot with an ankle sprain. He had an ankle injury all that year. When he was on the field, he was pretty good for someone who was dealing with the ankle injury. Still, he played in the AFC Championship Game against the Ravens— played well in that game. Didn't have a touchdown, but he was pretty good.

Off the field, Aaron tried to continue living a double life.

In public situations, he remained gracious and kind, and projected a warm personality. He famously donated $50,000 to a charity run by the family of Patriots owner Robert Kraft. Whenever Aaron was interviewed and the topic of his generous donation was raised, he expertly projected an "aww shucks" modesty. He said his $40 million contract still felt surreal, and that he was determined to use that money for good in the world.

He also—to all outward appearances—took another step in becoming a family man. He became formally engaged to his girlfriend Shayanna, and she gave birth to his daughter: Avielle Janelle Hernandez.

Yet acts of charity, family, and modesty were the only things ingratiating Aaron to the fans that seasons. With a couple of exceptions, his play remained a frustrating disappointment.

In hindsight, for observers like Joe Kayata, the season was doubly disappointing because so many fans and observers had hoped that the good fortune he'd experienced would allow Aaron to turn his life around.

Says Kayata:

He was getting his life back on track—that's what everybody thought. Because I think everybody knew of his issues and stuff. As a fan, you're like, all right, this is a good moment for this guy. He's getting paid. You can kind of look at your life and say this is the defining moment where I'm going this way. I'm going the right way. I'm going to live a good life. And why wouldn't you, because you have everything in front of you. But of course, that's not what happened.

Personally, that's what I struggle with the most with this story. I know how hard you have to work to get to this level. The sports business is incredibly competitive and it's tough to even get to the pro level. So that's why I'm always surprised when you see the mighty fall. I'm like, wow, I just don't even understand how you could have that kind of a contract, $40 million, seven years. And that's not enough to keep you on the straight and narrow?

It's like sometimes when you hear these stories, and they're like, well, why would somebody do that? They have everything. They have the life. They have the fiancée. They have the baby. They have the contract. They're a New England Patriot, you know. Why would you let it all slip away? But sometimes, something else is going on.

In fact, Aaron had *several things* going on in his life that served to undermine his many successes. One of the biggest was the gradual souring of his relationship with Bradley. Since the night of the shooting in July of 2012, things between the two men had grown strained—this might have been a natural reaction to the stress involved in concealing their roles in a murder. Furthermore, now each man had something on the other. Each man could, theoretically, turn the other in. Each man had something to lose. . . but of course, Aaron had infinitely more.

Even so, they still hung out, went to clubs, and played video games—and Bradley was still Aaron's main dealer and source of drugs and guns—but the tone between the two men had changed, and not for the better.

Then, one morning in early 2013, Aaron and Bradley found themselves headed home together after a raucous night at the same club—Cure Lounge—they had visited on the night of the shooting. It was well after midnight, and Bradley was driving Aaron's SUV. They passed a police officer while Bradley was speeding and driving erratically, and were pulled over.

This was precisely the kind of situation that Aaron had always been able to navigate without any real consequences. (Though there's equally little doubt he was furious at his friend for speeding.)

But when the police officer stepped up to the car and asked for a license and registration, the magic that had always worked in the past suddenly failed . . . and the consequences came hard and fast.

Bradley was found to be driving while intoxicated and was arrested on the spot. Aaron, as the passenger, escaped a criminal charge, but suffered a fate that was at least as shameful and embarrassing. This was because the police report—which was soon splashed all over the news—contained details of how Aaron had tried to use his status as a star on the Patriots to convince the police officer to let them go.

It was a dark time for Aaron. Not only were Pats fans expressing doubts about the wisdom of signing him to a $40 million deal, but now they turned up their noses at the tight end's arrogant attitude and belief that he was above the law.

Psychologists tell us that people with psychopathic personalities are often unable to blame themselves for their own poor judgment. They just can't do it. And so it was with Aaron. Unable to blame himself, he looked around for another source of his misfortune—and the only suspect he could see was his friend and fixer, Alexander Bradley.

CHAPTER 8

"Bill Belichick is the number one person that teaches teams. Don't listen to the media because most of the time they make up stories and they're rarely true. I wish he practiced what he preached. Especially coming to me, throwing me in the, in the, in the dust in the wind."

—AARON HERNANDEZ, JAILHOUSE RECORDING

There's a saying about keeping your friends close and your enemies closer. But what was Alexander Bradley to Aaron Hernandez at this point? Enemy, or friend?

Logically, there must have been a time when he stopped being one and became the other. We cannot know precisely what Aaron was thinking at each moment, but it seems clear that in February of 2013, a change occurred. This change coincided with a trip. Aaron and Bradley had flown together down to Belle Glade, Florida, to visit Aaron's friends from his Gator days—chief among them Deonte Thompson, who would go on to have a solid career in the NFL, playing for several teams including the Baltimore Ravens and New York Jets.

Maybe the changeover happened on the plane.

As Aaron and his erstwhile friend left the airport and drove to their destination, Bradley's fate may have already been sealed.

Belle Glade was a short drive west from Palm Beach, but a world away in terms of what could be found there. Belle Glade was known as a rough and struggling community. With an official population of around 17,000, it had from time to time ranked near the top in the country for any small city when it came to rates of HIV infection and number of violent crimes. It had a reputation as a bleak and bare sugar cane town, where people were desperate and might do almost anything for a dollar.

In short, it was the kind of place where Aaron felt right at home.

Once the visitors from New England arrived, Aaron, Bradley, and Thompson began a raucous week of partying, using Belle Glade as their home base but traveling throughout the area. They drove to surrounding cities, drinking and going to strip clubs. Though they should have been having fun, as the week wore on, Aaron looked distracted and became increasingly paranoid. He mentioned to members of Thompson's crew that he believed they were being followed by law enforcement. (Though Aaron was certainly anxious and paranoid, he may still have been correct. Having Aaron shadowed after the murder of de Abreu might have well been within the purview of law enforcement at this juncture.)

As the days of partying stretched on, the group found themselves at a Miami-area strip club called Tootsie's Cabaret. It was one of the largest and most opulent places of its type in the entire United States. At more than 60,000 square feet, it was less a strip club and more like a Vegas casino—billing itself as an "adult mega club."

On their first night at the club, Aaron and this crew partied in the VIP room and racked up five figures worth of charges as remarkable as that might seem. Though the group had fun, the night was not without tension. Aaron still seemed paranoid, and repeatedly voiced concerns that a pair of men in the club were actually undercover police officers shadowing him.

The next night, the crew returned to Tootsie's. That was when things really began to spin out of control.

On that second night, the group partied hard and consumed many drinks. Aaron remained aloof and paranoid, but his paranoia morphed into anger as the night wore on. He began arguing, loudly, with Bradley. (The subject of their argument has not been shared by witnesses, so we can only conjecture. However, by this point, the relationship between the two men had degenerated to such a degree that they might truly have been fighting over nothing.) Aaron got so heated that he left without paying his bar tab. Bradley immediately followed after Aaron. Still fighting, the two men got into a car and Aaron drove off in a fit of rage.

What happened next was shocking and would change everything else in Aaron's life—forever.

Just a few minutes after leaving the strip club, Bradley lay in a nearby parking lot, shot in the face.

There were no external witnesses to what occurred, but the evidence strongly points to one—and only one—scenario.

Bradley and Aaron quarreled in the car. Aaron pulled over, and they continued to fight. Then Aaron took out a gun and shot Bradley in the face, leaving him for dead.

That was the best guess. But to this day, no one knew what *really* had happened.

Except for Bradley... who was not quite dead.

Although he would lose an eye and require extensive surgery, Bradley's wounds were not fatal. Aaron's bullet had passed through parts of his skull and face, but missed his brain.

Bradley was found by a local truck driver who saw what he thought was a dead body lying next to a chain link fence. The truck driver pulled over to take a closer look.

It turned out that Bradley was not only still alive, but coherent enough to ask the truck driver to call 911 once he was roused, which the driver did. As they waited for emergency services to arrive, the driver tried to apply pressure to the gaping wound in the front of Bradley's face. A few minutes later, the police and paramedics showed up.

As they tended to his wounds, the police asked Bradley what had happened and who had shot him. Though he had been grievously injured and his survival was far from assured, he still began to obfuscate and lie. He told some of the responding officers that a group of African American men he did not know had shot him. When speaking to different officers, he simply said he could not remember, or that it hurt too much to talk.

The truck driver who found Bradley was also questioned by the police. He said he remembered seeing an SUV in the area, but not much else.

He certainly did not describe anybody matching Aaron.

Miles away by that point, Aaron was—of course—still paranoid. As it turned out, he had good reason to be.

As the rest of that day unfolded, Aaron made hasty plans to leave Miami. He also wondered if Bradley was dead. We know this because when Aaron arrived at Miami International Airport, he called the mother of Bradley's child and asked if she had heard from him. She had not.

Meanwhile, Bradley was undergoing emergency surgery. His right eye was destroyed, but his other eye would be fine. More importantly, the bullet had gone through his face but missed everything else significant. He would not be in mortal peril, and his functions would remain more or less intact. Once out of surgery, he was able to speak just fine. Yet this did not mean he would cooperate with the police officers who now sought to solve this crime.

As he recovered from surgery, Bradley backed off of his crime-scene claim that it had been a group of African American men. Now he simply said that he was not able to say who had shot him. It would be dangerous for him, he said. He just couldn't do it.

But as soon as he had recovered enough to use a phone, Bradley immediately began calling and texting Aaron.

After what must have been a remarkable surprise for Aaron—messages seemingly from beyond the grave—an epic barrage of voicemails and texts ensued.

Who can imagine how low Aaron's heart must have sunk when he received that first text from Bradley? He probably thought he had gotten away with it; "solved" his problem. But now, less than a day after the shooting, Bradley was not only alive but well enough to communicate.

The only relief for Aaron must have been that Bradley made it clear in the texts he had no plans to go to the police. But it was also clear that he was—understandably—furious.

Bradley told Aaron that this attack would not be forgotten. Just as Bradley had been physically scarred for life, so had Aaron's life. Everything would be different. Though there was no clear resolution to their text conversation, Bradley made it clear that he would never forget what had happened, and never forgive Aaron.

We do not know precisely how Aaron spent the next seven days back in New England, but it must have been a time of intense paranoia. A new Sword of

Damocles was hovering over his head. If Aaron scanned the news—which he probably did—he would have seen nothing about the police following leads in the shooting, but it was not the police who concerned him. It was Bradley's connections in the criminal underworld. Aaron had more than just Bradley to fear. A man who could seemingly conjure all manner of guns or drugs out of thin air—seemingly at will—should certainly have the juice to have someone like Aaron murdered.

At the end of what was probably the most nervous week of his life—so far—Aaron reported to the NFL combine in Indianapolis. There are rumors that at the combine, Aaron told Coach Belichick his life was in danger and that he needed to be traded. While Belichick and team owner Robert Kraft have declined either to confirm nor deny this, Aaron's agents confirmed that he *did* have trouble in his personal life during this time and was looking for a change of venue.

Whatever the situation (and whatever they were actually told), Belichick and Kraft decided not to pursue a trade. Even though his previous season had been a middling disappointment, they had made a great investment in him. It might pay off yet.

Belichick and Kraft did not provide Aaron with an answer right away. Perhaps seeking to call their bluff—and show that he was serious—Aaron had drinks with representatives from other teams in conspicuous places during the combine. He sat in prominent locations in local restaurants and bars, making these meetings hard for the Patriots to miss.

The combine ended with no firm decision from Belichick and Kraft. While the Patriots seemed to mull the situation over, Aaron reached out to his agent and was forthcoming about at least some of what had transpired during his Florida trip. The agent preemptively engaged a criminal defense lawyer (though as it turned out, the lawyer's services were never needed).

Aaron also recruited a new friend from the criminal underworld—Bo Wallace—to replace Bradley as his assistant and fixer. Wallace was paid $1,000 a week by Aaron, ostensibly for being his "driver." Yet, of course, Wallace was to have other important jobs: providing a constant stream of drugs and guns and protecting Aaron from Bradley should he ever resurface in an act of retribution.

A few weeks after the combine, a compromise seemed to be reached with the

Patriots. Belichick's and Kraft's heartstrings may have been pulled—not by the threat to Aaron, but his fiancée and daughter. The compromise was that Aaron would not be traded but would go to California for the bulk of the offseason. This was where Tom Brady often spent a good part of his summers. Just as the coaching team at Florida had hoped that keeping Aaron around Tim Tebow might have a positive effect, there may have been similar reasoning used here.

It is important to note that Belichick and Kraft did not alert any authorities to what Aaron had told them (or how much he told them). This is revealing. (Most of us, if someone we know says they're fearing for their life, we would go to the police right away.) As powerful, important members of the community, Belichick and Kraft would have received while-glove service from Boston's finest. (They also had the means to hire all manner of private security for Aaron, had they so desired.) But the fact remains that they did *not* go to the police.

This leaves open only a handful of possibilities:

- They did not believe Aaron was actually in danger.
- They did not care about Aaron and/or whether or not he was in danger.
- They knew that going to the police would reveal the criminal elements of Aaron's own past and present.

If Aaron had been a literal Boy Scout all his life—or someone with the reputation of a Tebow or a Brady—there might have been reason to suspect Aaron was unfamiliar with the criminal world and exaggerating the threat to his life. But Aaron was a fish who swam in these waters every day, and Belichick and Kraft could see it from a mile away. They knew he was telling the truth. When Aaron said he was being threatened, he was being threatened.

So, what if they didn't care about him? But who simply "wouldn't care" about a $40M investment? Even if you divorce all humanity from the scenario and look on with the cold calculation of someone who did not care whether a person lived or died, he was still a valuable asset to the team. There simply is no way that Kraft and Belichick would have allowed him to be harmed before he provided what they'd paid for.

That only leaves the final option. Belichick and Kraft knew that law enforcement asking questions about the people Aaron associated with was the *last* thing they needed. It would bring the wrong kind of attention, and God knew what kind of things would be uncovered.

This is, really, the only option that makes any sense. Belichick and Kraft might have told themselves that Aaron was a man mending his ways, but they weren't willing to risk kidding anyone other than themselves. Neither of them wanted to risk cops looking underneath the rock that was Aaron Hernandez. The things underneath it were just too horrible.

So Aaron made the move to California.

Despite the encouragement of Kraft and Belichick, he ended up spending very little time around Tom Brady, whose life with supermodel Gisele Bündchen seemed the complete opposite to his world. (Brady, for his part, is said to have never taken to Aaron. Former Patriot Brandon Lloyd has told how Brady once told Aaron to "F*** off" after he was laughing and acting inappropriate during a pre-game walk through.)

> Tom keeps a serious walk through. Tom says, "Shut the F up. Get the F out of here." In this particular walk through he's been calling Bill Belichick "Daddy."

He rented a house in Hermosa Beach, and moved in with his fiancée and baby daughter. Yet, though the scenery might have changed, Aaron remained alarmed, paranoid, and agitated.

As police records show, on the night of March 25, 2013, Shayanna called 911 and said that Aaron had slit his wrist and lost a lot of blood.

The police responded, and Aaron was not found to have serious injuries. Later, however, Shayanna hinted that Aaron had not injured his wrist intentionally, but that it had happened as a consequence of his punching through a window. Whatever the actual circumstances of the injury, a volatile Patriot was showing clear evidence of inner turmoil.

In subsequent days, the Hernandez household would be the subject of other

911 calls, but these came from neighbors. Several times, police arrived to find Aaron drunk, loud, and upset. They asked him to keep it down, but never concluded that he was a danger to his fiancée and child, or to himself. (Aaron kept guns and drugs in his residence in California, but they were never discovered by law enforcement.) Despite police visits, loud, violent fights became a regular thing. Aaron was a man stretched to his last nerve, and he may have been taking it out on the only person present—even though Shayanna was clearly not the cause of his problems. Rather, Shayanna was an innocent bystander caught up in proximity to the madness Aaron brought with him.

There is one clue to what may have kept Aaron so very agitated during this time. Though he had physically removed himself from the East Coast, he had kept the same cell phone, and records show that he was still receiving texts from Bradley about the shooting. These texts may well have been the triggers for his violent outbursts.

It was rare, but Aaron sometimes texted Bradley back. In their messaging, they guardedly allude to the shooting. The topic of money or other compensation is often raised. Does Aaron owe Bradley? Will Bradley try to extort Aaron? Can their differences ultimately be resolved? Sometimes, threats of violence seem to emerge. Yet surprisingly—at the same time they are having these heated, belligerent exchanges—the duo also used these texts to make vows of brotherly love for one another.

They pledged a kind of strange fealty and loyalty, and they seem to find no contradiction in it. They could threaten each other one moment, then emphasize the bond between them in the next.

It's not clear if these exchanges with Bradley "got better" over time, or if Aaron became less agitated as their communication grew. From all outward appearances, the Patriots star remained very agitated and paranoid. At one point, he placed an order for an armored personal car—presumably to protect himself from assassination.

Yet, in the end, cabin fever got the best of him. Aaron could have decided that being in mortal danger was worth it if it meant he was no longer trapped in a tiny house with his fiancée and a baby, in a city where he knew almost no one.

We do not know precisely when he left the Golden State, as he was sighted in May back in Providence, Rhode Island, drinking at a bar. Soon, he had returned full-time to his old haunts.

A man like Aaron could not be in exile for long. He was a man from the streets, and it was there he seemed determined to return… even if it would mean his life.

CHAPTER 9

"I'm like dude, I'm trying to live till I'm at least 28."

—Aaron Hernandez, jailhouse recording

The return to the East Coast meant a return to the familiar, but Aaron Hernandez still felt paranoid and unhappy. His anxiety was through the roof, and his drug use—probably increased to temper that anxiety—also reached heroic levels. And all that summer, he continued to maintain a double life.

In public, Aaron said he was hopeful that the Patriots would have a great season and return to the Super Bowl. He gave interviews to the local media in which he seemed positive and carefree. He was also honored by the national Pop Warner football program during this time, and given their Inspiration to Youth Award. (Those who knew Aaron intimately thought it was crazy that a murderous, drug-using criminal like him would be in line to receive such an honor, but Aaron himself did not question it. There were no contradictions for him. To be one person in front of smiling kids, and another in the club with his crew, came so naturally it was like breathing.)

Yet Aaron was not perfect at compartmentalizing his life. Sometimes, even in public situations, he lost control.

Journalist Michelle McPhee shares one of the most outrageous stories of Aaron's behavior during this time, which she believes serves as a harbinger of the even more unbelievable conduct that was to come:

> One of the stories that always bothered me about Aaron, the one that
> really tells you who he is, is during this time he went out to a bar on

Atwells Avenue in Providence with Ernest Wallace. He had a gun on him. They had to ditch it under a car, but somebody [in the bar] yelled out, "Patriots suck!" And Aaron went outside and pulled out his penis and urinated on the window of the bar in front of everybody, as an NFL star.

Now, if that doesn't tell you the mentality of this guy, what does? This is not a good person. This isn't a good human. Aaron is not a good human. If you're representing the New England Patriots and you are in New England and you are pissing on the window of a bar, that doesn't bode well for your persona, and the persona that the Patriots like to hone of we're an all American, clean guy team. Look at Tom Brady and imagine Aaron Hernandez having dinner with the Bradys. That does not go. That is not happening.

Meanwhile, Bradley's texts continued to torment Aaron like a bothersome pest that just wouldn't die. He sent Aaron a steady stream of messages. Some made veiled references to the shooting, and others made veiled threats. Others still took a tone of tentative reconciliation, and seemed to hint that the two men might be able to "work something out." (Aaron, again, occasionally texted back, but his messages were usually evasive and noncommittal.)

Aaron didn't know it, but Bradley was also in the process of filing an explosive lawsuit against him during this time. Yet no sooner was it filed than Bradley had it quickly withdrawn. So, given what we already know to date, one has to ask themselves why?

Observers have speculated that Bradley hoped more than anything that Aaron would give him a large cash payment to settle the score between them. Using the courts to get at this would be a long and expensive approach. It would be far better if Bradley could convince Aaron to pay him the money informally, using the type of street credentials the pair was used to.

Bradley could only have introduced and removed the lawsuit so suddenly for one reason: that Aaron finally appeared ready to bargain.

Via text, the two men haggled like traders at a flea market. Bradley wanted as much as $5 million for his pain and suffering, but hinted that he might settle for as little as half of that. But Aaron—probably as a strategic move—kept Bradley dangling on the line, sending out figures and then recalling them. Occasionally, he threw out numbers so low that he had to know Bradley would reject them. Then, when Bradley did, Aaron would go silent for a while. (This probably made Bradley crazy, and/or made him consider refiling the lawsuit.) But Aaron never broke off negotiations entirely. Though he might go silent for an extended period of time, he always resumed the negotiations.

These texts show that Aaron had a deep understanding of his former associate, and that he was willing to use it to manipulate him. Whether Aaron's "negotiations" with Bradley are genuine or not is something we can't know for sure. But, either way, they had the effect of managing Bradley and stalling for time, which is precisely what Aaron wanted to do. While he tried to figure out how to rid himself of Bradley for good, Aaron kept him just interested enough. Bradley could smell a cash settlement in the wind. Even if it never materialized, it always felt close. Aaron's manipulation of his old friend was masterful.

While he was keeping Bradley dangling on the line, Aaron was also making other moves. He expanded his base of operations by renting a run-down two-bedroom apartment in a dodgy neighborhood about half an hour away from his mansion. This apartment was to become his new secret hideout—a trap house, or drug den. He kept it secret from nearly everyone in his life—including his fiancée. Only his close crew of criminal friends—and, as it turned out, one Patriots organization employee who helped him find the place—knew about it. Critically, the supposed love of his life, Shayanna, had no idea it existed.

More than anything, the apartment was a place for smoking weed. The neighbors in the building got used to a permeating marijuana odor. Aaron sometimes told people it was his uncle's apartment. Most of the time, though, he didn't talk to visitors about how he had come to be in possession of it. The less anyone knew, the better.

In addition to providing a place to light up whenever he wanted, the apartment could also be a safe space for Aaron to express his sexuality free from guilt or prying eyes. He may have been burned too many times at lounges, bars, and strip clubs. Those were places where people could see things and get the wrong idea. They were also places where violence could happen. Where you could be disrespected. Taking this view, Aaron seems to have chosen to make the secret apartment into his own private nightclub.

No longer did he need to go to the club. Now—at least occasionally—the club was going to come to him.

Aaron had always been careful when it came to hiding the fact that he was bisexual. Yet the stress of his impending war with Bradley, the threats of law enforcement catching up to him, and other problems in his life seem to have triggered something. He began to express himself sexually in ways that he never had before.

In startling new interviews conducted for this book, it can now be revealed that Aaron's closeted lifestyle reawakened in strange ways during this period. Not only that, but the steps Aaron took in order to conceal his sexuality set him on a bloody path... *to even more murder.*

Chad (who asked we not use his real name in order to protect his real identity) was a male stripper working in the Boston area at the time. A serving US Marine, he started stripping in his spare time after a friend shared just how much money could be made. Most of Chad's work involved appearing at bachelorette parties, but he occasionally performed for male audiences as well. Most of his private stripping jobs were found through the Craigslist website.

Chad first met Aaron when he was home on pre-deployment leave, and was picking up a few grand a week stripping on the side.

The night he met Aaron started just like any other.

Chad answered a Craigslist posting for what he was told was a bachelorette party. Yet the surprises started as soon as he arrived. . . and they didn't stop.

"I walk up the stairs and I knock on the door, and this guy opens the door—and I'm like, all right; it's probably their friends or whatever," explains Chad. "I'm thinking there's going to be a bunch of girls inside. But I get inside and realize it's four dudes. . . and that's it."

The stripper had been summoned to Aaron's secret new den of vice. There was no bachelorette party. There were no women at all.

Chad was not hesitant about expressing his confusion and concern to the men who had tricked him. As he tells it in a world exclusive interview:

I'm like, "Hey, man. You guys said it was bachelorette party."

And these are some pretty beefy, big dudes. Do you know what I mean? I'm like, not the biggest guy. I don't think the situation is too safe in my head, so I'm trying to get more information the best I could.

And he was like, "Oh, yeah, man. It's just us. But if you're willing to stay, we'll give you $2,800 right now and $1,200 at the end of the night."

And I'm like, "Well, the money sounds right to me." Do you know what I mean?

So they're like, "All right."

We were drinking and stuff and I'm doing my thing, walking around in my little Chippendales outfit. And then they just started busting out the alcohol and I'm like, "Cool, cool, cool."

They were kind of feeling me out. I don't know if they thought maybe I was like—because with Craigslist you never know what you're going to get and stuff like that.

According to Chad, the men were a mix of races—while, black, and Hispanic. Though they were physically intimidating gentlemen, he did not recognize any of the men as celebrities. Yet he could tell that something was "up"—a strange vibe pervaded.

"As the night went on, it seemed like there was an anxiousness in the air when I was in there," says Chad. "I don't know if they didn't trust me or what."

Perhaps to calm their nerves, the group of men began smoking marijuana while Chad danced for them. They invited Chad to participate in the drug use, but he declined, citing the fact that he might be drug tested by the military—an excuse the men seemed to accept. Chad had never seen people smoke so much marijuana, as the men inhaled copious amounts.

Then, after the marijuana, cocaine was proffered. Again, Chad turned it down, citing the fact that he could be drug tested. But he looked on as the men did massive bumps.

As the drug use ramped up, Chad became even more nervous. Perhaps this was visible on his face, because—seemingly to calm him—one of the men reminded the dancer that he was being paid handsomely for this gig. . . and paid him more than half of his fee.

[He reminded me that] upfront I got $2,800. And at the tail end they were offering me $1,200. He's like, "Hey, man. This is the money right here. We're going to give you this $2,800 now, and you get the $1,200 later." And I saw the money. Do you know what I mean? I saw the $1,200 in this envelope.

Chad was handed $2,800 by a man he later realized was Aaron Hernandez. *The* Aaron Hernandez.

Tense minutes passed and Chad continued to perform for the men. According to the stripper, they became somewhat calmer—genial and talkative—probably from the drugs they had ingested. Yet just when things seemed to be relaxing into a comfortable groove, a man—Aaron—summoned Chad over for an intimate lap dance.

[Aaron Hernandez] was like, "Hey, man, come here." And he's like sitting down, all sprawled out. And I go over there and I started grinding on him and dancing on him and stuff. It wasn't my scene, but at the same time, the money is right. And he was pretty gone at this point. And he started touching on me and stuff. He grabbed my ass and touched my dick. I was like, "Hey, man. You can't be doing that. You're crossing the line a little bit, man."

And how did Aaron respond to an admonition to be less "handsy?" As Chad recalls:

He started getting more aggressive, and then I was like, "Yo, chill. Chill the fuck out."

And he was like, "What the fuck?" Do you know what I mean? "We're paying you."

And I'm like, "Well, you're not paying me for that. I don't think there is any kind of money that's going to get you that."

So I get off of him and I go and drink some more. I'm trying to avoid him a little bit. And then I overhear them arguing and stuff. And they were talking about, "Oh, this guy, Odin, he [stole] my medication. I can't be having that get out. I can't even send anyone to go get my meds anymore. He knows. He knows."

Chad was unaware at the time, but he had just overheard a bombshell.

The "Odin" whom Aaron was referring to was Odin Lloyd, a semipro football player who was then dating Aaron's fiancée's sister, Shaneah. Lloyd played for the Boston Bandits, a local team which was part of the New England Football League. They were nowhere near the level of the New England Patriots; their "home field" was a high school football stadium. All of the Bandits players had day jobs—Odin Lloyd was an electrician and day laborer. (At the same time, most of the Boston Bandits dreamed of moving to the NFL one day. It was not unheard of, but very rare.)

Odin was a 27-year-old immigrant from Saint Croix in the US Virgin Islands. He had always been an athletic guy, and also had a capacity for criminal mischief and illegal dealings. Because of this, it had been easy for Aaron to welcome him as a potential member of the family. He and Aaron had become close with one another, and when Aaron had moved back from California, Lloyd had quickly become a regular member of his posse.

Mostly, Lloyd did small favors and errands for Aaron. Because Lloyd seemed to have no compunction about criminal activity, the Patriot had him perform tasks he did not want to do himself. Lloyd sometimes procured guns and drugs, but other times might simply do a task that could have gotten Aaron mobbed by Patriots fans—such as picking up food at a restaurant.

There was one area, however, where Aaron excluded Lloyd, and that was his bisexuality.

It's likely that Aaron kept this part of his life separate from Lloyd because the two men were dating a pair of sisters. (Shayanna's understanding was that Aaron would discreetly see other people—yes—but did she know that sometimes extended to men? Moreover, did her sister know about this understanding? Probably not.) So while Aaron might have Lloyd along when the itinerary included having drinks and smoking weed, Lloyd was discreetly left out whenever the group's activities might betray Aaron's sexual orientation.

And the night that Chad was hired to dance was *definitely* such an evening.

As Aaron grew furious because of the news he was learning over the phone—that Odin Lloyd apparently had taken something and "knew" something—Chad stayed silent and played dumb. Like exotic dancers all over the world do every day, man or woman, Chad never revealed that he understood something important and dire was being discussed right in front of him.

Privately, though, Chad was quite aware of what was happening. (Or as aware as he could be from hearing only one side of the conversation.) Aaron eventually hung up the phone, and for a while nothing more was said. Chad continued to dance and the men around him continued to drink and use drugs.

As the evening wore on, however, the men eventually returned to the topic. It seemed that whatever this Odin Lloyd guy had done, it was very bad and very serious. And, most importantly, the men in the room with Chad felt it needed to be concealed at all costs.

At one point, Chad recalls Aaron saying: "Yo, man. I'd rather go to fucking jail for fucking murder than have that shit get out."

Chad continued to dance, but now his military training kicked in:

[I can tell Aaron is] hiding something, just the way he animated his body. I like to think I'm [good at] reading people posture-wise. It's something we had to do [in the Marines]—when you're in another country, you've got to read people and make sure someone who is dressed like a regular person is not going to pull an AK out of their robe, do you know what I mean? And [Aaron] was postured up like, "Hey, man. I am down to kill somebody to keep stuff under wraps."

It was a scary moment for me, man. . . I've gotten shot at a fair amount of times. And I felt safer in an environment like that, than in that environment.

Chad realized that the danger around him was serious and real. All of his training told him that these were the kind of men who would kill to keep secrets—and they were speaking about doing that very thing. Could their plans to keep things quiet include killing *him*?

As he danced, Chad observed the men's clothing more closely. What he saw did not lessen his concern.

"I didn't see any [guns] firsthand," Chad informs us. "But some dudes were 'printing.' Printing is like if you're conceal carrying, you can see the outline of something in someone's pants, or in their shirt and stuff. You see the outline of something there. And these guys. . . no one carries stuff in their waistbands, unless it's a gun or a weapon of some sort."

Chad began to think about the idea of a nonspecific "medication" that had been stolen by Odin. His mind raced for what it could be. Was it illegal steroids? All of these men we so muscular, they definitely looked as they could be steroid users. Or was "medication" a euphemism for something else—perhaps an illegal drug?

Chad's mind continued to race, and he noticed other strange things about the situation. Chief among them was that the muscular, moneyed men did not seem to fit with the shabby apartment where he was dancing:

> In my job in the Marine Corps, we had to do a lot of, "Hey, you need to read people and understand what the dynamics are for stuff."
>
> So I was like, these guys. . . They have nice clothes on. They've got their fucking jewelry on, and shit like that. And nice watches. But the apartment didn't get the money vibe. I did not think that they had a lot of money coming in. So the couch, it looks like they pulled it out of a dumpster. Mattresses on the floor. But the alcohol is high-end stuff, brands I didn't recognize. And then you've got this apartment that doesn't match the people. Do you know what I mean? I kind of reminded me of a college dorm, but a lot more drugs and alcohol.

The dissonance between the wealthy-looking men with the expensive liquor and drugs and the dingy fraternity-party apartment sent Chad's mind down another rabbit hole.

As a private dancer, he had seen into many people's secret lives. He knew that— for a variety of reasons—many chose to keep parts of their personalities and sexuality hidden from view. Chad deduced that these men had to be part of a lifestyle in which they could not be openly gay or bisexual. (Secret evenings with dancers might be the extent of their ability to express themselves openly.) With this in mind, Chad reframed his hypotheses about a secret "medication."

Perhaps, he reasoned, it was for HIV.

As festivities began to draw to a close, Chad reports that Aaron began growing difficult, hostile and aggressive once again. The young dancer got a decidedly bad feeling about where things might be heading, or what might happen when the music literally stopped.

Then the phone rang once more, and the evening came to an abrupt and dangerous end. As Chad relates:

> So the night started coming to a close. And everyone is fucked up, and Aaron is fucked up. And he's like still getting touchy-feely. Then suddenly he ended up taking another call, and all you hear is like, "Yo, this is bad, man. There's a mole. I'm fucked. I can't have this getting out there. Odin knows about the meds. We've got to take care of it! We've got to make sure that this dude is just silent, this shit disappears."
>
> I still didn't really understand what they were talking about, so I'm trying to piece it together. I wasn't trying to eavesdrop on that shit. Because as soon as I heard, "There's a mole," and that guy Odin got brought up again, it's like I'm trying to fucking stay the fuck away from this.
>
> So I'm like, "Hey, guys, I'm going to go. Can I get the rest of that money?"
>
> And [Aaron] is finally off the phone and says, "Okay. I'm going to go get it from my car."
>
> And I'm like, "What do you mean you're going to go get it from your car?"
>
> And he's like, "Yeah. My money's in my car."
>
> And I'm like, "Okay."
>
> And he leaves. But I'm like, "Oh, shit, dude. That fucking money

envelope is right there. I'm like, I've got to get the fuck out of here, man. This is not it."

So I dipped out, took a different exit.

I went out the front door and I walked down to the set of stairs like I did the first time to make sure I was going the same way. And I was out of there, because he could have gone to his car to get a gun. He could have just left to go do anything. And I was like, "I'm drawing a line here, man."

As the young Marine exited the party—with only $2,800 of the $4,000 he had been promised—he was bracingly aware that his nose for danger might have possibly saved his own life.

Bo Dietl is a former New York City Police Department detective and founder of one of the nation's premier private detective services. He is intimately familiar with the story of Aaron, and through this investigation, has been made privy to Chad's account of what transpired that evening.

Interviewed for this project, Dietl attaches special importance to the phone calls because Aaron had a pattern of going off the deep end after getting bad news over the phone. That was fully on display here.

Dietl tells this author:

[Aaron is] making moves. He's grabbing this guy's junk. The phone rings. And someone's on the phone telling Aaron something about this Odin guy about the meds. Again meds. They're not using the word drugs. It's meds. The word meds comes out. The name Odin comes out again. And then he just changes his whole demeanor. He's getting crazy. And then our Marine here, all of a sudden sees that things are going crazy there. Aaron and his pals are upset and they're losing control of the situation. The dancer's getting panicked, so he wants to get the hell out of here.

So this is a witness to the name of Odin coming out again. Whatever was on that phone call, they don't know if the dancer overheard it or what was being said. But he's a witness. He smartly knows he has got to get the hell out of there without collecting the rest of his money. 'Cause he doesn't like the way it looks right now. And he sees the craziness going. They were high, drunk, cocaine. Everything going down over here.

Dietl also attaches considerable importance to the words used when making the phone call.

Now this, in my detective nose, "meds" don't mean drugs. Meds mean medication. That someone knew too much, and there was a rat amongst them. He mentions that there was a rat amongst them that knows about this. And then the name Odin comes out. Makes me believe that's the first time that they find out that Odin might be knowing about these meds. The possibility of meds for HIV. . . that's definitely a motive. That's the beginning of this right now. I personally never heard [street drugs] used that way, as "meds." Never in my whole career. I've never heard the word "meds" [in that context]. And I was a homicide detective for 15 years.

What unfolded in the days ahead would only confirm both Chad's and Dietl's suspicions.

Chad's sixth sense had told him that Aaron was a killer who would not hesitate to take lives in order to protect himself. And he had overheard Aaron and his friends discussing all manner of secret things, and he'd also watched them use illegal drugs. It was no stretch to imagine Aaron being more comfortable with getting rid of Chad than risking leaving him alive.

Although the dancer escaped into the night, his ordeal was not yet over. Several days later, Chad received a mysterious phone call. As he tells it:

It was a blocked number. They were like, "I want to apologize for what happened the other night. We would like to compensate you for your troubles. Could you please meet us at this address?"

I'm like, "All right, sure."

They were like, "Okay."

He gave me the address. I'm like, "I'm not going to this place alone. I'm not making that mistake again."

So I had one of my boys come with me. He's driving. We drive up and we're driving through a sick neighborhood, man. I'm talking about these houses are super nice. Shit's real nice out there. Do you know what I mean? We roll up to this house and I checked the address to make sure I'm in the right spot. Because I'm like, "I just met this motherfucker in like a trap house. What is going on here?"

It just screams like power moves. Do you know what I mean? People who have power like that, if you want to disappear, man, you're gone. Think about it. The celebrities, they don't lead the lives that people think they do.

Chad began to suspect that the men had ulterior motives for wanting him to come back around.

I think that Aaron [Hernandez] was concerned about both the dances—his sexuality brought into question—and whatever conversations happened that I did hear and didn't hear. There's two ways you can tie up the loose ends. Pay the person off, or put him in the ground. That's the only two ways to silence somebody if you think about it.

Despite his fear, Chad walked up to Aaron's house and knocked on the door—and what happened next was like a scene from an action movie.

I go to knock on his door and the door opens. He grabs me by my forearm and drags me in his house. He slams the door behind me, and I'm like, "Oh, fuck, dude." So I like posture up and I grab him by his shirt and I'm pushing against him. He throws me up against a wall, and he's like, "Did anyone follow you? Who the fuck is with you? Are you alone?"

I'm like, "What the fuck?" It's the dude from the other night.

My boy's outside, but he's obviously not going to be able to see what's going on in the house. He'll be able to tell people when I'm dead, or when I don't come out. But it's, obviously too late for that.

I'm like, "No, dude. My friend, he drove me here." He was like, "What do you mean, your friend? Why doesn't he come inside? Tell him to come in." I'm like, "No, man. That's not how this is going to work out. I'm just here to get compensation, but he's there for my protection. Do you know what I mean? You have to understand that."

That probably saved my life.

As Chad explains, he soon realized Aaron was not alone. There were other men in the house. And despite its tony address, the mansion had been converted to a drug den.

At this point Aaron became suspicious, and began to search Chad.

He's just being fucking paranoid. I'm thinking this is a fucking schizo, dude, and a fucking weirdo. He goes through my wallet, looks through all my fucking shit. He puts all the shit in a shoebox, and he throws it in a fucking black bag.

I'm like, "What the fuck?"

He's like, "Follow me."

We walk through his house. It's super-dark in there. A lot of the lights are off and blinds are closed, and there's just … The first thing I'm seeing is a coffee table kind of deal, coke on it, shotgun. I'm talking about a fucking brick, dude. I've never seen a brick before in my life—a brick of cocaine, wrapped up in cellophane.

Remarkably, it was only at this moment that Chad had his first inkling of who Aaron might be.

Once I walk past that table, we're walking through the house. Then we start going into this basement area, and I see trophies and I see pictures. I see him in his jersey. I'm like, "Oh my fucking God, dude. This guy is a fucking football player." Everything just started fucking coming around and making sense. I now know that this dude is a pro football player.

Next, they entered the basement where more of Aaron's friends were waiting. Many of them were armed with guns. Aaron's paranoia then went on full display for Chad.

> We end up getting down to this basement, and he's just all over the place. He's talking to his boys. He's like, "Yo. They fucking know, man. They're fucking looking for me."
>
> [Aaron would react to] any fucking creak in that fucking house. If someone's phone went off, the guy's all over the place, super-paranoid. He's like, "Yo, do you hear that?"
>
> A car would drive past.
>
> "Do you hear that? Is that a helicopter? Are they coming?"
>
> He kept looking at his phone. I think maybe he had cameras in the house that were hooked up to his phone or something. I don't know. He keeps checking his phone constantly. He's just all over the place, paranoid, out of his fucking mind. That's scary, especially in the situation I'm in because people who are scared make rushed and not-the-best decisions.

Chad was directed to wait in the basement—surrounded by the imposing Aaron and his crew—for about twenty minutes. Upstairs, Aaron's associates were talking with Chad's friend who still waited outside the house. Eventually, the men upstairs seemed to reach a conclusion. They called Aaron on his cell phone as he waited with Chad.

> So I'm sitting there, and the call comes in. It has to be the guy from outside that was talking to my friend, and he's saying, "Hey, man. This isn't going to work. I've been talking to this kid. The situation is just way too hot. We're not going to . . . It's just not going to play out like the way we want it to."

[Aaron] is like, "Fuck." He's like, "Fuck-Fuck-Fuck." He's hitting himself in the head.

He looks at me, and he's just fucking pissed. He talks to his boys some more, and they're arguing.

He comes up with this envelope. He looks at me in my fucking face, and he's like, "If you don't disappear, I'm going to make you fucking disappear."

As I'm leaving, he's like, "Keep your fucking mouth shut, or I'm going to fucking find you."

On his own accord, Chad left in a hurry, and remained well aware that he had just narrowly escaped death.

It is probable that Aaron's plan had simply been to invite Chad over on the pretense of paying him the remaining money owed, then taking him into the basement and killing him. Aaron and his crew would then dispose of the body, and the young Marine who moonlighted as a stripper would never be heard from again. Aaron was more than willing to take his life if it would eliminate the risk of Chad telling anyone what he'd seen and heard.

Only the lucky chance of Chad having brought along a friend—specifically, a friend who had elected not to go into the house with him—had saved Chad's life.

Yet even that was not the end.

Several days later, Chad received another phone call:

I ended up hearing from [Aaron] again. It was a phone call. A [bought] number. It was probably … I don't know how many days past it was, but I get this phone call.

He's like, "Remember what I fucking told you. I will take care of you if I fucking have to."

To this day, Chad is haunted by how close he came to being killed. The whole experience remains bewildering:

Going to that house was fucking—literally Russian roulette. It could have been multiple reasons why they didn't do it. Maybe they knew I wasn't going to fucking talk. Maybe it was a combination of that and my boy being there, or maybe it was the neighbor seeing it. But I made it, and . . . This is just some shit.

Chad's shocking account shows that Aaron's double life was spiraling to new heights of insanity. He was indulging in booze, drugs—and perhaps most tellingly, other men. What's more, he also had a secret so sordid that he was willing to kill in order to hide it from the world.

Was it that he had contracted HIV from homosexual activity?

Many experts believe this is possibly the shocking secret that Aaron strove so fervently to conceal.

Noted Assistant District Attorney Jarrett J. Ferentino would review materials and medical record requests related to Aaron when the football star went on trial. In an exclusive interview for this book, Ferentino reveals the shocking conclusions that lead him to believe concealing an HIV diagnosis may have been directly behind Aaron's motivations.

Explains Ferentino:

> I've reviewed documentation from Aaron Hernandez's attorneys. They requested medical information from the New England Patriots. First, they requested it via letter that the information be voluntarily provided to them. It included in that packet a signed release from Aaron Hernandez. That information was not provided willingly by the New England Patriots, according to those records. The next step was Aaron Hernandez's attorneys sought to subpoena those records through the court system. In that documentation, they've requested the following information. One, his physical health records. Two, his mental health records. And three, any drug testing or drug record. [There was no request for] any HIV or STD testing or diagnostic record.
>
> I would say there are three possible scenarios why that particular HIV/STD information would not be sought. One, Aaron Hernandez

may have instructed his attorneys that, in fact, that information is nonexistent, that he did not have HIV or any STD. Two, they did not want to request that information because checking that box would create the inference that that information exists and he may or may not have that disease. Or three, he was aware that there was a record and didn't want it to come out.

Ferentino believes that this is strong evidence for the possibility that Aaron had HIV and was willing to kill to conceal it. He also believes it is "fair game" for further investigation for anyone with the goal of getting to the truth. He told this author:

> I would say this puts the entire clinical picture of Aaron Hernandez, his medicine, any diagnoses he has, an HIV/STD diagnoses. . . any diagnoses. At that point, it's fair game, because we are trying to solve the motive [for his behavior].

Chad the exotic dancer was not the only one to step forward with a terrifying account of how unhinged Aaron could become when he felt concerned his status could become exposed.

He is also not the only person to have an encounter with Aaron that specifically foreshadowed the murder that would end his football career forever.

A precocious young drug dealer who went by the handle "Q" was also uncovered as part of our research, and he provides us with an exclusive look into his own perspective on an out-of-control and secretive Aaron.

Q has never before been interviewed publicly about his connection to Aaron, and like Chad, refused to give up his identity for fear of recriminations.

The pair first met after Q snuck his way into the VIP section of a club where Aaron was hanging with his friends. That night, his only intention had been to sell drugs to as many people as he could. As he describes this first encounter:

> I noticed [Hernandez in the VIP area] and I thought it was pretty dope. I started talking to him and shit. We bullshitted for a few minutes.

Then his homeboy started hollering at me about some shit. So I noticed they had [some cocaine] and shit. So it was like, "Hey, you do coke?"

I was like, "Yeah, I do coke." So they busted out theirs; I busted out mine. You know, I did a few lines with them.

Then his buddy took my phone number down. I told him if they ever needed some just holler at me.

But what started like any other new relationship between a dealer and customer got intense very quickly. Q continues:

The next time I heard from him it was June 6 [of 2013]. His buddy was like, "Yo. It's Hernandez's boy."

I was like, "What's up?"

Then he told me to meet him, and I was like, "How much you need?"

He's like, "How much you got?"

"I have how much you need."

"Bring 500 dollars' worth."

"All right, homey. You got the money?"

"Yeah, I got the money."

He gave me the address. It was this cemetery.

He was like, "Come alone," this and that. So at first I was kind of sketch, but I can understand it from a drug dealer's perspective, you know, wanting to come alone with all that kind of shit. Fucking—you know, you're famous. The name is big out there.

Despite his finely honed street senses, Q had little inkling of what he would truly encounter when he reached the graveyard.

I came [to the graveyard]. I met up with him, and [Hernandez and his crew were] in a big-ass, black Suburban. The car was full of people; there was only one seat left. Aaron Hernandez was sitting in the front passenger seat. They called me over, and the window was like halfway down so I could just, like, see somebody's eyes, and they told me to get in. So I got in. Then, you know, I showed them the shit, and they handed me the money, and then they was bullshitting for a minute.

Then Aaron Hernandez got a phone call … around like 9:00 p.m., and he started like freaking out on the phone. I just ignored it for a little bit; started talking to his homeboy that had hit me up.

Then it started escalating. Hernandez started really freaking out. He was talking about he saw this dude named Odin a couple blocks up the street. At first I was like, "All right; it's probably just [some league shit] he's got going on." I really didn't know; it wasn't none of my business to ask. Unless they told me about it, I'm not going to ask about it.

I'm still there, bullshitting with his boys, and then he gets off the phone and starts talking to his homeys. He's like, "Yo, fucking Odin is a couple blocks up the street." At this point I was sitting back, chilling, just listening to the conversation. You know, wondering if they're going to tell me, "All right, bro; appreciate you bringing the shit." Then I'd leave and they'd hit me up some other time, you know?

A couple minutes go by and they're talking amongst themselves and everything. Then Aaron starts getting mad. He pulls out a gun and hits the fucking dashboard with it. Then he's waving it around, like hollering at his boys and shit, talking about, "We got some shit to handle." You know, "We got to fucking get rid of this shit."

Everybody was strapped. Everybody had guns. That whole group in the car.

He's like, "Y'all either on my side or their side. There's no changing sides. I was like—well, I mean—at first I was just like listening to what was going on. As long as he ain't talking to me directly, I ain't got nothing to do with it.

Then he started like yelling and shit, and hitting the dashboard again, and then he saw a cop roll by. Everybody got quiet, like deathly quiet. We were all just sitting there. The cop rolls by in his patrol car. real slow. Everybody's pretending to be chilling. Then the cop just keeps going. We sit there for about two more minutes after that, just quiet, nobody talking.

Then Aaron Hernandez starts talking again. He's like, "Oh yeah. So, you know, we got to do this. We got to roll out. We got to go take care of this." You know. I was like, you know, I finally asked them; I was like, "What's going on?" He told me a story about the fucking pills, like him knowing shit, this and that, and I was like, "I don't know what to tell you." Somebody had stolen some pills from him, or something like that. Like if he knew that that information had gotten out, you know, he was in a state of mind where he wasn't about to let that happen. Like no matter how he had to do it, he was going to take care of his.

At this point, Aaron and his crew concluded their transaction with Q and pulled away. Yet they had revealed too much. Combined with the account of Chad, a vivid portrait is painted that contains means, motive—and opportunity.

Odin Lloyd almost certainly knew that Aaron was taking medication for a secret illness—perhaps even HIV, as homicide expert Jarrett J. Ferentino speculates. Were it to be HIV and this to get out, it would endanger all the core aspects of Aaron's life—his reputation, his job, and his romantic relationships.

Dr. Jeff Gardere is one of America's most respected clinical and forensic psychologists who has spent many years working on cases like Aaron's, and who is intimately familiar with the case of the fallen New England Patriot. In exclusive analysis for this book, he notes that, because of the numerous physical exams given to NFL players, an embarrassing condition might have been something Aaron had assiduously devoted himself to keeping beneath the radar. . . at least so far. However, in addition to HIV, Gardere believes it could have been medication for something else.

He explains:

> Certainly, if it was, God forbid, if it was some sort of cancer or some sort of other illness, the team would know about it, I would think, due to the numerous physical examinations that they do and his performance on the field—noticing if something was wrong. I would think it is a medication that may be tied to some sort of stigma; that may be

tied perhaps, to something that could be extremely embarrassing, or that can be career-ending. Something that [makes him feel] that the public would turn on him or that would cause him a lot of eyeballs, a lot of trolls.

If we are looking at something that is extremely embarrassing, then I think you could rule out an illness that might have been treated by the team that they knew about. Because obviously, he didn't want the team to know about it, it seems to me. And so what are we looking at here? What causes some of the major issues as far as stigma?

Could it be a mental health issue, where maybe, it is some sort of antipsychotic medication? Because a lot of people get depressed, and they are on antidepressants.

In Aaron's world, would a diagnosis of depression be something to kill to conceal? Unlikely. Would it be a sign of weakness so great that he would commit murder over it? Unlikely. Or did it need to be something more?

Gardere continues:

Well, if it is an antidepressant, is it worth killing for? No. Anti-anxiety? No. If it was an antipsychotic medication? Perhaps, he may not want people to know that there may be some sort of an issue where people think he's crazy or there is some sort of psychosis. But I think we also have to look at is it something—especially when we look at stigma— around chronic sexually transmitted diseases.

Let me be very clear: anyone who is taking medications for any of these things, whether it be for a depression or psychosis or a cure for hepatitis C or taking their daily medications for being HIV-positive or having AIDS, there should be no stigma with that.

And even though we know that being gay is normal, there are a lot of people who still view it as something that needs to be put away— closeted away—especially in professional sports. That professional sports is supposed to be about being rough and tough and a real man. And so there are many players who are closeted and would like to

come out. And have started coming out. But feel that they may be stig-
matized by business, by endorsers, by their fans. So it is a very different
situation for players to be able to come out.

Many different people are HIV-positive. But, of course, in the public's mind, they will tie that much quicker to someone who is gay,
because of how we have shown this in the media; our attitudes about
it, which are very, very negative. And whether you are gay or straight
or bisexual, let's be real, a lot of people tend to think that being HIV
positive makes you "less than."

As Dr. Gardere sees it, while there ought to be no stigma attached to these medical conditions, it does not replace the fact that a disclosure of a diagnosis for
Aaron might have been ruinous. His pro career, his endorsements, and his reputation—both on the field and on the streets—were all in danger.

However many lives Aaron Hernandez had, *all* would be negatively impacted
by such a medical diagnosis being revealed.

When it comes to the question of whether or not Aaron would kill to protect
his reputation, Gardere responds:

Given the right circumstances or the wrong circumstances—that self-
hate, where you don't even care about yourself anymore—who knows?
Who knows?

Sportscaster Joe Kayata supports this possibility, but also notes the impact of
Aaron's general paranoia at the time:

There's belief that with Odin [Lloyd] there may have been something
to conceal that was embarrassing to Hernandez. That information he
maybe wanted to hide. But, at that point, with Aaron's drug use, he
could also become incredibly paranoid and thought, he could have
thought you were out to get him. Who knows what he was using. It was
possibly hallucinogenic drugs. The stuff that he was taking, law
enforcement says it makes you batshit crazy. Which [makes it]

surprising that he could play so well. Again, when we parallel his doc-
umented drug use with [his performance], I'm like "How is this guy
playing football?"

So Aaron had reason to kill. However, as we uncovered as part of this investigation, in this particular case, Aaron also had the wrong man.

He was fueled by an inner paranoia, and by a murderous instinct to kill to
protect his own interests. He had already used lethal violence in response to the
smallest slights, and was known to take violent umbrage at the slightest disrespect. For Aaron, taking the life of Odin Lloyd probably felt like a no-brainer.

But that night in the graveyard—as Aaron and his crew left Q behind—they
were headed in the wrong direction. As we reveal here for the first time, Aaron
had it wrong. Either his tip was incorrect or he was too late. Aaron and his crew
headed to a place where Lloyd no longer was, and possibly never had been.

But did they still kill someone when they got there?

All signs point to a frightingly great big yes.

In the world of underground criminal violence, things have a way of not always
going to plan, and Aaron was about to be reminded of that firsthand.

CHAPTER 10

Friend: "Man, Wilker's been in the paper trippin' on Belichick."
Aaron: "I heard, I heard, I heard."
Friend: "He went ham like he controls the players."
Aaron: "For real. That's what Bill does! He tries to program everybody!"

—AARON HERNANDEZ, JAILHOUSE RECORDING

On the night that Aaron Hernandez left Q to go and "take care of" Odin Lloyd, a man named Jordan Miller—who bore a great physical similarity to Lloyd—was gunned down in a seemingly motiveless murder, less than a mile from the cemetery.

Nine shots were fired at Miller through the window of his building.

His murder—to this very day—has never been solved.

Miller came from a poor family, and was likely involved in illegal activities himself. He carried guns and used drugs. He may have also run in some of the same social circles as Aaron... or Odin Lloyd.

In an exclusive for this book, we connect again with former New York City Police Detective Bo Dietl—who served from June 1969 until he retired in 1985, and was one of the most highly decorated detectives in the history of the police department, with several thousand arrests to his credit—about the strong, under-reported possibility that Aaron and his crew may have also murdered Jordan Miller that night in a shocking case of mistaken identity.

On the night in question, Miller was shot inside his house at 633 Cummings Highway. It was dark, and the shooter(s) may only have been able to see his outline. (An outline that—everybody agrees—looked an awful lot like Odin Lloyd.)

Dietl imagines just how easily Aaron and his crew could have done the job:

> It sounds like Hernandez gets a tip from one of his goonies. That Odin Lloyd is at this location. They drive, there's this kid was shot through the window in a drive-by, in an unidentified vehicle. Jordan Miller shot inside his home, from a drive-by shooting through the window.

The facts of the case also lead Dietl to wonder if there might be another scenario for how things unfolded. Could Lloyd have been acquainted with Jordan Miller and also in the apartment at the time of the shooting? What's more, because it was a quick drive-by, Lloyd might not even have known that Aaron and his crew were the ones to blame.

> I would want, as a detective, to try to make a connection between Odin Lloyd, the deceased, and the other deceased, Jordan Miller, see if they knew each other. Because it's very possible that Odin Lloyd could have been in that apartment when they shot Miller, and if they look similar, which I believe they do. They shot the wrong guy at that time. Obviously a week later, Odin Lloyd is murdered. Now what I'd like to see, and again we're not saying that Aaron Hernandez did the actual shooting, but it's very possible that he did the actual shooting, or one of his little cronies. I don't care if he pulled the trigger or not, if Aaron Hernandez was involved with the conspiracy to murder Odin Lloyd, and Jordan Miller, it's the same as pulling the trigger. If you're working for me and I tell you, go kill him over there, that's a conspiracy to murder, and you're as guilty as the person pulling the trigger.

After he was shot in the drive-by, Jordan Miller did not die immediately.

Dietl believes this is important to understanding the timing of the case.

> Being that they transported Jordan Miller to the hospital, where he died, they were giving him CPR. That means that there was some life left in him; that doesn't mean he could have been shot three hours prior, and sometimes you survive for three hours, and you're internally bleeding. The fact is if he died on the floor of his apartment, you would have rigor mortis set in, in so many hours that you would be able to validity, and you would see the blood flow down to the bottom of the body. In this case, you wouldn't get that because he was still obviously somewhat alive; they took him to the hospital. They didn't pronounce him dead on the floor.

Miller surviving to the hospital helps us to understand when word may have become available that Jordan Miller had died.

And for Aaron to learn that *Jordan Miller*—not Odin Lloyd—had been killed by him or by his associates.

Going on his honed police instincts, Dietl further imagines a scenario in which Aaron becomes aware of this misfire, and has the means, motive, and opportunity to see that the murder of Miller is never connected to any other killing.

Put bluntly, Dietl believes that Aaron may have tried to "make it right" by paying off Miller's family. They were not wealthy by any means and could have desperately used the money.

Additionally, as Dietl also speculates, if Miller's family accepted the money, then it may explain why they have not been more insistent that law enforcement catch the perpetrator.

> When you have people involved with drug dealing and all these types of crimes, it is not uncommon that someone would offer them money just to drop everything? I work in a world of real, factual evidence. It's not innuendo. It's a chain, it's a direction of thought. Is it factual? We don't know that, we don't know that for a fact. But could it be? I'd like

to certainly re-interview the family. In reality, if we could prove that Aaron Hernandez was involved with the death of your relative Jordan Miller, there's certainly an opportunity for money there. That you could possibly recover from his estate on a civil case, against his estate for the wrongful death of your loved one, Jordan. That is if we can show that Aaron Hernandez was involved one, either a conspiracy, or in the actual shooting. That could be a motive for someone to say, I want to talk to you. All of a sudden, we can determine if Jordan Miller was killed with a conspiracy, or by Aaron Hernandez, there certainly could be some lucrative money coming to you in a civil case. That would be a good direction for a detective to take.

If I went to that family and said, look, whether you took money or not, it has no bearing on the fact that your relative Jordan Miller was murdered. We really feel as though we have enough evidence, and we're looking in the direction of Aaron Hernandez, who has an estate loaded with cash, this could help in a wrongful death suit against his estate. We feel your relative Jordan Miller, we feel as though could have been murdered by some of his goonies, or by him. If we could prove this—and regardless if you accepted anything, including money—we have a case. You have a right to take money. There's no crime in that.

So Dietl believes that the family of Miller could be reluctant—even today, when Aaron is dead—to assist the Boston Police Department due to the fact that they could have accepted money from Aaron. Even though their having accepted money from Aaron would not *necessarily* make them criminally complicit, Dietl believes they are probably too frightened to pursue the matter. They would prefer to let it rest.

Of more importance, however, is the prospect the BPD could link the two crimes. Ballistics in the Jordan Miller shooting were never compared to those in the Odin Lloyd case—but Dietl believes this "cold case" might be solved if they ever were.

He hopes fervently that this can be done someday.

Certainly, when you have an open case, a cold case murder, I want to find out if there is evidence. It's feasible enough to determine that there was anger going on that night of June 6, you heard Odin being over-heard by "Q" in the graveyard, talking about he's got to do something with him now. It was anger, and it was craziness, just happened to be someone get killed that night, I want to find out if in fact possibly this has a connection.

Why does Dietl believe this is so important?

You know, after watching and reading everything that I have [about the Jordan Miller case], this is a bombshell. Because what you have is, you have "Q" as a witness that is bringing together the possibility of yet another murder that Aaron Hernandez was involved, or his goonies were involved in, in a total conspiracy. You have the motive behind the murder of Odin. You also have the very strong possibility of Jordan Miller being mistakenly killed that night.

What we have to do is bring this evidence to the Boston Police, the homicide department, that had been working on it. One, we need to find out if there's any credible ballistics—or there's any credible connection between Jordan Miller and Odin. Now as far as the motive goes, we also now have why Aaron Hernandez wanted to kill Odin for these pills, whatever these pills are. It is very obvious that was brought up. It was so distinctive about him and these pills, him and Odin and these pills. We've got to do something now, and it just happens that blocks away we have another murder. So, in reality, this is something of a bombshell, as far as for that fourth unknown until now murder. Also, again, we have established the motive on the Odin murder.

Thus, Dietl is able to see it both ways. Miller could have been killed accidentally, but his murder could have also been intentional. In either case, he believes that the victim's family could still have a right to seek compensation from Hernandez's estate.

You know, looking at everything here, it's very possible that Odin came into possession or got knowledge that there was medicine involved, possibly for HIV. That Aaron Hernandez was taking that medication or was in possession of that medication, which is normally taken to treat HIV. This certainly would be a real motive for Aaron Hernandez or his goons to kill whoever knows about it, i.e. Odin. Then, all of a sudden, you might have had Jordan Miller being caught up and mistakenly murdered. I'd like to find out more from Jordan Miller's mother. I'd also like to find out more from these witnesses. Again, the witnesses to the fact when they made these statements, these witnesses, would they come forward? Because this could certainly be a good case for the fourth murder. Also to substantiate, to re-convict, re-convict on the appeal of Aaron Hernandez murdering Odin. Because here's your motive.

If Aaron Hernandez committed these murders or was involved in the conspiracy to commit these murders, these families have a recourse, civilly, to go after Aaron Hernandez's estate. If one of my family members were murdered by this creep, I would certainly want satisfaction—and that's their right.

So, on that fateful night as left the graveyard, did Aaron makes moves that ultimately killed Jordan Miller in a horrific case of mistaken identity? The answer is almost certainly yes. However, the surprising part isn't that this murder is now coming to light. The surprising part is that we have not heard of many additional cases like it. Boston metro area law enforcement has a respectable clearance rate for murders—most years, they make arrests in more than half of cases—but when you segment it out, the statistics tell a different tale. The number dips to more like 40 percent when you remove people who are Caucasian. (Almost everyone with whom Aaron associated was Hispanic, African American, or mixed race.) It dips even more if you remove murders in middle to high-income neighborhoods. And those numbers plunge even further when you remove cases where the victims did *not* have prior arrest records.

That is to say, if you were looking to murder non-white people with prior arrest records in the poor parts of New England in the 2010s, you had a better chance of getting away with it than not.

Terrifyingly, Aaron could have been so quick to use violence simply because he knew he could get away with it, or because he had gotten away with it in the past. It is very possible that beyond what we already know about—and beyond cases like Jordan Miller's that are just now coming to light—there may still be other instances of murder by Aaron that remain, for the moment, unknown.

A source close to the investigation told this author:

Unfortunately, I think all that we've learned through this investigation and through this entire case, is that there's more. There is more beyond what we know now, and all you have to do is ask around 'cause [Hernandez's crew] said many times that every time there was a new story of violence, there was a story of someone that being threatened with a gun. You know, he talked about shootings all the time. I'd be flabbergasted if there weren't more shooting victims that Aaron Hernandez pulled the trigger on that we'll never know about.

CHAPTER 11

"They, they talking about like people in gangs gonna, um, gonna try to shank me this and that because to move up to move up in the gang this and that I'm like, come on man like, do you not know me, man I'm not worried about that."

—AARON HERNANDEZ, JAILHOUSE RECORDING

A week after the shooting of Jordan Miller, Aaron Hernandez was ready to try again.

We can deduce that Aaron probably believed Odin Lloyd was unaware of what had actually happened to Miller. This is because of what happened next.

Aaron asked to see Lloyd again, and invited him out.

Lloyd agreed.

On June 14, 2013, Aaron took Lloyd out drinking at a Boston-area club called Rumor. Aaron could have still been attempting to gauge Lloyd's knowledge of the situation. How much did he really know? Was he going to bring up the shooting of Miller? Was he completely unaware, or going to act oblivious?

Some who have investigated this case believe that this evening may have been Aaron giving Lloyd a "final chance." If Lloyd had stolen something—such as HIV medicine—perhaps he would return it. If he had become aware of an embarrassing medical condition that could sabotage Aaron's career and persona, perhaps he could be convinced to swear that he would never reveal it.

Aaron prepared for this evening with Lloyd almost like he was going on a date. He dressed to the nines. He paid for all their drinks. He even rented Lloyd a black Chevy Suburban to drive.

Little is known about what words passed between Aaron and Lloyd at Rumor, but it certainly did not end well.

Witnesses who were at the bar that night report seeing Aaron and Lloyd arguing. It didn't come to blows, as was the case on so many occasions prior, but voices were indeed raised. If Aaron was trying to get Lloyd to do something—or to promise something—it was clear that Lloyd was resisting. This made Aaron furious, and he eventually stormed out of the bar.

Lloyd didn't know it—as he stood at the bar and finished his drink—but from that moment on, he was, for all practical purposes, already dead.

Two days after taking Lloyd to Rumor, Aaron accompanied his fiancée to a fancy dinner in the city. Once they arrived at the tony restaurant, Aaron began ordering round after round of cocktails. What followed was a crash course in serious alcoholic indulgence. Even for a man of NFL-player proportions—who was also a practiced inebriate—the number of drinks Aaron consumed that evening alarmed the bartenders and servers—all of whom remembered that detail when later questioned about the evening by authorities.

After consuming a heroic amount of booze, Aaron then stunned onlookers by momentarily excusing himself for a smoke break—but it was not tobacco he was smoking. According to witnesses who passed him outside the restaurant—and the servers and patrons who smelled him when he reentered—the Patriot had clearly been smoking massive quantities of marijuana.

This kind of indulgence was not common for the "public" version of Aaron Hernandez—especially not so early in the evening. It was almost as though he needed liquid (and THC-based) courage. Like he was mentally and physically preparing himself for something big.

And he was.

Throughout their dinner—as his fiancée later testified—Aaron was distracted, sending a massive barrage of text messages while they ate and drank. Now under the calming gloom of alcohol and weed, Aaron was using these texts to solidify his plans for later that night. He was summoning his associate Bo Wallace and another criminal friend named Carlos Ortiz. He was also reaching out to Odin Lloyd.

It was not unusual for Aaron to reach out to his boys for a late-night meet up, but something in the air this evening was different. Odin, especially, seemed to sense it. He might have guessed that he was in danger, and that this day might signal his demise.

Even so, the plans were underway, and there was no stopping Aaron now.

Aaron and Shayanna left the restaurant and headed back to their house. At about 12:40 in the morning, Wallace and Ortiz arrived.

At about 1:10, the three men—Aaron, Wallace, and Ortiz—departed the house with Wallace driving.

For the next hour, the men drove around, discussing what was going to happen next. Phone records show they also called Lloyd no less than five times to make sure he was available to meet.

At half past two, Aaron and the others picked up Lloyd at his home. The vehicle they drove was a rented Nissan Altima. The car was intentionally a "nothing" car—nondescript, something nobody would look at twice. They drove for some time. About thirty minutes into their trip, Lloyd texted his sister to make sure that she knew who he had left with.

When the sister texted back to ask who, Lloyd sent the now infamous one-word text: "NFL."

Then, at 3:23 in the morning, Lloyd sent a follow-up message. It was the last text he would ever send.

"Just so you know."

Authorities estimate that just after this final text was sent, Wallace piloted the Nissan off the main road and into a quiet industrial park that was roughly half a mile from Aaron's house. (It is probable that during the ride Lloyd believed Wallace was driving them to Aaron's compound.)

At 3:27 in the morning—just four minutes after Lloyd had sent his last text—the Nissan pulled back into Aaron's driveway, where it was recorded by security cameras. Now there were just three men inside it.

Lloyd was back at the industrial park. Or rather, his lifeless body was. He had been shot six times in the back and the chest. An execution-style murder.

Aaron had gotten what he'd wanted.

Odin Lloyd was dead.

Not only had Aaron committed the murder—personally pulling the trigger—but it turned out he'd left evidence of his guilt everywhere. He had been unbelievably sloppy, and taken almost no pains to conceal his crime. Perhaps this is because he thought himself untouchable. Perhaps it was because he had been intoxicated at the time of the killing. Perhaps it was because he felt no need to take further precautions, as this was just the kind of murder he'd already allegedly gotten away with several times before.

Between Aaron leaving his house and returning home, Odin Lloyd was shot in cold blood and his body left dumped by the road. The question that keeps coming is simple. Why? To try to understand just what happened that night, we sent our team of investigators to the scene of Odin's murder.

Among them was Detective Sergeant Michelle Wood—a highly trained Chicago law enforcement officer who previously worked in a Special Victims Unit focused on homicides, gangs, and sex crimes. She has more than 300 arrests to her name.

Detective Sergeant Wood frames the crucial questions this way:

> What information did Odin know about Aaron Hernandez that was important enough for Aaron to kill him? This was definitely a premeditated murder. However, the actual execution of the murder was done so sloppy. And one has to think, what was actually going on in Aaron Hernandez's head at that point? What information did Odin have, that Aaron was willing to risk everything so that it wouldn't get out?

Traveling to the scene of the murder—even though it has changed somewhat in the intervening years—told Wood that there had been no attempt to conceal the dead man.

She declared:

> They didn't even make an attempt to hide his body afterwards. They shot him multiple times and left him there to die and just basically discarded him like garbage. I mean, Odin knew Aaron Hernandez and what he was capable of. Can you just imagine the dread and terror?

For Wood, the lack of motivation on Aaron's part to conceal the scene of a murder speaks directly to the pride and hubris that would eventually be his undoing.

As Detective Sergeant Wood puts it bluntly:

> Aaron Hernandez had all this publicity and everything throughout his life and that is what allowed him to do stuff like this because he didn't give a fuck. He didn't give a fuck.
>
> He didn't care about anyone but himself. It just doesn't make any sense to me.
>
> What's more, it's not just that. It's not just the fact that he thought people were going to find out he was gay. There's something else. This whole story makes little to no sense.

The evidence Aaron and his compatriots left behind was so immediate and compelling that police might have been forgiven for first thinking someone was trying to frame Aaron. It was too easy. Too perfect. All the clues led straight to him.

First of all, there is the proximity. The Boston area is full of industrial parks that are empty at 2:30 in the morning. But there was only one in a fancy neighborhood near where an NFL star lived.

Within the park were bushes—some, less than 50 feet from where the body had fallen. A killer aiming to conceal his deeds could have easily dragged a body into them, and probably delayed the discovery of the corpse by days or even weeks. Yet the body had been left just where it was. In daylight—or just in the glare of a pair of car headlights—it would be practically unmissable.

Aaron had also left five shell casings at the scene of the crime. (It would have been easy to pick them up; they were not hard to see and were clustered together, on the ground right next to Lloyd's feet.) Then, when Aaron returned home, his own home security footage captured him holding a gun that matched the shell casings. Though Aaron tried to destroy his home security video in the days that followed, he didn't get all of it.

All in all, it was the kind of shooting that might have confounded police in a bad neighborhood, where NFL players *didn't* live, and where people were scared to talk to the police. Aaron might have moved to a fancy address, but his skill at avoiding detection had stayed low-rent. It was a distinction that was about to be his undoing.

The next day, Lloyd's body was found by a jogger who immediately alerted law enforcement. Odin's mother, Ursula Ward, was informed shortly thereafter.

Ursula was a single mother who had always struggled to make ends meet; she had raised Odin single-handedly. In recent years she had dealt with ongoing unemployment. Odin was the one good thing in her life, and his death destroyed her, as one could imagine.

For the rest of the day, police gathered evidence and went through the many clues that had been left behind.

In another instance of sloppy thoughtlessness, Aaron had left Lloyd's cell phone in the dead man's own pocket. Initially, seeing the many text messages between the two, police had worried that Aaron might also be in danger; that whoever had killed Lloyd might be gunning for the star Patriot next. But when they took time to actually read over the messages, the likely role of Aaron had become clear.

A little more than 24 hours after the actual murder, police realized that Aaron was their main suspect. They began putting together what was needed to bring him into custody.

Meanwhile, Aaron was doing his best—in a muddled, second-rate and amateur way—to cover his tracks. But, as he would soon learn, it was far too little, and far too late.

Aaron's goal was to get as much incriminating evidence as possible out of his house. He guessed (correctly) that his home might soon be the subject of a police search warrant.

In this connection, he gave his fiancée, Shayanna, a mysterious garbage bag with orders take it somewhere and throw it away. She obeyed, not knowing what it contained. Investigators later surmised it contained tapes from his home security system.

Aaron also used the day after the murder to call a cleaning service to come to his house and clean it top to bottom. Presumably, he was hoping that any physical evidence he might have missed would be concealed through a good scrubbing.

Aaron then took the rented Nissan Altima back to Enterprise.

Records show that Enterprise noted that the vehicle had been dented and that one of the mirrors had been broken. This might have been connected to a last-minute scuffle as Lloyd fought for his life, or might merely have been the product of sloppy driving. Whatever the case, Aaron had no trouble paying for the damage to the vehicle.

And all this time, the police were still closing in.

Perhaps no one can speak with more authority to the physical area where the murder of Lloyd occurred than Jason Case, who owns the industrial park where the body was found.

Many Americans remember Case and his beauty queen girlfriend Amy Diaz as winners of the twenty-third installment of *The Amazing Race*, which aired on CBS in 2013. Ironically, at the time of the murder, Case himself was briefly considered a candidate to be a suspect in the killing because—per his contract with CBS—he could have no outside contact with the rest of the world while he was taping the show.

Largely unaware of this, authorities were initially suspicious when told the owner of the property was "completely off the grid" and untraceable.

In an exclusive interview, he characterizes his experience with the police investigation unfolding on his property in the hours that followed.

Case shares the questions he was asked when he arrived on the scene:

> The questions that were asked to me [by the police] were, "Could the potential murder weapon be found anywhere on the site?" We had a construction operation going at the time that we had to shut down. It certainly was impacting our business. We needed to cooperate with the investigative team as much as we could. So, there was a lot of questions. The police initially looked at me as a suspect, [but] I was with people and had an alibi at that period. So, I was good.

Once he understood that he was not a suspect, Case took in the horrible nature of the crime:

> When you think of a tragedy like that—and that's pretty much what it

is, and then you find out the details of how it happened—I believe they had come down a dark road, shot someone in the back—shot multiple times I believe because there was about, I think, five rounds of ammo found at the scene of the crime—and that was it. Open body, I think. Face up, wallet left. It's just an eye-opening experience because you're never safe, and I think that's what the community starts to feel when something like this happens.

Case—like the cops on the scene—was also struck by how the murderers had made virtually no attempt to hide the body (or other evidence), even though the property gave them more than ample opportunity to do so.

There was plenty of holes dug already [on the property]. All you had to do was throw him in it and throw some dirt on it. Maybe [the perpetrators] wanted to get caught. Certainly [the sloppiness] provided enough evidence to trace it back to [Hernandez] within minutes. So, I don't know. It does put a question in your head: Is he just a dumb criminal? Or was there something else where the truth lies beneath?

So, of all the places to dump a body or murder someone so close to the proximity of his house. Literally across the street. He could walk here in five minutes. So, it's … it adds a lot of questions. Virtually five football fields away.

When Case learned how close his property was to Aaron's house—by his own estimation, about 500 yards—he found himself guessing how the site might have come easily to mind for Aaron as he tried to think of where to do the murder.

Literally, to get on 95 the highway, you have to drive through this industrial park from where his house is located. So, he probably did drive by this location a number of times during the week. And it's an abandoned construction location, a lot of woods, vacant land.

You've gotta put yourself in [Hernandez's shoes] and see through the lens of that night. Why else would you be driving into a vacant

The front view of Aaron Hernandez's North Attleborough, MA, home
(Commonwealth of Massachusetts; official crime scene evidence)

Inside Aaron Hernandez's basement in his North Attleborough, MA home
(Commonwealth of Massachusetts; official crime scene evidence)

Aerial view of the industrial park where Odin Lloyd was murdered
(Commonwealth of Massachusetts; official crime scene evidence)

Photograph of a tarp covering the body of Odin Lloyd at the murder scene
(Commonwealth of Massachusetts; official crime scene evidence)

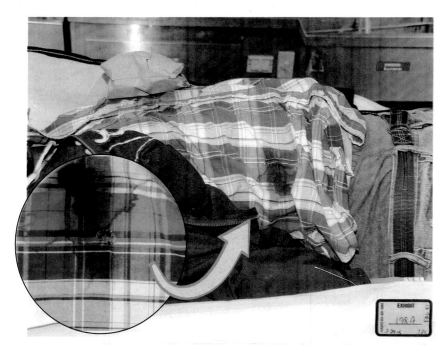

A closer view of one of Odin Lloyd's five fatal bullet wounds (Commonwealth of Massachusetts; official crime scene evidence)

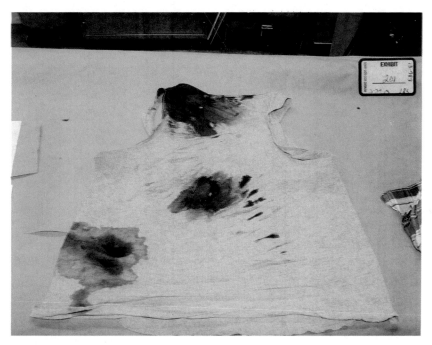

Odin Lloyd's bloodstained tank top (Commonwealth of Massachusetts; official crime scene evidence)

The rear view of a black Chevy Suburban rented by Aaron Hernandez. The keys to this car were later found in Odin Lloyd's pocket after he was murdered. (Commonwealth of Massachusetts; official crime scene evidence)

A handgun that was recovered in the woods near Odin Lloyd's body, but not believed to be the murder weapon which to this day has yet to found. (Commonwealth of Massachusetts; official crime scene evidence)

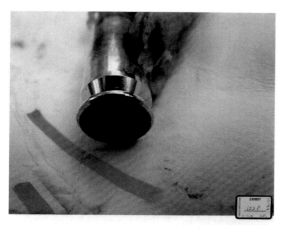

Bubble gum stuck to a bullet shell casing that was discovered in a car Aaron Hernandez had rented (Commonwealth of Massachusetts ; official crime scene evidence)

The bubble gum, bullet shell casing, and a child's doodling that were found in a rental car belonging to Aaron Hernandez (Commonwealth of Massachusetts; official crime scene evidence)

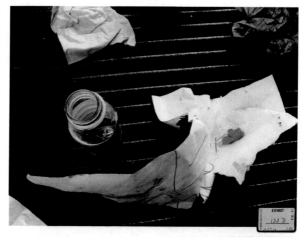

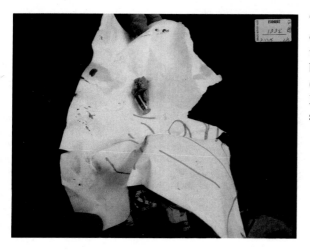

The bubble gum, bullet shell casing, and a child's doodling that were found in a rental car belonging to Aaron Hernandez (Commonwealth of Massachusetts; official crime scene evidence)

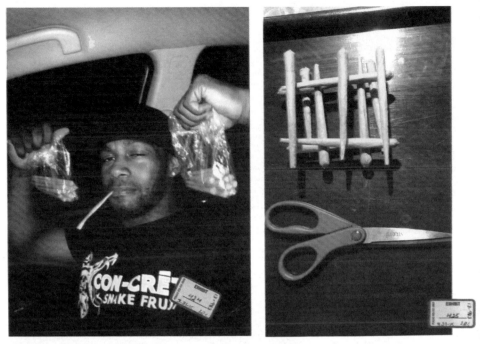

LEFT: A friend of Aaron Hernandez holding bag of blunts (Commonwealth of Massachusetts) RIGHT: Photograph of blunts stacked up on a counter next to scissors (Commonwealth of Massachusetts; official crime scene evidence)

The entrance to Aaron Hernandez's trap-house where he partied and hired the male stripper, Chad (Commonwealth of Massachusetts; official crime scene evidence)

After a long thorough search through Aaron Hernandez's North Attleborough, MA, home, Officer Donald Jackson finds illegal substances believed to be cocaine in the ceiling of the basement. (American Media)

Photograph of an array of pistols (Commonwealth of Massachusetts; official crime scene evidence)

EXHIBIT

322

An aerial view of Aaron Hernandez's North Attleborough, MA, home showing the media fanfare that occurred once he was a person of interest in the Odin Lloyd murder. (Commonwealth of Massachusetts; official crime scene evidence)

piece of industrial land, pitch-black, down a dirt road? You have to know what's going on around you. Why take that risk?

In the subsequent days, as the police presence waned, Case explains that he experienced a new kind of visitor to his property. The industrial park became a horrible kind of tourist destination.

It was eerie, and it reminded local residents that a murder could happen absolutely anywhere.

This site was just flooded with people; not just with investigators or people actively looking for a murder weapon. But fans, people that have interest in what was going on. The press, the media—they were there too. It was a pretty big event, and still to this day they come down, they do almost a pilgrimage down here. I don't know if it's the family, but they usually call me and ask me if it's okay to come to the scene of the crime to maybe pay homage to his resting spot. Basically, in other words, the wanted to see the place of his murder. Some people have reached out to me and they usually come as an annual thing.

A murder, in general, tears apart the fabric of a community. But when you throw in all the variables of a Patriots' player, living in a million-dollar home, family man, signed a $40 million contract. You start adding all these things into that pot and, yeah, that makes it a bigger impact to the community because it's more questions. It's more speculations. It makes you wonder. Is the guy living next door to you a murderer?

Meanwhile, as some police were busy checking out the likely site of the murder, others were looking a little closer to Aaron's home.

Aaron's next-door neighbor was Joe Judge, a Patriots special teams coach. Police knocked on Judge's door and asked him about Aaron, and specifically if he had seen him in the last 48 hours. Judge responded he had not seen Aaron since the last Patriots practice.

The police had no further questions for Judge, but they parked an officer outside and began watching Aaron's house and his every move.

Upon returning home from Enterprise, Aaron noticed that he was being surveilled. He didn't like it, and he called his agent, Brian Murphy, to tell him about it.

Murphy, in this case, appears to genuinely have had no idea of how dire a situation Aaron was in. Murphy said the police monitoring was inappropriate, and that his client shouldn't stand for it. He advised Aaron to walk outside and confront the police officers.

"If you haven't done anything wrong," Murphy advised, "they shouldn't be bothering you. It's okay to just walk up to them and ask what they want."

So Aaron hung up the phone and did exactly that.

The officers outside Aaron's house were in plain clothes, but he had seen enough police in his day to know the difference.

As one of the officers in the car—North Attleboro Police Detective Daniel Arrighi would later testify at trial—as soon as Aaron walked over and hailed them, the cops decided to go on the offensive. They immediately asked Aaron if he had recently rented a Chevy Suburban—the car that he had given Lloyd to use.

Aaron said that he had, for his friend "O."

Immediately, as Arrighi later testified, Aaron became "agitated and upset." The reason why is no mystery when all is considered. The police had just shown him that they already understood he was connected to Lloyd. (They had—in the same breath—also shown him what a lousy job he'd done of covering his tracks. In addition to the man's cell phone, Aaron had left the keys to that Suburban in Lloyd's pocket.)

According to Arrighi, although Aaron was angry, he did provide a few additional details. For example, Aaron disclosed his relationship to Odin Lloyd—specifically, that Lloyd dated his fiancée's sister.

However, Aaron soon clammed up entirely when the officers hinted they might like to have a look inside his home.

"You aren't coming in here," Aaron declared—motioning to his house—then stormed away from the officers.

Tellingly, Aaron had not asked the police any questions of his own, such as why they were at his house in the first place or why they were asking him about a vehicle being used by Odin Lloyd.

The police officers did not have to be Sherlock Holmes to know that this was not how innocent people usually acted.

In that moment, because of his actions, Aaron officially became a person of interest.

Arrighi knew he needed to talk to Aaron about what was going on. The tight end needed to be formally questioned, and soon. Arrighi relayed this to his superiors who called Aaron's lawyer. Aaron's lawyer, in turn, called Aaron himself, and advised him to cooperate.

Some moments later, Aaron exited his house once more. He walked over to Arrighi and said he was willing to come to the police station.

After going back inside his house for a few moments to prepare, Aaron got into a car with Shayanna and their daughter, Avielle, and Shayanna drove them to the police station. The officers followed them there.

Shayanna dropped Aaron off at the station, and drove away. Yet as cell phone records later revealed in court show, Shayanna did not return home and stay there. Instead, she drove back to the house briefly, but then pulled away again, driving to numerous locations near the edge of Rhode Island. Police would later deduce that she was probably disposing of weapons and other crucial pieces of evidence from Aaron's household.

Meanwhile, Aaron was joined inside the police station by his lawyers; there is no evidence that he talked to the police in any meaningful way before they arrived.

In a sort of anticlimax, the police then informed Aaron that he was a person of interest in the case—that he should not leave town because they might need to talk to him again. However, they said he was free to go as long as he was willing to cooperate.

He said he was.

Aaron was then allowed to walk out of the police station without being questioned and without being placed under arrest.

Several hours later, the police informed Aaron's lawyers that the matter involved the murder of Odin Lloyd. The police shared that they knew Lloyd was the boyfriend of Shayanna's sister, and that the keys found in Lloyd's pocket matched a vehicle rented by Aaron. The police volunteered nothing more, and Aaron's lawyers did not confirm nor deny these facts.

In the background, the investigation continued.

The following day, the police went to the Enterprise car rental office Aaron had used, and investigated the vehicles he'd recently rented. They learned of the Nissan Altima Aaron had been using the night of the murder and how it had been returned damaged. However, it appeared that any useful evidence was long gone, since Enterprise had already cleaned and repaired the car.

The police also questioned proprietors of businesses in the surrounding vicinity of the industrial park owned by Case. Specifically, they asked for video surveillance recordings that might show vehicles in the area on the night of the murder.

The local businesspeople were helpful, and more than one was able to provide footage showing the neighboring area on the night of the murder. And in more than one case, that footage showed a Nissan Altima matching the one rented by Aaron arriving near the time the murder was suspected to have occurred, and departing just after.

Though no neighbors had cameras trained on the precise spot where the shooting happened—and Jason Case himself had no cameras—the police had just become even more confident that Aaron was their man.

The day after that—June 18, 2013—the police finally showed up to Aaron's house with a search warrant.

Up to this point in the investigation, Aaron's lawyers had been able to keep things quiet; there was no official word about what was happening. No websites or news outlets were carrying the story, and even locals chatting about the police presence at the industrial park did not have many details.

Now, however, that began to change. People were beginning to talk, and mentioning Aaron by name. After all, when a Patriots player is dropped off at a police station for questioning, people notice. Those people tell other people. Soon, word begins to spread.

After presenting their search warrant at Aaron's front door, the police began searching the house and seizing items as evidence. The police seemed uninterested in finding a literal smoking gun, and instead focused on electronics. They confiscated Aaron's computers, phones, tablets, hard drives, and everything they could get their hands on that might record video. This included all components related to his home security system. The police then departed as quickly as they had arrived. Their total time inside the house had not been more than a few hours.

The day after that, June 19, Aaron was summoned to Patriots headquarters. This may have been instigated by his own lawyers notifying the organization of what was happening, or it may be because the police tipped their hand to Bob Kraft regarding what was going on. (Even if they had *wanted* to contain the rumors, the police realized that would soon be impossible for *anyone* to do.) Aaron drove to Gillette Stadium, where he had a private meeting with Kraft and other senior members of the Patriots organization. By all accounts, Aaron swore up and down that he'd had nothing to do with this murder; he insisted on his innocence. For the moment, the Patriots were still willing to take him at his word, and Aaron left the stadium with his job intact.

Later that same day, the news media began arriving at Aaron's house en masse. Officially, he was still only a "person of interest," but this fact alone still qualified as news. Correspondents did live remote crosses to their studios from the street in front of Aaron's house. News outlets began to run stories that wondered openly if Aaron might be involved in the death of his close friend.

Three days later, Aaron was presented with what must have felt like another bombshell. He was delivered a summons notifying him that Bradley had again filed a lawsuit against him for shooting him in the face. It sought considerable monetary damages.

Beyond what the lawsuit itself might mean, this was damning for Aaron because—at what must have felt like his lowest moment—it indicated that his months of attempting to placate and mend fences with Bradley had all been for nothing. Bradley was not—and would never—be his ally.

On top of that, it signaled that Bradley probably smelled blood in the water. Aaron looked like he was going down, and Bradley wanted to "get his" while there was still something left to get.

Almost immediately, the media began reporting on Bradley's lawsuit.

Right and left, the forces of the universe seemed to be turning against Aaron. It must have been a long night in that household.

The next morning—June 23, 2013—the street in front of Aaron's house was crowded with news trucks. *All* major news and sports networks were now reporting on the events involving the superstar Patriots tight end.

It is easy to imagine someone in Aaron's position wanting to stay hidden inside his home under such circumstances, but for unknown reasons, upon rising, Aaron decided to go back to Gillette Stadium. It is possible that he had been informed of something new over the phone and wanted to speak with the Patriots about it in person. Yet it is also just as likely that Aaron felt under attack—surrounded by a hostile press—and sought to find refuge at the one place where he was admired, loved, and supported.

The one thing we know for sure is Aaron was *not* summoned there by Kraft or Belichick.

Aaron braved the glare of the flashbulbs in his front yard, got into his car, and drove to the stadium. However, once he arrived, representatives of the team intercepted him in the parking lot. They spoke to him at length. After the conversation, Aaron turned around and drove back home. It was clear to the media (and all other observers) that the one-time prodigal son had been turned away. Sent home. He was no longer welcome at Patriots HQ.

Aaron returned to his house. A few hours later, there was a knock at the front door, and Aaron was greeted by a second group of police officers with a second search warrant. This time the police focused more directly on items of potential violence inside the home, confiscating a gun and many rounds of ammunition.

At the same time police were conducting this second search of Aaron's home, police headquarters received a remarkable phone call. It was from an employee at the Enterprise car rental that their suspect had used. The employee on the phone claimed to have been on the crew that had cleaned Aaron's Nissan Altima after it had been returned. She said local news coverage of allegations against Aaron had reminded her of an important detail. On the night she had cleaned the Altima, she had found a shell casing from a bullet. At the time she had not thought much of it, and did not currently know where it was.

The police went back to Enterprise to see if the shell casing was still in the dumpster where Enterprise put its trash from cleaning cars.

It was.

And it perfectly matched the others that had been found beside the feet of Lloyd's corpse.

Not only that, but it had a piece of chewing gum attached to it—chewing gum that could be tested for Aaron's DNA.

The noose, at this moment, continued to tighten.

Next, police reached out to Carlos Ortiz, the criminal friend who they knew had been with Aaron on the night of the murder. On Monday, June 24, Ortiz was taken in for questioning, but not placed under arrest. During this questioning, police asked Ortiz if he knew about the ongoing investigation involving Aaron. Ortiz said that he did. The police then began hinting that they suspected Ortiz had been present at the scene of the murder but that he had not pulled the trigger. Using time-tested police tactics of pitting one suspect against the other, they pointed out that Aaron had the money to afford the finest defense lawyers in the country. What kind of lawyers could a low-level street fixer like Ortiz afford?

They let that hang purposefully.

But Ortiz remained uncooperative. He would confirm nothing, and would not talk about his friend.

Sensing a more powerful truth serum was called for, the police next showed Ortiz footage captured by the security cameras near the industrial park on the night of the murder. Ortiz could not—and did not—deny that the cameras clearly showed him inside the Nissan Altima on the night in question. And, moreover, that the footage showed four men in the care as they approached the industrial park, but only three inside as they left it.

This evidence—and other police tactics—began to work their magic on Ortiz.

Retired New York City Police Detective Bo Dietl is an expert on the approaches that investigators use at this stage with a possible accomplice like Ortiz.

He knows every angle open to the detectives, given that Ortiz was not the only one present during the crime. Explains Dietl:

> Whenever you're doing an investigation on a murder like that, you like to get collaboration. In other words, you like to get more than one witness or accomplice. In reality, you use what we kind of call ruses. We have another witness that said, "You saw this." Another witness is

giving us this information, so all you're doing is substantiating what we know already. That's a tool in investigation that we use all the time. It's a good tool for the fact that you make a person feel as though, "Oh, you're not the only one testifying," where they have fear that there's gonna be retaliation against you. When you have two witnesses and you're comparing the same information, "Oh, the car was an SUV. We saw it down the block. In Aaron's case, two guys were in there," and then you have another witness. This is collaboration, as far as I'm concerned.

Confronted with this evidence—and the fact that his cohorts might one day testify against him—Ortiz concocted a strange explanation.

He said that while he had indeed been inside the car on the night of the murder, he had been deeply asleep. He had seen and heard nothing until the vehicle had arrived back at Aaron's house at the end of the night. He was sorry, he said, but he could be of no help when it came to revealing what had happened off-camera in the industrial park.

The police asked if he would take a polygraph.

Ortiz agreed.

However, his story of being asleep throughout the car ride was found to be untruthful by the polygrapher. Confronted with this, Ortiz again became more forthcoming.

He said that he *had* been awake, that he *did* remember traveling with Aaron to the industrial park, and that there *had* indeed been a shooting. And after it, certainly, Lloyd had lay dead on the ground.

Yet as the police leaned in closer—anticipating that Ortiz would now settle the matter beyond any doubt—the criminal invented a new excuse for why he could tell them more.

Someone had done the shooting, Ortiz said. But the night had been dark and murky. Foggy. Misty. Once outside of the car, shots had been fired. He heard them loud and clear. . . but he could not see them. Because of the murky fog, he had been unable to see precisely who had done the shooting. It might have been Aaron, or it might have been Wallace. He just didn't know.

And—Ortiz hastened to add—because he could not see what was going on, he was also unable to say if the shooting had been done in self-defense. Perhaps Lloyd had pulled his own gun and fired first, but the weapon and shell casing had been stolen from the crime scene by neighborhood kids before the police arrived.

While getting Ortiz talking was progress, this particular response must have produced enormous eye rolls on the part of the police as their net was closing in. To their certain knowledge, no meteorological phenomenon was present in the industrial park on the night of the murder. There was no fog or murk. It was not even raining.

After leaning on him further—and emphasizing that his "fog and mist" story had no basis in fact—the police *were* able to get Ortiz to confirm one further detail about what had happened. Though he still clung to his claim that it had been too murky to see very well that night, Ortiz admitted that he *had* been able to see Aaron holding a gun in his hand.

Ortiz would say no more, but he didn't really have to. Based on all the other evidence they were gathering, the police were starting to feel as though they had an airtight case.

There was virtually no explanation for what had happened that night that wasn't a shooting with Aaron directly involved. If he had not pulled the trigger himself, he had at least been present. And what Ortiz *had* confirmed left no room for theories that the murder scene might have been staged by one of Aaron's enemies—that it was "too perfect" to be real.

This was looking just plain real.

The police circled their wagons and shared what they had with prosecutors. Law enforcement knew that they only wanted to move forward if they were 100 percent sure about their case against Aaron. Moving forward prematurely—or with circumstantial evidence that Aaron's lawyers would render unconvincing in court—would be a disaster, especially with such a high-profile suspect. If someone with the stature of Aaron were charged with murder and then found *not* guilty, it would be disastrous. Prosecutorial careers would forever be ruined.

But when police and prosecutors looked at their cards—again and again, from every angle they could think of—all they could see was a winning hand.

They had him locked, and they knew it.

So, nine short days after the actual murder, on June 26, 2013, the police showed up at Aaron's house to take him into custody. He was officially charged with the murder of Lloyd.

A mere ninety minutes later, the Patriots announced that he had been released from the team. They issued a prepared statement, which read in part:

> Words cannot express the disappointment we feel knowing that one of our players was arrested as a result of this investigation. We realize that law enforcement investigations into this matter are ongoing. We support their efforts and respect the process. At this time, we believe this transaction is simply the right thing to do.

As Aaron's became the 28th NFL player arrested since the end of the previous season, many found it ironic that the Patriots had any room left to claim that they were doing something because it was "the right thing to do." The Patriots had all but made an institution out of looking the other way when it came to the transgressions of their players, especially the behavior of Aaron. Indeed, after the Arizona Cardinals released wide receiver Michael Floyd on December 14, 2016, following a DUI arrest, the Patriots claimed him off waivers the next day. He played for the Patriots thirteen days later. Now, suddenly, they claimed to have found a conscience.

As word of the shocking events rippled through both traditional and social media, very few were fooled by the Patriots' PR stunt.

Perhaps seeking additional damage control, later that day Bill Belichick made his own statements at a press conference about the matter. He seemed to take a "you win some, you lose some" attitude, and to claim that this had always been his approach.

As Belichick said in part:

> Our players are generally highly motivated and gifted athletes. They come from different backgrounds. They've met many challenges along the way and have done things to get here. Sometimes they've made bad or immature decisions, but we try to look at every situation on a

case-by-case basis and try to do what's best for the football team and best for the franchise. Most of those decisions have worked out, but some don't. Overall, I'm proud of the hundreds of players that have come through this program, but I'm personally disappointed and hurt in a situation like this. Moving forward consists of what it's always been here; to build a winning football team, be a strong pillar in the community, be a team that our fans can be proud of. That's what we're here for.

After making this statement, there are accounts from Patriots players that Belichick commanded them never to speak Aaron's name again. Former Patriot Dane Fletcher remembers the coach saying, "It's not going to be spoken of. Aaron was released on this date, he is not part of this team. He will not be spoken about in this locker room. It was kind of that understanding with everybody."

They were not even allowed to reference his past accomplishments. He was dead to Belichick—and the organization. It was as though mere banishment was not enough, and Belichick wanted to—figuratively—sentence Aaron to something worse than death. He wanted to sentence him to never having existed as a New England Patriot in the first place.

Events immediately subsequent support this desire of the club to "unmake" Aaron.

The Patriots announced to fans that they would be able to return any Hernandez jerseys they had purchased from the stadium and receive a refund or exchange, no questions asked. (Journalist Michelle McPhee shares that a friend who traveled to a poor country in Africa years later saw children running around in "No. 87 Aaron Hernandez" jerseys. All the Patriots' remaining stock had been donated to charities, a long, long, long way away.) The Patriots lost $250,000 accommodating these exchanges. Aaron was also dropped by all of his sponsors. He was digitally removed from video games that had featured him. His name was physically taken off of almost everything it adorned.

As former footballer Dereck Faulkner observes, this treatment of Aaron was not limited to the Patriots organization, and may not have even come from them, but from the NFL itself.

According to Faulkner:

> At the end of the day, we can speak on how the league really is trying to disappear this entire image of him. They got rid of his jerseys. They totally stopped the sale. So really, it's like a—it's a black eye, but at the same time, it's like a black eye they're trying to like fade away, in a sense. So they don't want to even really bring up Aaron Hernandez's name anymore.
>
> Like they took all of his—all of his photos were taken down in Florida, definitely in New England. You'll never see an Aaron Hernandez jersey anywhere, so they definitely did a job in the sense of like PR-wise control.

Sportscaster Joe Kayata muses that Belichick's approach to the issue was accepted by most people because the so called "Patriots Way" had indeed seemed to work in many previous cases:

> They have the Patriots Way, and it's their way or the highway and you follow their rules, and if you don't you're gone. And if you do you'll succeed and you'll go to Super Bowls and you'll win Super Bowls and that's what I think everybody wants. But, if you don't, they'll get rid of you quickly. And I think, for the most part, he did his job and he did what he had to do and I think it's good that he was there, because it was a controlled environment. Where some of these teams it's [a] free for all. You do whatever you want, and you're the king of the city. Whereas, the Patriots, it's not that way. It's the Patriots Way or the highway.
>
> Following Aaron Hernandez's arrest, I think [the Patriots] just went into camp, and it was just a weird scene because nobody wanted to talk about it, and it was just weird because he [would be] going through a murder trial. Something that's really never happened in this area before. It was a difficult environment to work in, because you're trying to do your job, which is to be a sports reporter, but at times big things were happening and the news wanted you to ask questions about their

response. Especially Gronk. And I felt bad for Gronk in this whole situation because they were linked together. They were like this tag team duo, the greatest tight end duo of all time and he was linked to him, and will be linked to him forever; because they came in the same draft class, and they were this dynamic duo, and then Gronk was constantly asked about it. At one point he was like "I'm not talking about it." And he stopped talking about it. I don't think we've asked him about it since—but I'm sure he would never talk about it.

The ripples from this impact were now felt all across the NFL. In locker rooms all over the league, players and coaches alike asked themselves if what they'd heard about Aaron could possibly be true.

Explains Faulkner:

I got the news about Aaron Hernandez's murder, or his murder charges, from a teammate of mine, and it was utter shock. We were both kind of shocked about it because you don't—you never think that you would hear about a guy who's on the top of the world and the top of his profession, one of the elite players in the league, being charged for murder.

It was like—it was utter shock. It was shock—it sent shockwaves throughout the entire league. For active guys and retired guys, it literally was something that you just don't hear of. The last time we heard of anything of that was like Rae Carruth [the NFL player who served 19 years for a murder plot against his pregnant girlfriend]. We heard about that—I heard about that when we were kids. You've got a guy who's an elite receiver, no different from Aaron.

Aaron was a Pro Bowler at that point, was an elite guy, and you're hearing about that. It was just a shock.

As Faulkner's reaction illustrates, being arrested was indeed something that might happen to a lower caliber of NFL player, but not to a giant like Aaron. Not to a superstar.

And when it comes to Aaron's swift canning by the Patriots, Faulkner is ultimately sympathetic.

> The New England Patriots, in cutting Aaron, they had zero choice. They had to act immediately. And most teams would have acted—or all teams would have acted immediately, and the league would have acted immediately. It just shows [laughs] the level of no-nonsense that they have and the level of cutthroat mentality that the league has in regards to your being able to damage the shield and damage the image of the league. Once there's a threat of you damaging the league, that's an ultimate no-no. So any guy, Aaron or whoever, who would find themselves in that position, would be out of the league immediately.

In the days after his arrest, a series of doors were slammed in Aaron's face. His team. His league. Most of his fans. Most of his friends. All of his sponsors.

It all went poof. Just like that.

He was left with a very small, core group of remaining supporters in his life. These included his mother and brother, his agents and lawyers, and his fiancée, Shayanna. (Shayanna herself was also the subject of intense examination by law enforcement. After all, she was living right there in the house with Aaron, and had opportunities to help him—and was asked to dispose of what was likely crucial evidence that tied her lover to the murder of Lloyd.)

So, it was with this tiny nucleus of remaining allies that Aaron began to plan his defense.

In all, Aaron faced six charges—five related to unlawful gun possession and use, and the last for murder. As Aaron and his expensive defense team began analyzing the evidence, they kept coming back to something—and that thing was a gun. The one thing the prosecution didn't have—for all their mounds of evidence—was *that* gun. They didn't have the one physical object that would tie Aaron most closely to the crimes, and which was necessary for the crimes to have occurred.

This was not insignificant. For Aaron and in his defense team, it meant they had some glimmer of hope.

In the following chapter, Thomas Hodgson, Sheriff of Bristol County, Massachusetts, will provide exclusive information about the circumstances surrounding the incarceration of Aaron while he awaited trial. However, Hodgson was also involved in the police work that went into quickly and definitively making the case against Aaron in the days after his arrest. Hodgson was one of the men involved in the search of Aaron's 8,000 square foot home.

He agrees that, going into the trial, the biggest difficulty for the prosecution was that the murder weapon itself was never found. (To this day, it is still missing.)

According to Hodgson, the gun used to kill Odin Lloyd is now likely "at the bottom of some river or some lake somewhere."

As the local media began gearing up to cover one of the biggest trials in New England history, the details about what Aaron had—or hadn't—allegedly done in the moments before, during, and after the murder began to seep out. The specifics of what the police had found slowly came to light. Some observers were concerned that, apparently, the murder weapon had not yet been located, but most still believed that the case against Aaron was going to be a cakewalk. Some feared that the trial would be almost anticlimactic, because the government's case against him would be, somehow, *too* good.

McPhee summarizes her own impressions—which many in the press were also feeling—as the two sides prepared for trial:

> I've watched him play, but to me, I came at this story as a crime reporter. I've been a crime reporter for a long time, and this was gonna be a massive story, and one of the things that had immediately stuck me when the story broke, was Aaron Hernandez was hardly a criminal mastermind. He's a guy who picked up his friend, Odin Lloyd, his future brother-in-law, and brought him back to a wealthy suburb, that had never seen a murder, and instead of dropping him in Dorchester, which there are sadly, are a lot of murders in Dorchester. He brings him back in to a tony suburb, and wacks him [very close to] his home. Who does that?
>
> Who leaves chewed up bubble gum in the rental car they use for the murder? Nobody, unless you're a dummy. Who leaves footprints and

video? Think about it. This guy left a bread trail for investigators. It didn't take long to figure out that this dumbass did this crime.

The evident contempt voiced by McPhee was shared by many in Boston at the time. Aaron's behavior had been disgraceful. He had brought shame to his city and his team. Fans who were accustomed to cheering Aaron on any given Sunday now felt disgusted with themselves for having supported an alleged murderer. They felt fooled. Bamboozled. And the worst part as that the person who had fooled them was clearly no criminal mastermind. Though sportswriters imbued his catching and blocking on the field with poetics usually reserved for the transcendent or religious, this upcoming trial laid bare that Aaron was not magical and definitely not some sort of deity. He was a not-very-smart criminal who had allegedly killed somebody over his own fear and insecurity. And what was more, he had not even been smart enough to halfway cover it up.

To fans in New England, Aaron appeared to confirm their worst fears. He was every negative stereotype of an NFL player come to life. He had been hiding right under their noses, and they hadn't even noticed.

Patriots fans might have hated themselves for getting duped by someone who was clearly no master criminal. But, as the date of the trial approached, they hated Aaron more.

When it came to bail, Aaron's lawyer argued that his lack of a criminal record, his celebrity status, plus his fiancée and young child made him a low flight risk.

Yet, the judge was not swayed. As court transcripts show, in the bail hearing, she called the evidence against Aaron "very, very strong."

Aaron would stay in jail until the trial.

CHAPTER 12

"I can't wait till all this mess is over with."

—AARON HERNANDEZ, JAILHOUSE RECORDING

Aaron Hernandez was held at the Bristol County Jail while awaiting trial. It was a sprawling facility that housed about 750 pretrial detainees. This move meant a kind of vulnerability that Aaron had not had to confront in many years. Would he be attacked by any of the other inmates? Would he be beloved by them? There were so many unknowns.

And while his strength would keep him reasonably safe in most situations, there were ways that Aaron massive physical size counted against him inside the jail. He was confined to a seven-by-ten cell. He could not move about most of the day. For such a large man, it must have been extremely claustrophobic.

The staff and administration at the prison were not overly concerned about Aaron's comfort, but his safety was foremost on their minds. From the get-go, it was assumed that he was a man with a target on his back.

Perhaps no one alive today can speak more definitively to Aaron's experience of being incarcerated than Sheriff Thomas Hodgson.

As Sheriff Hodgson explains, knowing his facility would house an inmate like Aaron brought many special concerns and considerations:

> I had to begin planning for such a high-profile person. It does require some careful thinking around where they're going to go. We obviously want to protect them. It's not uncommon when high-profile people come into a prison facility, there's always at least one person in there

that wants to make a name for themselves by targeting the high-profile person. So you have to take certain precautions to make sure that doesn't happen.

For this case, I wanted to make sure that we had the right staff in place. We had young staff that could have been fans that might do things or they are tempted to do things that Aaron Hernandez might ask for in the way of special privileges or what have you.

So I want to make sure we had experienced people, my superintendent talked to my medical people, where we were going to house him, but for how long? Because obviously we were concerned too about his transition from going from a stadium, if you will, on Sundays with thousands and thousands of people cheering him on, revering him, with two numbers on the back of his jersey to a place where he was not going to be revered a whole lot by many people.

And there'd be just one of many where he would have a much longer number and a much smaller living space.

Hodgson also makes clear that his jailers were aware of the potentially damning psychological toll Aaron might experience. Some inmates came from housing situations that had been poor to begin with. Small, shabby bedrooms. Joint living arrangements with other men.

But Aaron was literally coming from a mansion.

It was a long, long way to fall.

As you can imagine, he's gone from an 8,000-square-foot home to a 7x10 foot cell. He's not walking from room to room. He was in Special Management. He didn't have the same amenities obviously, and so he is in the general population. So that's a big transition, so we have to be careful to make sure that, number one, his mental state is going to be okay. He's going to transition okay and so forth. That requires us to take these steps that occur when you have a high-profile person.

Hodgson also explains how he and his team at the prison were forced to strike a strange balance. They had to accommodate someone with Aaron's special back-ground... without being seen to give him special treatment.

Hodgson had an entire jail to think about, and hundreds of prisoners who weren't Aaron. If word got around that a former NFLer was getting things a cer-tain way, then morale in the prison could quickly go south. Prisoners could com-plain, or riot, or worse.

Even though it was going to be a challenge to maintain a sense of normalcy around Aaron, he and his crew understood that that was now exactly what they were tasked with doing.

Hodgson says that Aaron was informed from the start he would receive no special treatment. Hodgson tells how he thought this so vital, he did it personally:

> I told [the jailers], "As soon as he comes in the door, make sure you let me know before he leaves that intake area, I want to speak to him."
>
> So when he came in, I was down at intake. I told him, "Look, I'm the sheriff here. I want you to know that you're not going to be treated any better or any worse than anyone here. If anybody is around you more than they're supposed to be, you need to tell the immediate supervis-ing unit and/or me, but you need to let us know that."
>
> I was surprised in how congenial he was. He had a very magnetic personality, somebody that was really easy to get to know. In a matter of minutes, you think he's a nice guy, smiling, seemed very warm and just a regular Joe.

Aaron was processed and taken to his cell. The routine of his days was explained to him. Word spread throughout the prison. The other prisoners gossiped. The rumors *had* been true. The Aaron Hernandez was joining them, and now he was actually here.

As the novelty of his presence slowly died down, Aaron adjusted to prison life with disturbing alacrity. A celebrity among the other inmates, he nonetheless spent most of his time alone, doing things like playing solo card games.

Although it left him confined and constrained—and took away almost all of his choices—the jail also removed Aaron's problems and stressors in a way he hadn't experienced in years. Over the course of his entire life, Aaron had always had things to worry about. As he aged, his problems had grown right along with him—in both size and number. But now that was suddenly over.

He no longer had to keep up with organizational expectations from the Patriots. He didn't have to worry about being murdered by Bradley or any one of his other enemies. And perhaps above all, he didn't have to worry about his public lives and his secret lives bleeding into one another.

In a way, it was a relief.

Aaron accepted his situation with a contemplative calm that was almost eerie. To quote Sheriff Hodgson:

> We were stunned at how easily he just sort of seamlessly transitioned into the prison setting—and he hadn't done time in prison. Our staff were sort of struck by that; I was.

Yet there is one area where Aaron might have maintained a secret inner life while waiting in the jail. Namely, in his health status.

Hodgson confirms that Aaron's arrival at the jail would have involved a medical physical exam. Every inmate got one. Aaron would have been asked very sensitive questions that would have included questions about what medications he was taking, and questions about diseases. He would almost certainly have been asked if he had HIV, as others have speculated in this book. However, Hodgson told this author that Aaron's responses, by law, will forever remain out of the public eye.

"The medical histories and the medications that people are being given are protected by law," explained Hodgson. "So we can't reveal anyone else's medical conditions or treatments."

Yet when pressed about the possible evidence that Aaron had HIV disease, Hodgson goes on to confirm the following:

> If *anyone* that comes to prison has a disease, and it was a communicable disease, they would not be put in a cell with someone else that

potentially can get infected. The medical staff would make those
determinations, and they would class the person either into medical
and keep them in medical until such time as they had a cell where the
person could be by themselves and not be able to infect other people.
But that's a very strict medical protocol that all prisons have.

It should be noted that Aaron was immediately given his own cell (though, in
fairness, this may have been because he was a high-profile inmate).

While his legal team prepared for trial, Aaron slipped so easily into prison life
that his jailers became disturbed. The abrupt removal of his day-to-day problems
and the strict routine of prison life had done something to Aaron's psyche. He was
almost like a religious pilgrim who was attaining some sort of deep spiritual
peace.

Which was, in a word, suspicious—especially to those who did not know
Aaron.

Hodgson relates that Aaron took to jail so easily that he became concerned that
the football player might be hiding something. Foremost on Hodgson's list of
suspicions was gang affiliation. In the experienced sheriff's perspective, it was
hard for someone to come from the places Aaron did and *not* be touched by gang
life. The fact that he was now an inmate with no serious problems only made
Hodgson more suspicious that Aaron was reconnecting with gang life—the
Bloods specifically—while on the inside. A cursory physical inspection of Aaron
was all it took to give those suspicions life.

Explains Hodgson:

> We had some concerns that Aaron was affiliated with the Bloods. He
> had a whole host of tattoos on his arms. He had tattoos on the web of
> his index finger/thumb, which is a common place for the Bloods to
> have their markings. He denied [gang affiliation] to my internal affairs
> people. They passed that along to me, but we still had concerns about
> it. My staff were still not certain.

But Hodgson knew it was vital for him to make the determination, and quickly.

Aaron's life could be in danger. Even if Aaron seemed at peace (or even legitimately felt that way), there was still the possibility that someone in a rival gang might try to be a hero and take him out. (To be clear, Hodgson was also acting out of self-interest. If anything happened to a high-profile detainee like Aaron, it would be disastrous to his career—as authorities came to realize in the aftermath of pedophile Jeffrey Epstein's suicide while incarcerated in August 2019, while awaiting trial on child abuse charges.)

As Hodgson elaborates:

> It was important for us to get to the bottom of whether or not he was in a gang or not, affiliated with Bloods because we have rival gangs inside our facility.
>
> We need to know everything as much as we can when it comes to gangs and intelligence, as to who the players are and where they're going to be because we also have intelligence on people who are already there. And we want to make sure that we're on top of it for a lot of different reasons, not just propagating fights and things like that. But those things can settle the riot if you don't have the proper background information.

But Hodgson's usual intelligence gathering brought up nothing definitive when it came to Aaron. The NFLer's celebrity seemed to shine like a blinding light that made it impossible to tell who was talking about him because of his fame and fortune, and who might be planning to do something sinister.

In the end, Hodgson decided to use a one-on-one interview with Aaron to get to the bottom of things. While Aaron never flat-out admitted which gang he belonged to, what the sheriff discovered was extremely revealing nonetheless:

> I explained to Aaron that we just wanted to know and understand [his gang affiliation]. But Aaron was one of these people that was very street smart. And Aaron would be suspicious of anything that I would be asking. That played out, and that's what brought us to this sort of defining moment where he needed to know—he thought he was better

than I was on being street smart. He understood that that wasn't going to fly, that ultimately, I was going to be at least as street smart as him if not better.

When I'm speaking to Aaron about his tattoos, the whole while I was speaking to him, he kept looking to his right because that's where the other officer was sitting.

And then I could see, although he was listening to me, also his mind was working around, "What's the [game] here?" There's another officer in the room. What's this guy trying to do? Is he trying to trick me? So after just a little bit, he said, "Can I ask you a question?" I said, "Sure." He said, "Did you wear that sweat suit in here to try to get me to relax so I'd talk to you?" I said, "What are you, a friggin' idiot?"

And I was smiling when I said to him, "You think I'm going to come in here dressed up on Saturday? This is my day off. Do you think I'm gonna get dressed up to talk to you? You've got to be kidding." And he kind of laughed, and he said, "Well, listen. I'm-I'm-I'm-I'm street—I'm street smart. Nobody's better than me at that." And I said, [Unintelligible] what you're doing?" and I said, "Really, you-you're that good?" And he goes "Yeah." And I said, "Well, you're not better than me." "Oh yeah, I am. Oh yeah, I am."

I said, "Nah. So let me ask you a question. What do you know about the key motivations in people? 'Cause there's three key motivations in people—that we all have. One of them is [unintelligible] the other."

"I don't know what you mean." I said, "Well, see, you're either auditory type or visual type or kinesthetic type. Primarily, you're motivated by one of those three. You may have a combination, but you're motivated [one by one.]

"And you're a visual type. How do you know that?" I said, "'Cause every time I talk to you, you say, 'I see what you're saying. I see what you're saying.' An auditory type, you would have said, 'Yeah, I hear what you're saying. It rings a bell with me.' And if you're a kinesthetic type, you'd say, 'That feels good to me' or 'I understand.' But see, you don't do that."

He goes, "Wow." And then I started talking to him about overcoming behaviors. "How do you do that, overcome my behaviors? How do you—how do you shatter that old behavior and replace it with a new one?"

And I started getting into that and he goes, "Wow, you're really good and, you know, maybe you are as good as me." And he started then to sort of establish respect. And then in some ways, he kind of started almost liking me because I was not judgmental about him.

Establishing this bond with Aaron was key for Hodgson in determining how best to understand his prisoner. There was no "eureka moment" when Hodgson broke through and got Aaron to spill his guts, but a rapport was built. Aaron seemed to show genuine respect to his jailer. He was legitimately communicative.

But were those communications true? How seriously did Aaron himself take Hodgson? There is room to wonder if the tight end took everything the sheriff said with a grain of salt. For example, this jailhouse phone recording made during this period exposes a cynical Aaron in an exchange with his Aunt:

Aaron: You know what the, what the sheriff said to me? He told me that, he told me you need to talk with your father throughout the days, so that the love can build up through your heart. And you won't think about all the things you don't have.
Aunt Jennifer: What the fuck? I think he needs therapy.

Aaron: That's what that nigga told me. Yeah. Yeah.
Aunt Jennifer: Alright, he needs to take some meds.

Aaron: For real. I was like, typical, typical uh, typical white person saying.
Aunt Jennifer: (laughs)

So when he was speaking to other people, Aaron dismissed Hodgson's attempts to meaningfully reach him. Yet that does not mean the sheriff's attempts to connect were a total failure. Aaron might simply have been uncomfortable admitting to the connection.

If Hodgson can be said to have made an error in his attempts to connect, it is grounded in the fact that he was concerned mostly about *external* threats to Aaron. And, in the end, we now know the greatest danger to Aaron's life was himself. Yet Hodgson is able to recall instances when he saw "flashes" of the "other Aaron Hernandez" threatening to peek through the genial football player personality.

In retrospect, Hodgson realizes these flashes ought to have concerned him more.

> The darker side was always sort of behind the scenes. There was only once where he went from zero to 60 with me, and that was when I had returned from Quantico from the [PI] Academy after two weeks of leadership training. And he had done something while I was away. I said, "I want to see him in an interview."
>
> I walked in, and I looked over at him because he was sitting at the table when I walked by. And I did this intentionally because I knew he sort of looked at me as a father figure. And I just looked at him, and I shook my head, and I said, "I am so disappointed." I went to sit down, and that set him off. So he started yelling at me across the table, screaming, "These guys had no right to look at my legal mail. They were searching my cell, yada, yada, yada."
>
> And I said, "Am I yelling at you?"
>
> [Hernandez said:] "No, but this is wrong," and he's really upset.
>
> So I said, "This isn't the Aaron Hernandez that I know. When I'm on the street, people ask me, 'What's this guy like?' You know what I tell them? I tell them he's one of the nicest guys you'll ever meet, easy-going, guy you'd want to go grab a beer with. But that's not the Aaron Hernandez I'm seeing here." So he started to come down a little

bit. And I said, "Look, if you were wronged, if anybody violated a policy here, they'll be held accountable."

I said, "Do you trust me?"

"No, I don't trust you." [Hernandez replied]

"Aaron, you don't trust me?"

"Well, I don't completely trust you. Like I wouldn't let you take flowers to my mother or something," which was kind of weird.

I never did understand exactly.

Because the situation of being incarcerated did not allow Aaron to "act out" in the ways he usually liked to, he used noncompliance and sudden anger to show his displeasure to Hodgson. Aaron might have been trying to throw Hodgson off his guard, or he may simply have wanted attention. Whatever the case, tiffs between the two men became a regular thing… and it extended beyond the sheriff.

As time went by, Hodgson saw Aaron's uncanny skill when it came to manipulating other people from a variety of perspectives.

Aaron was a master manipulator. He was a master at it. He was very, very good, knew how to use his personality to get what he wanted. My instructions: If ever he used the first name of any officer in the unit where he was, that officer was to be removed and reassigned because I knew at that point he'd already broken the officer down. And he had a really easy way of doing that. The other thing about Aaron that really was very evident to me was he had a metal trap for a mind.

Anything he did not want to penetrate that trap, he wouldn't. He would completely control it. So all the realities swirling around him, he would pick and choose what he wanted to be reality, and that would exist in that metal box that he would think about every day, and everything else could never get in.

Aaron, in my mind—I'm not a psychologist—but he displays every indication he's a sociopath. Sociopaths dissociate themselves with the act soon thereafter. If you recall, after he killed Odin Lloyd, there's

film of him here throwing the baby up in the air, playing with his child
as though nothing happened.

In addition to his quest to understand and "read" Aaron, Hodgson nurtured a
relationship with him that had genuinely touching aspects—at least one of them
involving "reading" in a very literal sense.

Michelle McPhee shares a detail she discovered about the relationship that
Hodgson himself may have been too modest to mention in his own interviews:

> Aaron got out of the University of Florida completely unable to read or
> write. He couldn't read. The cops had to read the warrant [when they
> arrested him]. They had to really help him with the language that was
> in the court documents, and in the search warrant, that they eventu-
> ally showed up at his house with.
>
> Think about it. Here's a guy, who got through [less than] four years
> of college, and when he left, he learned how to read with the help of the
> Bristol County Sheriff, Tom Hodgson, and the book, *Tuesdays With
> Morrie*, which ironically, he would pass on to his good friends, the
> Pouncey twins, 'cause they, too, got out of the University of Florida
> without knowing how to read or write.

Hodgson's goal of helping Aaron learn to read may have been undertaken out of
a genuine concern for the young man, or it may have been yet another tactic to
help the sheriff connect to his new inmate and understand what he was all about.
Either way, we would probably not have Aaron's final, telling suicide notes if not
for Hodgson—because Aaron would have been literally unable to write them.

During his time in jail, Aaron spent plenty of time talking and working with
Hodgson, but these were interactions Aaron assumed would be forever
private.

Hodgson is only talking about them today because Aaron is dead.

For the rest of his time, Aaron chose only to pursue communications he
believed would stay outside of the public eye. He turned down all requests to be

interviewed by the media, and/or to tell what would unequivocally been his own shocking side of the story.

When he was forced to be in front of a camera because of a public court appearance, Aaron remained silent and always let his lawyers do the talking. He did not smile nor acknowledge the cameras trained on him. He mostly just kept his head down.

Part of this silence came from the fact that Aaron did not want to be asked about the relationships he had severed—the one with the Patriots foremost among them. Aaron had been deeply impacted by what happened with the Patriots during his time behind bars. Namely, that the team did not fall apart without him. With a few minor adjustments, they continued to win and win big—retaining their spot as perhaps the most dominant team in the NFL.

As sportscaster Joe Kayata puts it:

> [With Hernandez incarcerated], you have to change your offense. And the Patriots did change their offense. They didn't go with that two tight end set that they had for three seasons with him that worked so well, so they had to change things up. And they went more to the slot receiver, and it changed. But, they were fine. They went on to win a couple more Super Bowls. So, the Patriots did okay without him, but to think about where they would be *with* him, and if he was still at his peak. I don't know if he would still be where he was.

Aaron was also dealing with the fact that many Patriots fans—who had held him in such high regard—had also shown no compunction about moving on without him.

Explains Kayata:

> The initial reaction was that he was guilty. It just came out so fast, and he was cut from the team, and all signs pointed to him being guilty. I think that all the fans took a step back and instantly—you know he was found guilty in the court of public opinion before he ever found guilty in actual court. So, I think fans kind of took a step back. But, I don't remember the actual moment right away, that the real fans

reaction to it. But, I think everybody was just shocked to be honest with you. That was the main thing of "How could one of the New England Patriots do this?"

And as to the press:

> [We members of the press] were more busy about covering the team. And they were going to the Super Bowl, and they played the Seahawks in Super Bowl XLIX. It turned out to be one of the greatest Super Bowls in the history of Super Bowls. Malcolm Butler has an interception at the end and that was it. And it was February 1st. And meanwhile, we have a crew at the Aaron Hernandez trial. So, that's what kind of stuck out to me is that, while this guy is trying to save everything he has in court, his former team is moving on and they're in Super Bowl XLIX.

Michelle McPhee also opines on the willingness of New England sports fans to quickly move on from their one-time hero. There was, she believes, a collective disgust that somebody who had worn the uniform that represented the city in so many ways would have sunk so low.

> [Fans feel that] if you wear a uniform of any type for my city, a police uniform, a firefighter uniform, if you're a member of EMS, if you're wearing any sort of uniform that represents my city, Boston—the New England Patriots and the Boston Red Sox and the Boston Bruins and the Boston Celtics, all of them—you have to behave accordingly. You are representing me. You're a diplomat for my city, and if you're out there killing people and shooting people and smoking [drugs] and doing all kinds of insanity, I don't want you wearing a uniform. I don't care how good you are on the field.
>
> If you are tarnishing the good reputation of my city and the people that work alongside you on a field, on a line of a fire truck, in a police car, I don't want you. So, that's the attitude. . . it doesn't matter how good you are. If you're dragging your girlfriend out of an elevator by

her hair watching her bounce across the room, then I think we get rid
of you because you don't represent us. You don't represent our values.
You don't represent our city.

It was crushing to have gone from a beloved public figure to a reviled one. (The
group of fans who stayed supportive of Aaron while he was in jail was very small.)
There was a part of Aaron who wanted to believe that the fans' love for him had
not ended. (Or that, if it had, he might one day be able to win it back.)

A remarkable trove of jailhouse phone recordings exist—released from prison
authorities to this author—that provide insight into Aaron's psychological state
during this period, and they also tell us something about the people closest to him.

Aaron's friends did their best to convince him that he still had some kind of
public support, because they knew that's what he wanted to hear. It is impossible
to know if this had the desired impact on Aaron, or was clearly—even to him—
just wishful thinking. This call between Aaron and a friend—made not long after
the start of the NFL season—is representative:

> **Friend:** Hey bruh, you know, let me tell you some-
> thing. One second thought bruh, hey, you know how
> like, we wore the hats and shit?
> **Aaron:** Yeah.
>
> **Friend:** Bruh. That's all everybody hollered bruh at
> the games bruh.
> **Aaron:** What?
>
> **Friend:** Free Hernandez bruh. Swear to God bruh.
> **Aaron:** No way!
>
> **Friend:** Bruh, swear to God bruh, and I was walking
> with my GM and they um, they were at the Hall of
> Fame you know all the fans were right there bruh,
> and they were just chanting that shit, chanting
> it. And I was like they ain't ever gonna let it go.

You're like the new O. J. Simpson of the town, of
the nation.
[Both laugh]
Aaron: That's crazy.

Whenever speaking on the phone, Aaron seemed mindful that he should also keep up the pretense of innocence. Whether either he or his friends took it seriously remains to be seen. Consider this exchange between the incarcerated star and a male friend:

Friend: You're staying positive though, too?
Aaron: Yeah, everything is great.

Friend: I gotchu.
Aaron: Great.

Friend: As long as you ain't lying to me.
Aaron: I wouldn't lie to you. Everything is great.
How could I not be free when I'm innocent? It don't
make no sense.

The only person who seems to have been willing to shoot straight with Aaron when it came to how he was being portrayed in the media—at least occasionally— was his own mother.

Though it contains hearsay and misremembered details, this example is typical:

Mom: And then today you know another thing coming
out in the papers and everything on the news
again.
Aaron: What?

Mom: Somebody named Chicago and they found a .38
gun, some shit.

Aaron: They did what?

Mom: They found a .38 caliber gun and somebody called Chicago, when a girl got in an accident, a 19-year-old girl got in an accident they found a gun in her car and they're tryna connect it to the double murder.
Aaron: What?

Mom: I don't know anything about it, it was all over the news last night I guess.
Aaron: Ugh this is weird. I don't even listen to all that media stuff.

[. . .]

Mom: What about this other 2012 thing that has me nervous I just read about that. Is that okay?
Aaron: What about that? Yeah I don't know, I know nothing about it. Except what people tell me.

Mom: Alright.
Aaron: Why's their stuff in the paper?

Mom: No just about the car being at the house.
Aaron: Oh I don't know. Honestly I don't, I have no clue about any of that but it's just the, it's what the police do they try to make shit up or something, I don't know.

[. . .]

Aaron: God writes straight with crooked lines, remember that.
Mom: Well this God is gonna go real straight.

Though she didn't sugarcoat the things that she said to her son, Aaron's mom remained tender and sympathetic, and that comes through in her tone. Reviewing the seemingly endless jailhouse recordings, there is the sense that Aaron at least looked forward to talking with his mother.

The same cannot be said for his fiancée, Shayanna Jenkins.

Reviewing the recordings of the time, it seems clear that talking to his fiancée was a stressor for Aaron. When they conversed, his replies to her were typically brief and terse, as if he was not encouraging her to continue talking.

Shayanna did not hesitate to give Aaron bad news, or to give him additional problems to deal with. She also did not hesitate to share the negative ways in which his actions had impacted others.

In his calls to his fiancée, Aaron heard from her—again and again—about the strain his arrest and actions had put his family under. In one typical recording, Shayanna Jenkins shared how Aaron's arrest has impacted her own life, despite her best efforts:

> **Jenkins:** Well it's not even me 'cause I mean I've been ignoring it and whatever and I don't go but it's like when I get around people or when I'm in that environment it's literally, it's all anyone talks to, even in the grocery store and they'll be like, Aaron Hernandez you know what I mean it's just random things and it's just like oh my God I cannot literally I had to go to Providence, literally in the freaking ghetto to do my grocery shopping the other day. Just to get away from everything, everyone knows who I am, everyone knows what the baby looks like, everyone knows my vehicle, so when I pull up they're already looking. It's not like we have privacy, it's not like we're hounded, but you know they're still talking about it and being assholes on purpose like you might be an aisle away and they know I'm in the next aisle

so they're gonna mention your name you know what I mean just to see my reaction.

Several of the calls between Aaron and Jenkins provide evidence of a growing frustration and emotional distance on the football star's part.

Aaron: Whoever's listening to this call - FUCK YOU!
Jenkins: What?

Aaron: I'm saying the people listening on the other line.
Jenkins: Your whole demeanor has changed.

Aaron: I know.
Jenkins: Why.

Aaron: Huh?
Jenkins: Why.

Aaron: What do you mean? I'm tired of that damn Bible.
Jenkins: My god.

Aaron: You didn't tell me you love me yet, or you miss me. You don't miss me? You're enjoying your time by yourself, huh?
Jenkins: Aaron, yes, I miss you but I'm not going to remind you every single day.

Aaron: You only see me once a week, what [do] you mean?! You can't remind me when you see me? The hell you talking about?
Jenkins: Listen. Listen, this is bringing flashbacks you need to slow your roll. Your whole persona right now.

Exchanges with his fiancée also make clear Aaron and Jenkins had very different expectations regarding what might constitute a speedy resolution of the case.

Aaron: In like eight, nine months I'mma be in court, and then they gonna say not guilty, after I've proved my innocence. And then I'm gonna be home with you guys, chilling, doing the, doing the *something*

Jenkins: No that's eight, nine months, that's a, that's a while from now.

Aaron: Not really.

Jenkins: What do you mean not really?

In these jailhouse calls, Aaron can also be heard giving an assessment of his treatment at the hands of the Patriots and Bill Belichick.

Despite being shunned by the team and essentially thrown away, there are times when Aaron still seems to recognize his old coach as an innovator and leader.

Aaron: Bill Belichick is the number one person that teaches teams, don't listen to the media because most of the time they make up stories and they're rarely true. I wish he practiced what he preached. Especially coming to me, throwing me in the, in the, in the dust in the wind. (laughs)

Friend: What?

Aaron: Word. Cause if he really believed that he wouldn't be listening to all these false accusations! 'Cause when I'm innocent, you know what I'm saying, it's gonna be, it's gonna be a whole bigger thing, you know what I'm saying, all these people

that are hating on me, when I'm innocent, what're
they gonna say now?

Yet, in another exchange with a friend on the same topic, Aaron seems to portray Belichick as inflexible, stentorian, and controlling:

Hernandez: That's what Bill does! He tries to program everybody but you know, some of them niggas
is like I'm, you ain't gonna program me, you know
what I mean? I'm myself. Yeah you don't like that.
You know what I'm sayin? That's why he got a problem with the. . .? You know what I'm saying? He's
like that. Bill wants you to say, talk how he wants
you to talk, do everything how he wants you to do
it, you know what I'm sayin?

While Aaron was ruminating on how he had gotten to where he now was, the world outside moved on without him, and his lawyers prepared for trial.

Though some of his friends and family tried to conceal it from him, in the eyes of much of the public, he was already guilty. The police eventually released footage of Aaron holding the gun they believed was the murder weapon—a .45 Glock—and also released many incriminating text messages between him and the other suspects involved. (Even though police did not have the gun itself, the fact that they had this footage seemed to be enough to secure a guilty verdict for many observers.)

Seeking to earn their astronomical pay, Aaron's team of expensive defense attorneys began fashioning arguments on their client's behalf. In addition to the cold, hard fact that the prosecution could not produce the murder weapon, there were several other circumstances that—if they did not exculpate Aaron completely—at least made a cold-blooded murder seem out of character for him. (This might be especially true for members of the jury who only knew Aaron from the all-American image of him the Patriots and the NFL hoped to project.) The most astounding among them was the simple fact that Aaron had never actually been convicted of anything before. He had no priors. Despite a life spent scoffing at the law, he had never been found guilty of breaking it in any serious way. Nor did anyone know of the potential that he had killed—or orchestrated the killing—of Jordan Miller in a case of mistaken identity.

And the brushes Aaron did have with the law? His defense team was ready to minimize them and make them seem like rare exceptions. A few traffic violations? A fistfight in college that got a bit out of hand? These were modest, venial sins. These were the sort of sins the members of the jury might well have committed themselves at some point.

If there was any flaw in Aaron's selection of a defense team, it may have been that he was the kind of person who believed that the most expensive always equaled the best.

Michael Maloney, an established local attorney who would later represent Carlos Ortiz, characterized Aaron's defense team like this:

> The defense attorney for Hernandez wasn't actually someone who had a great deal of criminal experience. It was someone that was employed from Ropes & Gray, which is the powerhouse law firm that the New England Patriots used to secure a lot of their contracts, like the $40 million contract.
>
> They don't necessarily know their way around the justice system. So when I saw some of these heavy hitters coming in knowing what they're charging, knowing what they're looking for and immediately attacking some of the—the integrity of the evidence—yeah. So the mental health components of this case really never, you know, saw the light of day because the defense attorney employed by Hernandez really took the approach as opposed to going after the mental health or this individual needs treatment or some sort of section or commitment like that, playing that angle.
>
> They really came after—we're going to pin it on Ortiz. Or we're going to pin it on Wallace. And you know, good, bad, or ugly, that was the theory that was employed by Hernandez's attorney. So a lot of the pre-trial motions were focused on suppressing. And what I mean by that is keeping various parts of evidence out of court, so the jury never

sees it. So a lot of the defense strategy and theory implemented by Hernandez's attorneys was keep out as much evidence as we can. And then, throw all the rest of the evidence—push that onto Ortiz. Push that onto Wallace. It was an unsuccessful theory.

While lawyers readied for a courtroom battle, Aaron received letters from fans and sometimes answered them. (His responses were usually filled will dull platitudes to be strong and believe in God.) He read the Bible (something he could now do, thanks to his literacy lessons from the sheriff). He also ate massive quantities of Honey Buns, the snack cakes that often served as a kind of jailhouse currency.

Aaron sometimes got into minor scraps with fellow inmates, but they were always relatively minor. Compared to many of the inmates around him, he was still close to a model prisoner.

As excitement for the trial built, the story received more and more national attention. It was reported outside of the New England press, and in media outlets that did not usually cover stories involving football players. For example, *Rolling Stone* published "The Gangster in the Huddle," an extensive article alleging that the Patriot was a habitual user of PCP.

Meanwhile, Carlos Ortiz and Ernest Wallace were both charged with being accessories to the murder of Lloyd. However, their trials would not start until Aaron's had concluded.

Then Shayanna Jenkins was charged with perjury related to having lied concerning the details of Aaron's actions and whereabouts on the night that Lloyd had been killed. These charges against Jenkins would later be dropped.

Jenkins and Aaron might have seemed—for all intents and purposes—to be essentially a married couple. Life partners. Serious about one another. But legally, they were only *engaged*, not married. This would turn out to be huge, as a married person cannot legally be forced to testify against his or her spouse. The same privilege is not afforded to those engaged. Shayanna made it very clear from the start that she did not want to testify against Aaron at the upcoming trial but knew that she could be legally vulnerable if she did not. What Jenkins would do or say—and how it might impact the fate of Aaron—was an open question as the proceedings got underway.

Aaron's. trial for the murder of Lloyd finally began on January 29, 2015. Press from all around the world covered it, and the families of those involved attended personally almost every day. The scene outside the court was one of chaos. Helicopters flew overhead and those attending court that day had to park up to two and a half miles away.

The stakes were unbelievably high. If Aaron was convicted, he would spend the rest of his life behind bars without the possibility of parole. Barring something like a presidential pardon, he'd die in jail.

For their part, the Patriots—and the NFL itself—were hoping that the trial would conclude as quickly as possible. (At various times, there had been evidence indicating that Kraft and/or Belichick might be called to testify. This must have added to the tension. Anything could happen when a powerful person got on the stand.)

Any what verdict were they hoping for? On the one hand, it was bad PR for the Patriots and the NFL to have employed a convicted murderer. However, this scenario had happened before, and would surely happen again. All manner of scoundrels had played in the NFL, and the league still remained intact. And what of the other scenario? What if Aaron were found not guilty of all charges? Would he want his job back? Would he demand it? This actually might have been a more terrifying scenario for the Patriots and the league. Aaron's name was going to be dragged through the mud by the prosecution, and everybody knew it. By the time the trial was over, even if the jury vindicated him, he was going to be so soiled that probably no team would want to be associated with him.

The Patriots looked on nervously at a spectacle they wished would very soon be over. Everyone knew that trials were like live theater: You never knew in which direction things were going to veer.

As opening statements began, the prosecution laid out its case in a clear, workman-like way. There were no real surprises.

According to the prosecution, Aaron killed Lloyd because Lloyd had become dangerous to him. A blabbermouth who might spill secrets. And prosecutors carefully used the text message trail Aaron had left behind to establish clear premeditation. Shooting Lloyd had been no last-minute decision stemming from a disagreement at the industrial park. Rather, Aaron had been planning to do this for some time. Lloyd was dead as soon as he'd gotten into that car with Aaron, Ortiz, and Wallace. (Most likely, he had been a dead man walking a long time before that.)

The prosecution danced around precisely *why* Lloyd had become so dangerous to Aaron. They characterized Lloyd becoming a "loose cannon" in Aaron's eyes. Of saying too much, and of being the kind of guy who would run his mouth.

However, the prosecution never became much more explicit than that. They never said which criminal activities Aaron was afraid Lloyd might talk about. There were lots of them, of course, so the jury probably had an easy time guessing.

It is important to note that the prosecutors *never* said that Aaron was afraid that Lloyd would share that he was bisexual or had HIV. The prosecutors never even implied it. But they certainly could have, if they'd wanted to.

By the start of the trial, it was well known that one of the first things law enforcement had done was explore a motive concerning Aaron's sexuality.

When the police and prosecutors got a search warrant to review Aaron's phone records, they had found a lot of sexually charged text messages between Aaron and a number of men. It had naturally become one of the avenues they found themselves exploring.

Many of the police conducting the investigation had had no idea Aaron was gay or bisexual.

In addition to monitoring Aaron's own jailhouse phone calls, the calls of Wallace and Ortiz had been monitored as well, and their statements also showed police that Aaron probably had a secret gay life.

For example, Wallace had been recorded making a jailhouse phone call in which he explicitly says of Aaron, "I wouldn't have helped him if I had known [that he was gay]."

Wallace spoke to one of our investigators from behind bars in a more in-depth interview. Still reluctant to discuss specifics of the Lloyd murder, he continued to defend Aaron and promised to tell the truth "one day"—a truth he has presumably kept from law enforcement the courts.

I still wake up every morning and can't believe that all this stuff happened … This whole situation is just the craziest situation I [have] ever been. Being with Aaron, the last thing that I thought was that I'd be in jail looking at a life sentence or even being in jail during the sentence that I'm doing now.

The way it played it out with all these allegations of him doing this, that that, the other cases, like the case that he beat before he passed away [the Boston double homicide], all of this shit is crazy. I can't believe it.

From what I'm hearing, it sounds like even Aaron's own brother put a negative mark against him. That's crazy. Aaron was a good kid. If he was your boy, he would take the shirt off his back and give it to you, "You know what I'm saying?"

Ever since this whole thing started, all you hear is negativity about him. I know and people that been around him know that he's not a negative person.

I have always wanted to have the opportunity to talk good about him, because nobody's talking good about him. Before all this happened, everybody was his best friend. Everybody was happy with him. Then all of a sudden, this happens and he was shunned him. To this day, people don't even know what really happened.

One day, I will get a chance to say my half of the story because they had him [Aaron] looking like a monster. Plus, they got me looking like his protégé monster too. It's not the case.

By the time of the trial, the prosecution had considerable evidence—not just hearsay—that Lloyd knew that Aaron was gay, if not also battling HIV. And Aaron was clearly afraid that Lloyd was going to reveal that fact to someone close to him, such as Aaron's girlfriend's sister.

While planning how they would come after Aaron, police and prosecutors had carefully considered whether to include this idea—that Lloyd knew that Aaron was gay, and that Lloyd might tell people—as a motivation for Aaron to kill him.

Prosecutors could definitely prove that Lloyd was one of the men who had had access to the secret sex apartment that Aaron kept on the side. (A strong theory among investigators was that Lloyd had either walked in on an encounter between Aaron and another man at the apartment, or that Lloyd had gathered some knowledge by talking to Aaron when Aaron was drunk. One member of law enforcement openly bandied about a scenario in which the two men went out drinking on a Friday night, Lloyd had a couple of drinks, and he might've off-handedly made a derogatory remark that Aaron took as homophobic. Perhaps this was even the crux of the disagreement at the club that some witnesses had seen.)

Prosecutors also thought that some of the text messages on Aaron's phone between him and Bradley could be characterized in court as indicative of a relationship that went beyond friendship. The way the two men spoke of their fraught relationship and their love for one another could also have been used to paint a picture for the jury of a secret sex life—whether it was real or not. And it would be no great leap to imagine Lloyd learning of these texts.

It's not known if Aaron's own defense team believed that prosecutors would bring up a secret gay sex life as a motive. But the actions they took show they may have intentionally concealed details of his sex life so that the prosecution could not use them—even if they intended to.

For example, at trial, the defense wanted to access Aaron's medical records. However, the form they filled out to access them—a long form with a series of boxes to check beside different medical conditions—has almost every box checked… except for four. One of those four boxes is for information relating to HIV or other STDs.

As detective Bo Dietl observes:

> This subpoena for the medical records for Aaron Hernandez by the defense team is very distinctive. There's four boxes here. Drug or alcohol abuse, social worker information, psychiatric information, and then there's HIV or sexually transmitted disease. This is not a mistake. Every box is checked *except* HIV or sexually transmitted disease. Why was that left out? You tell me. Every box is checked except that one.
>
> So, they didn't want to know. It's very obvious they didn't want to

know if he had HIV or not. They didn't want the evidence there. That certainly could be checked by the police to substantiate the motive. To substantiate the fact that that's why he killed Odin. So I, as a detective [if I had been in charge of the case], would request the blood to find out if he had HIV. Because that could put my whole puzzle together for establishing the motive for killing Odin.

As a detective or prosecutor, right now you have to look for the motive. If he had HIV and that was going to be released to the public, that would certainly be a motive for murder. Very simple. There's no question about it. It's not the idea of if he was gay or not gay. That's not the problem right here. The problem is you got to have motive—and by not checking this, by not revealing that he had HIV, because HIV would be the motive for killing the person that knows and could let the secret. Maybe he was blackmailing Aaron? Who knows.

Dietl also hastens to make clear that even though Aaron was *afraid* that Lloyd could or would tell the world about his HIV disease, there is no actual evidence that Lloyd planned to do any such thing.

We have no real concrete evidence that Odin said, or was going to release any of this information about these meds. We don't know that for a fact. The only thing that I feel very uncomfortable about is that we have to realize we don't know, again, what Odin was going to do, if anything. So he's a true victim at this point right now.

Of all the people interviewed for this book, no one has more intimate knowledge of Aaron's sexuality than Dennis SanSoucie, his closest friend and occasional sexual partner from high school. What are his thoughts about the potential impact of Aaron's need to keep his gay life a secret? As SanSoucie explains:

It is a motive for him, if that was the case, and that he didn't do the shootings. I do strongly believe it was a motive because what we don't know is maybe there were video clips of him engaging in gay activity.

Maybe there were pictures. Maybe there was more than just someone going to step up and say "Yeah, do you know the Patriots tight end? Yeah, he likes guys." I think there was a little bit more to it, but I think it was something that Aaron could not live with if the truth was out. This is why I say the "reverse psychology". He needed to act so gay around people because he was involving himself in that activity, but he needed to have his mind say that, "Oh, other people have kind of seen this, but I can kind of just play it off that I'm having fun. Even if people think I really am, no one really knows the truth. So, if I could just talk about it then maybe it's going to be easier for me to deal with."

The Aaron Hernandez that I know, just like the Dennis [SanSoucie] that I know, didn't want anyone to know the truth. The only reason the truth has come out is because he has passed away.

Though Aaron's need for a secret sex life might have been an excellent motivation for the murder, prosecutors made the decision never to bring it up in court.

In the end, their reasons for this omission were several:

- "Outing" Aaron in court might make him seem like a victim, and make him more sympathetic to the jury.
- Patriots fans were everywhere (even on juries), and the idea of "dragging Aaron's name through the mud" by invoking *any part* of his sex life was also likely a way to turn sentiment against the prosecution. Bringing up his sexuality might make it seem the prosecutors were using unsavory, inappropriate tactics. The case was disturbing enough, and there were almost certainly jurors would find a secret gay life even more upsetting.
- Finally, the prosecution felt like they had such a strong case against Aaron that they didn't *need* to bring up his sexuality. Sticking to the facts of the night of the murder was a battle the prosecutors felt confident they could win. Adding new elements to the trial—like motivations stemming from a hidden gay sex life—would move the fight to uncertain ground, where potentially anything could happen.

So the prosecution stuck to the facts.

The evidence showed what Aaron had done. There were multiple reasons *why* he had done it, but the facts made clear he *had* done it.

They let that be enough.

When it came to granular and explicit details regarding Aaron's motivation, the prosecutors would let the jury use their imaginations.

Even though his sexuality was left out, observers seemed to find the prosecution's version of events very compelling.

Michelle McPhee shares the courtroom's reaction to the presentation of the basic facts in the case:

> It becomes very clear this weekend [of the murder], that Aaron Hernandez gets an idea in his head, that Odin Lloyd knew something about him that he didn't want out, and the very next night time's changed. Instead of being best buds, Aaron Hernandez has these two wackadoodles, essentially his bodyguards. One was on angel dust. Who even does angel dust, in this day and age? But one of them is a dust mop named Carlos Ortiz, and the second guy is Ernest Wallace, who he had to hire, Ernest Wallace, because he shot his last bodyguard, Alexander Bradley, in the head and left him in an industrial lot, very similar to the one in which Odin Lloyd was found dead.
>
> So, here is a guy. This is not a friend you want to have, because if you don't pay your share of the stripper tab, he'd shoot you in the face. If you said something derogatory about his, you know, divulged his sex life, he shot you in the back [several] times, and so, clearly, Aaron had this hair triggered temper, and on Saturday night, he picks up Odin Lloyd, who clearly sensed that something wasn't right, 'cause he texts his sister, "Did you see who I left with?" "Nfl." And Aaron Hernandez installs a security surveillance system, and this idiot is caught with the murder weapon on his own cameras, which he thought he could smash with a baseball bat, and the cops wouldn't be able to retrieve the data that had already been uploaded on it. So, he's not exactly the smartest criminal we've ever come across.

Wackadoodles, indeed.

It was clear from the prosecution's opening that Aaron had associated himself with many shady characters who might potentially play roles in this story. The jury settled in for a tale that would involve many bad decisions by Aaron, and the choice to associate himself with many bad people.

When it came time for the defense to present its case, the approach must have caused Kraft, Belichick, and the whole NFL to breathe a collective sigh of relief.

Rather than trying to excuse Aaron's actions because of the pressures of the NFL (coupled with regular blows to the head), his lawyers argued that the current trial was the result of sloppy police work by incompetent cops.

The defense team claimed that Aaron had been targeted merely because he was the most prominent and famous of the men who had been in the car with Lloyd that night. They argued that while Aaron lived in a shadowy world of criminal types, any one of the men present that night could have killed Lloyd. Ortiz and Wallace were not angels. Did they have a score to settle?

Law enforcement, the defense claimed, had selected Aaron to throw the book at him because he had celebrity status. Because he was the first one of Lloyd's associates who came to mind—no more, no less. The defense claimed the prosecution would not be able to prove beyond a reasonable doubt that their client had been the one who pulled the trigger. They would not be able to prove who had pulled the trigger at all.

SanSoucie recalls his impression of the defense's argument at the time:

> So if Aaron was at a scene of a crime and a murder had been committed… there's some ties to that. So yeah, there's a 33 percent chance that he did commit the crime, but with two other people. [Prosecutors] point the finger. Here's the NFL star. Point the finger. I mean, this is something that could've been in the works to be set up. And I don't know how it would've went down.

The defense said that all the prosecutors could prove was that four bad actors had driven into an industrial park, and three had driven out. Beyond that, said the defense, the other side had nothing. They had no confession. They had no video or audio recordings. They did not even have a murder weapon. *All* they had was some lazy cops who thought it would be easy to pin a crime on a celebrity.

Yet, as opening statements concluded and witnesses began to take the stand, the defense had a hard time portraying the officers who testified as incompetents who were obsessed with celebrities. Their investigations had been by the book and top notch. And, time after time, the officers showed how they had carefully pursued *all other* avenues of possibility before being forced to conclude that the evidence pointed *only* to Aaron. Again and again, they pointed out how difficult they knew it would be to charge Aaron. As the jury listened attentively, the cops emphasized that charging Aaron had not been done lightly. Instead, they said, it had been done because the overwhelming evidence of his guilt left them with no other choice.

During cross-examination, Aaron's lawyers tried to show that the police had targeted the Patriot from the beginning. Not only that, but also that the police had left glaring holes in their investigation. (Holes through which the "real murderer" might have slipped.) The defense *was* successful in identifying minor paperwork errors committed by the police in the preparation of search warrants, as well as during the cataloging of evidence. But that was it. There was a general sense in the courtroom that these were soft body blows; the defense had landed no solid punch that anyone could see.

During the course of the testimony, the jury was taken to view Aaron's house and, more than once, to view the industrial park where Lloyd's body had been found.

Jason Case explains what this process was like:

> The jury came down a number of times. We were very cooperative. We had to block off the street. All the police officers were around. A lot of media, a lot of press always here when they catch wind of somebody coming to visit the location or the scene of the crime. And it's a little eerie because it brings back all that. It brings back what really took place on this property and brings you back to a real situation that's eye-opening.

To augment their firsthand visits to important locations in the case, the jury also heard from experts in DNA, ballistics, and crime scene investigation. They were also shown videos by the prosecution that were taken from Aaron's cell phone. These videos showed Aaron cavorting on the night of the alleged murder; acting erratic and strange. Acting, in short, like somebody who might be preparing to commit murder.

Then the prosecution called a surprise witness—Aaron's own fiancée, Shayanna Jenkins. They wanted her to settle one of the most crucial questions in the case: Where was the murder weapon?

As the jury had already heard, though Lloyd had been shot with a Glock .45— and an expert who worked for Glock had testified for the prosecution that the gun Aaron had been seen holding in the surviving home surveillance footage was indeed a Glock .45—nobody had been able to find the weapon itself.

Aaron's defense team believed it would be hard for prosecutors to win a murder trial without a murder weapon.

But that was where Jenkins came in.

Under oath, she testified how, shortly after the murder, Aaron had asked her to dispose of a black box in his basement. The trial transcripts reveal precisely what she said under oath:

> **Prosecutor:** Ma'am, do you recognize the area of your home here?
> **Shayanna:** I do.
>
> **Prosecutor:** And what area is this?
> **Shayanna:** The back patio.
>
> **Prosecutor:** When you receive these calls from the defendant that he asked you to do something?
> **Shayanna:** Yes.
>
> **Prosecutor:** What did he asked you to do?
> **Shayanna:** To remove a box.

Prosecutor: Did he indicate to you what was inside
the box?
Shayanna: No.

Prosecutor: Did he say why he wanted you to do
this?
Shayanna: I believe he said it was important I'm
not too sure.

Prosecutor: Okay. And with regard to why it was
important, did he further describe that? Why it
was important?
Shayanna: No.

Prosecutor: After you had put the box in the
trunk, what did you do?
Shayanna: I left.

She had not looked inside the box, Jenkins claimed, but had dutifully taken it out of the home and discreetly thrown it away in a public waste receptacle. She said the box was very heavy. At the time, Jenkins believed it contained only several pounds of marijuana.

She also testified that she knew Aaron kept a gun in the house; in a drawer. She often noticed it whenever she opened the drawer. She testified that after throwing away the black box, the next time she opened that drawer, the gun was gone.

All along, Jenkins claims that she doesn't know anything, but if she truly didn't know, why did prosecutors give her immunity?

Detective Michelle Wood and undercover investigator Sargent Don Jackson, who worked together in attempting to answer so many unresolved questions, find Jenkins's lack of curiosity as disturbing as it is unbelievable.

Jackson: She can hardly testify and think anyone
is going to believe her when she says, "I knew
what was in part of the box, but not all of them."
Not at all. You know what's in that box if you're

putting clothes inside that box. Her sister's boy-friend is killed, brutally killed by her boyfriend, fiancée. She's just going to carry a box out.

Wood: Her sister's boyfriend is brutally murdered not far from [her house]. She's not worried that perhaps this person is going to come back after her? This person is friends with her boyfriend and presumably may know where she lives. So there's a killer on the loose and she doesn't care at all? She doesn't question it one bit? When her boyfriend Aaron Hernandez tells her, "Here, take this box and get rid of it?" Yeah, complete nonsense. She should be worried that am I next, is Aaron Hernandez next, but she's not. Her concern is sim-ply getting that box out of the house. If this were me, I'd be freaking out and using all those cam-eras that he has propped around the house to ensure that you were secure.

Jackson: Absolutely. Her sister's boyfriend is killed, her future brother-in-law. The police show up here to confirm that Aaron is okay because they tied the car, Odin, and this house together and all she's worried about is covering up a box walk-ing out the door, not saying she knows what's in it! She doesn't know what's in it. We watched her put stuff in it. It's baffling.

Wood: She should be worried. Am I next? Is Aaron next, but she's not. Her concern is simply getting that box out of the house.

Jackson: Getting rid of the box.

Wood: If you actually think about it, that murder was half a mile from here.

Jackson: Right up the street.

Wood: If this were me or anyone for that matter, we'd be freaking out and using all those cameras that he has propped around the house to ensure that you were secure.

Jackson: I wouldn't be walking out the back door.

Wood: They certainly weren't worried. Did she look worried when she was walking out of the house?

Jackson: No.

Wood: The only thing she was worried about was getting caught.

It was clear that the prosecution wanted the jury to conclude the gun had been in the box. (After the trial, some journalists have speculated that the gun was later obtained by associates of Aaron—who had watched Jenkins dispose of it—and taken to Georgia where it was thrown into a swamp. Others merely believe it now rests in a garbage dump somewhere in New England.)

Jenkins had not named the make or model of the weapon while telling her story. However, a Glock .45 was presented to her at the end of her testimony. She confirmed that, yes, it appeared to be the same gun that Aaron had kept in the drawer.

Then, in what must have been extremely awkward for the engaged couple, Aaron's own defense team went after Jenkins.

The defense challenged her recollection of the events. They challenged her memory of when she had last seen the gun in the drawer. And, most of all, they challenged her knowledge of firearms and her ability to identify a Glock .45. (The prosecutors had shown her only one gun and asked if it matched the one from the drawer, and Jenkins had said it did. But this was nonsensical if Jenkins did not "know guns." Perhaps she was only affirming that it was a handgun, not a rifle. Or that it was an automatic, and not a revolver. There were many different kinds of guns.)

Jenkins did not waver under cross-examination, but neither did she score many points. She gave muted, quick answers, and appeared to be unable to recall many details.

Jenkins's testimony let prosecutors present an explanation for where the missing gun was. But it was only that—one explanation. It was certainly not proof.

The day after Jenkins stepped down from the witness box—with, probably, the Patriots and the NFL collectively holding their breath tighter than they had in many years—the team's owner, Robert Kraft, himself was called to testify.

Kraft's testimony was short, but damning to Aaron.

Kraft told the story of how Aaron had come to visit him immediately after the murder and sworn he'd had nothing to do with it. It was very clear to the jury that Aaron had almost certainly been lying to Kraft. Beyond the details of the night of the murder, there were other things Aaron had said to Kraft that just didn't add up. What's more, if Aaron would misrepresent himself to his own employer, might he also be doing that—here, today—in front of the jury?

Kraft was asked about nothing further. After telling the story of Aaron's claim of innocence, he was allowed to step down.

NFL executives from coast-to-coast must have, again, breathed a collective sigh of relief.

Kraft was followed by another major witness for the prosecution—and a familiar if not confronting face for anyone who'd been following Aaron's saga thus far: Alexander Bradley.

The twist was that, because of a legal ruling, Bradley was not allowed to mention that Aaron had allegedly shot him in the face, despite being clearly disfigured.

Even so, Bradley still found a way to deliver meaningful testimony that put another nail in Aaron's coffin.

Acting as a kind of character witness, Bradley told the jury how Aaron had bought marijuana from him on a near-daily basis for many years. He also testified to the range of other drugs that he saw Aaron use on a regular basis. Without speaking about his own shooting, he told stories that made clear Aaron possessed an ever-ready willingness to use violence. Bradley also confirmed that he had seen the same mysterious black box in Aaron's house that Jenkins had later disposed of.

* * *

What, then, really happened to the missing gun?

Not content to let the question linger, in the course of our investigations for this book, we took the unprecedented step of renting the North Attleboro home of Aaron and Jenkins to conduct our search for the murder weapon.

Why did we do this? What made us think we might find something that the government missed?

The answer is in a jailhouse phone call between Aaron and Jenkins, which has only recently been made public after being unearthed for this investigation.

In the conversation, Aaron tells his fiancé: "Just sell the house, honestly … We're selling the house—everyone knows where we live. The only thing they have on me is finding those things in my house."

Because of this, we were convinced that the gun could still be there, hidden somewhere in his home, waiting for us to find it.

We conducted a thorough search of the mansion. We surveyed all the key locations where Aaron's security cameras had been trained. We spent an extensive amount of time searching the furnished basement where Aaron kept his pool table, and where he often "held court" with his friends. The space is nearly 8,000 square feet. There were more surveillance cameras in the basement than in any other location.

In this basement, we found empty safes that had been "drilled out" in the course of the investigation. We did not locate the murder weapon. However, we did discover a significant amount of cocaine—missed by law enforcement—and an iPod.

Why was this important? If we found cocaine, and police had not in their initial search, was the investigation botched from the outset?

What's more, one of the major scandals of the trial was that Bradley originally claimed that he and Aaron had recorded a music video of themselves bragging about committing murders. However, the video was saved and password protected, and Apple refused to unlock it on his phone. In the end, a potential superweapon for the prosecution was disarmed. The video was never shown to the jury.

As Michelle McPhee explains, many who were passionate about seeing justice done were accordingly furious:

> That's one of the reasons I don't have an Apple iPhone, because Apple refused to help the investigators unlock that rap video that mind have changed the jurors' mind. And there are dozens of cases where Apple was resistant to assisting in homicide and terrorism investigations, which is why I have a Samsung.

Could the video that Aaron and Bradley recorded also be on the iPod we discovered in our search of Aaron's house? Excited by this possibility, we sought to have it forensically examined by an expert. However, to our dismay, we learned that it no longer works and cannot be salvaged or repaired.

Nevertheless, the significance of our finding this potential cannot be overestimated. At the very least, it indicates the initial search by police. It also strongly hints that the investigation was thorough from the outset.

But the story of our investigation into the missing gun does not end there.

After we seemed to hit a roadblock after not finding the gun in the house, Aaron's co-defendant's attorney, Michael Maloney, revealed an unexpected bombshell—the murder weapon, he confessed, was dumped in Connecticut.

Read as an on-the-record interview between our investigative team and Maloney—ostensible about Aaron's defense counsel—wends its way to this revelation:

> **Maloney:** The defense attorney for Hernandez wasn't actually someone who had a great deal of criminal experience. It was someone that was employed from Ropes and Gray, which is the powerhouse law firm that the New England Patriots used to secure a lot of their contracts, like the $40 million contract.

They don't necessarily know their way around the justice system. So when I saw some of these heavy hitters coming in knowing what they're charging, knowing what they're looking for and immediately attacking some of the—the integrity of the evidence—so for example—I don't know if you're familiar with—but there was actually—the box was thrown out. It was—which weapon was it that was thrown out via motion to suppress?

Interviewer: That was Wallace's that was found in the basement, I think.

Maloney: Yeah. It wasn't the g—was it the gun? There was something—

Interviewer: It wasn't the murder w—it was a gun. But—

Maloney: It was a gun but not the gun because the gun wasn't found.

Interviewer: They never found the gun.

Maloney: Yeah. The gun—

Interviewer: It could still be in this house.

Maloney: I don't think it is. I have a pretty good idea where it is. [laughs]

Interviewer: Really?

Maloney: Yeah.

Interviewer: Where?

Maloney: In Connecticut.

Interviewer: In that box [she] took out?

Maloney: Yeah. Yeah.

Even without the video, Bradley's testimony sent the defense into a tailspin; the attack on *his* character seemed to be working. Aaron's lawyers could see it on the faces of everybody in the courtroom. The jurors were beginning to understand what kind of man Aaron was. The idea that the police had done shoddy work and selected the tight end out of spite and proximity was getting harder for them to swallow.

The defense could feel the trial slipping away. They knew they needed a new approach.

In what must have seemed like a last-minute Hail Mary, the defense next confirmed that Aaron *had* been present the night of the murder. However, they claimed that he had not killed Lloyd.

The defense stated that Aaron had not stopped Wallace and Ortiz because he feared for his own life. They claimed Wallace and Ortiz had taken large amounts of PCP on the night of the crime, and it had made them act violently and unpredictably. Aaron, they said, had been afraid for his own life, and unable to stop the crazed drug addicts from murdering Lloyd.

To make this case, the defense called Dr. David Greenblatt, an expert on the effects of PCP. He confirmed that if large amounts had been ingested, it might indeed have had the kind of effects on Wallace and Ortiz the defense team now described.

Next, the defense called DNA expert Eric Carita, owner of Ace Forensic Consulting Services, LLC. He had collected the DNA found on the piece of gum wrapped around the shell casing found in the back of the Enterprise car. That DNA had been identified as belonging to Aaron. The defense wanted to demonstrate that simply because Aaron's DNA was on the fired cartridge casing, it did not necessarily mean he ever handled the weapon.

Interviewed exclusively here, Carita shares what he told the jury.

> My job, in this case, was actually the collection of DNA from a piece of evidence that was originally not tested. The defense decided, "Hey, listen. I want to have a certain piece of evidence tested for DNA in order to potentially answer a question."
>
> I think the defense wanted, in this case, the question of whether the partial DNA profile that was detected on a fired cartridge casing could have come from a piece of gum that was stuck to it. And with gum

being a rich source of DNA and fired cartridge casings having very little to no DNA profile from them, this is what is typically known as secondary transfer.

Basically, what the theory was is that Aaron Hernandez chewed gum. It was left in his vehicle.

After bringing back the rental car to Enterprise, an individual took what appeared to be paper with a little child's drawings or writing on it and picked up the fired cartridge casing and the piece of gum together, combining them, forcing them to touch, forcing them to come together. Then it was discarded in a garbage bag, which went into a dumpster.

After learning about this, law enforcement then returned; asked where this garbage was; collected the piece of evidence and tested the fired cartridge casing. It came up with a partial DNA profile, which was consistent with Aaron Hernandez's DNA profile. But the gum that was stuck to it was never tested.

So in that case, the defense requested that I collect a swabbing or collection of DNA from that piece of gum and have it tested for DNA.

Since Aaron Hernandez's DNA profile was detected on the fired cartridge casing, the defense wanted to demonstrate in fact that simply because Aaron Hernandez's DNA was on the fired cartridge casing, it does not necessarily mean he ever handled that bullet.

If I had chewed the gum, we'll say, and left it in the car and then the gum and the fired cartridge casing were smushed together, my DNA could be on that fired cartridge casing. Even though I had nothing whatsoever to do with the fired cartridge casing but only the gum, my DNA can be transferred onto that.

There are strengths to DNA, and there are just as strong limitations to it as well. These are some of the things we have to realize when we're performing DNA testing or testifying on behalf of DNA.

As the jury listened rapt, Carita explained what the evidence at the scene led him to conclude:

Allegedly, Mr. Hernandez purchased the gum; chewed the gum; left it in the car. And there was a fired cartridge casing in that vehicle as well.

Later on, an employee from the Enterprise car company found the paper, the gum, and the fired cartridge casing and combined them together when they were not originally combined.

Basically, the fired cartridge casing and the gum came in contact with each other, but they were never originally in that way.

Carita also reminded the jury that the piece of paper found in the back of the car by Enterprise employees was scratch paper—containing a series of aimless doodles, probably made by Aaron's daughter. In one sense, the doodles were not important to the case. Meaningless markings, they did not contain names or information. But the fact that they were made by Aaron's daughter may have reminded the jury that the murder took place on Father's Day, which could have unnerved them. It certainly unnerved Carita.

> That's a little disturbing. . . knowing that it was Father's Day; he got out and potentially had been involved in this crime; left his daughter's drawing in the back seat, and then it ends up crumpled up with a bullet casing and gum—I don't know why it bothers me, but it bothers me.

Even so, it was clear how Aaron's lawyers sought to characterize this evidence, and what scenario they wished the jury to imagine.

Explains Carita:

> Since they did come in contact with each other, the fired cartridge casing and the gum, the goal for the defense was to demonstrate that in fact the DNA could have been transferred onto that fired cartridge casing when they were smushed together basically by the Enterprise employee.
>
> Aaron Hernandez's DNA profile was already determined because it had been tested by the Massachusetts State Police Lab. So we knew Aaron Hernandez's DNA profile.

[But] when you have two pieces of evidence like this, the limitations of the testing basically don't determine. . . it doesn't prove in fact whether Aaron Hernandez ever handled that bullet.

Even as he explained to the jury about the uniqueness of DNA—sharing that nobody could have an identical DNA match outside of literally identical twins—the defense used this to create doubt in the minds of the jury (just as O. J. Simpson's dream team used the complication of understanding DNA to confuse jurors). The defense wanted the jury to understand that simply because Aaron's DNA was on that bullet, it was not proven that he had fired the gun.

Neither was it proven that he had handled the gun, or even loaded it.

The defense painted a scenario in which Aaron had merely chewed some gum and dropped it on the floor of his car. Later, a shell casing fired by someone else in the car had also fallen to the car's floorboard. The gum and the casing might have been then accidentally intermingled by the Enterprise employee.

Carita also showed that—though the same brand and flavor—there was no way to verify that the chewed gum found in the car was the same gum Aaron had been seen purchasing on the night of the murder. He also could not verify that the gum had not been chewed days before the murder. DNA, Carita conceded, "is resilient"; it will hang around on something like chewed gum for quite a long time.

Carita understood his testimony was intended to make the case against Aaron shakier. He was also well aware of the so-called "CSI effect" that came from jurors watching television shows in which DNA evidence was always so definitive that it immediately proved guilt or innocence beyond a shadow of a doubt.

What you're dealing with a lot of times on the stand is one side—we'll say the prosecution—is trying to support their theory. The defense is trying to support their theory. And what you have is the forensic evidence in the middle. But what the forensic evidence is there for is to basically say, "Here's what we got. Here are the results, and here is what it could or could not mean."

Forensics has many, many strengths. [But] it has many limitations as well. And I think the jury needs to understand that there are strengths and there are potential limitations. You don't want to get—you could say—overwhelmed by the CSI-effect.

Jurors have to be reminded that forensics is always important in cases, I believe. Forensics is one aspect, one piece of the overall puzzle. You have crime scene investigators. You have police. You have prosecution. You have defense. And forensics is one of the pieces of the puzzle.

So the defense showed that a piece of gum Aaron had once chewed had come into contact with a shell casing that any number of men in that car could have touched. As Carita stepped down from the witness stand, some in the courtroom sensed that things could be turning in Aaron's favor.

The final witness called by the defense was Jennifer Smith, the technician at the lab that had processed Aaron's DNA sample. She echoed what Carita had already told the jury, emphasizing that DNA can be transmitted from one object to another. She said it was extremely likely that DNA could have been transferred from the gum to the shell casing in the scenario described.

The defense also reminded the jury that a previous witness earlier in the trial, Jennifer Mercado, had testified to seeing Wallace and Ortiz smoking PCP earlier in the night.

Then, to almost everyone's surprise, the defense rested.

They had called only three witnesses, and their total time in front of the jury had been much shorter than the prosecution. But just as time of possession did not always determine the winner of a football game, the defense knew that the side making the lengthier presentation was not always the one the jury agreed with.

Aaron's defense team may have taken their clipped approach to project confidence, and to telegraph that the DNA ambiguity should definitively settle the matter, as it did with O. J. Simpson.

However, privately, it is much more likely that—to use another football term—they had called a last-minute audible. That this approach had been composed on the fly out of necessity, and they had done the best that they could to stitch together a new approach given the circumstances.

Whether Aaron personally understood the state of his defense is anyone's guess. He may have still believed he was likely to be acquitted when all was said and done.

During the entire trial, the jury never heard from Wallace or Ortiz. If they had, the two accomplices would probably have painted an even more damning picture of Aaron. Attorney Michael Maloney would represent Ortiz in his own murder trial, which took place after Aaron's. (Ortiz—who was not offered to "cut a deal" and testify for the prosecution—is currently serving a six-year sentence for being an accessory after the fact.) However, Maloney explains what jurors *might* have heard from his client:

> Ortiz was told repeatedly, "If you say anything, you know, you'll be next." And in fact, at one point [at a meeting after the murder at Hernandez's house], you know, he *is* put in that position—actually, he's sitting in the kitchen—right behind us, sitting in the kitchen.
>
> And Hernandez looks at Ortiz, whispers in his ear and says, "Look back there. See those woods. A lot of space to hide stuff back there." And the insinuation was one where, you know, you talk, you're next.
>
> I mean, that's what Ortiz experienced. Listen, there are a million things that Ortiz should have done differently. But he was also in a situation where he was physically domineered and physically threatened.
>
> And when he was told that—you know, he wasn't outright threatened. The language wasn't, "I'm going to kill you. I'm going to do this to you." But the insinuation, the context, the message was clear as day. You talk, you'll be in the woods.

According to Maloney, not only was Aaron guilty of killing Lloyd, he was also prepared to kill Ortiz and Wallace if he felt either of them might not keep his secrets. Aaron made that abundantly clear to both men.

And a jury would have known all about it had Ortiz taken the stand.

But that, of course, never happened.

After presenting their DNA experts to the jury, the defense rested.

The trial then moved to closing remarks. Aaron's lawyers chose a member of their team named James Sultan to deliver them—the last words the jury would hear in Aaron's defense before beginning their deliberation.

Sultan's remarks further revealed that the defense team may still have been grasping for a new angle that would throw the case their way. In their final words to the jury, they seemed to be arguing that Aaron simply had no motivation for doing the deed.

Sultan reminded the jury that Aaron and Lloyd had been close friends for many years. Sultan reviewed all the strong connections the two had—from football, to a rollicking lifestyle, to the fact that they were on course to literally become members of the same family. Sultan argued that Aaron and Lloyd didn't hate or distrust each other. To the contrary, they were best buddies. They loved each other. They were lifelong friends and (shortly) literal relatives.

And what offense had the prosecution concocted so dire that they believed it would cause Aaron to murder such a close friend? Sultan took the jury back through all the tiffs and disagreements between the two men that the jury knew about. He characterized them as minor, and tried to make it seem ridiculous that someone could ever be moved to kill somebody over them.

Aaron got into disagreements with people all the time, Sultan said. He got into serious disagreements and even fights—the lawyer said—and with people much less close to him than Lloyd. And yet Aaron didn't go around killing *those* people. So why on earth would he kill Lloyd? Why would he kill somebody so close to him over something so minor?

Of course, Sultan left out a good deal of Aaron's history.

He left out the many, many times that Aaron *had* been moved to violence over the smallest slights—naturally, as a defense attorney would do to create perception of their client to jurors. He left out the fact that Aaron had *often* attacked complete strangers at the slightest provocation—or even with no provocation at all. And he certainly omitted that fact that the only other relationship in Aaron's life similar to the one he'd had with Lloyd—his relationship with Bradley—had ended with Aaron's shooting Bradley and leaving him for dead in a parking lot.

The jury, of course, would hear none of this.

Sultan concluded his closing remarks by saying that even if Aaron *had* planned to kill Lloyd, there was no way he would have done so in the way prosecutors had lain out. Sultan seemed to be arguing that for Aaron to have done the crime as alleged, he would have to have been very stupid. (This was probably a tactical error on Sultan's part. None of the witnesses thus far—on either the prosecution or defense list—had testified that Aaron was very intelligent.) Sultan pointed out that no smart murderer would kill his victim so close to his own house—and he certainly wouldn't leave traceable car keys in the victim's pocket, or a cell phone with incriminating texts. What's more, he *certainly* wouldn't have brought along friends who would be witnesses. Sultan said Aaron was just not that stupid.

The prosecution argued he was.

In their own closing arguments, the district attorney made the case that all evidence showed Aaron was guilty. He had done this crime, and everything pointed to that fact. There was no other scenario that even made sense.

The theory that Wallace and Ortiz had done the deed was, they said, asinine.

After the night of the murder but before his arrest, numerous witnesses had seen Aaron palling around with Wallace and Ortiz. In public or private, they were convivial and chummy. If the two men had killed Aaron's brother-in-law-to-be on a PCP bender, Aaron ought to have been furious with them. He ought to have told the cops, or exacted revenge himself. (Or at least avoided the pair for a while.) Aaron did none of these things. He stayed tight with Wallace and Ortiz. Why? What was the only explanation? It was because—the prosecution argued—Aaron had wanted Lloyd dead and had pulled the trigger himself.

The prosecutors also made clear that poor planning, lack of forethought, or just plain stupidity were not exculpatory. Committing a crime in a very, very stupid way did not mean you hadn't committed it. Being stupid did not make you innocent. People committed stupid crimes all the time. Probably, *most* murders were committed stupidly. The prosecutors went after the defense's idea that Aaron was innocent because a real murderer would have made it harder for the police to catch him.

Whether he was smart or dumb didn't matter, said the prosecutors. What mattered was that he'd committed the crime.

And with that, the case went to the jury.

In the end, it took the jury six days to convict Aaron of first-degree murder. Though jurors have not come forward to discuss their deliberations, this length of time likely means they weighed all the evidence carefully, and perhaps even had some disagreements and discussions.

But in the end, their verdict was unanimous. Guilty as charged.

When the verdict was read, there was a burst of emotion inside the courtroom. Some people cried, while others embraced. For some, the conclusion seemed natural for the jury to reach. Yet many others—who believe the prosecution had never established a clear motive for the killing—were shocked when the defendant was found guilty.

Aaron, however, was eerily stoic.

According to witnesses, he mouthed only one word: "Unreal."

Who can know what Aaron was referring to? Was the verdict unreal? Had he really believed the last-minute, slapdash defense strategy his lawyers had concocted was going to work?

Or did the word "unreal" refer to something else? Perhaps Aaron was referencing the entire experience in total. Maybe he was referring to the fact that not so long ago he had been a young NFL superstar with many years of success in front of him… and now, only prison and a grave awaited.

Adding to the surreality for many Bostonians was that the Aaron trial had been going on concurrent with another major trial—that of Dzhokhar Tsarnaev, the bomber from the Boston Marathon. On April 15, 2013—just a couple of months before Aaron had killed Odin Lloyd—Tsarnaev had set off a bomb that killed two young women and an eight-year-old boy, left 17 people amputees for life, and seriously maimed another 260. The manhunt afterwards to catch him had left a city on edge. In many ways, it was Boston's own 9/11. Bostonians felt a horrible mix of emotions as both trials were reported on. In the Tsarnaev case, they were forced to relive one of their city's most harrowing and horrible moments. And in the case of Aaron, they had seen not an outside attack by a foreign element, but—perhaps even more horribly—one of their own turned against them.

A hero revealed as a villain. A source of pride transmogrified into a source of shame.

Aaron had been a Patriot. The Patriots were a symbol of the city. The Boston Bombing had literally occurred on Patriots' Day. Now, one of the Patriots was himself on trial for being a killer. The emotions of many were roiled as they looked on at these trials and tried to make sense of their world.

After the verdict was delivered in Aaron's case—and the city began the process of finding emotional closure—Lloyd's friends and relatives were allowed to deliver victim impact statements in front of the court with Aaron present. They spoke of how much they would miss Lloyd, and how much his horrible murder grieved them. They spoke of the gaping hole left in their lives, and how they feared they had lost the ability to feel happy again. These statements may have been cathartic to those delivering them, but it was all for show as far as the judge was concerned.

Because of state legal statutes, there was only one sentence that the judge could pronounce after the statements had been delivered.

Everyone already knew what it was.

Aaron would receive life in prison without the possibility of parole.

CHAPTER 13

Friend: "Everything, you're staying positive though too?"
Aaron: "Yeah, everything is great, Ry."
Friend: "I got you."
Aaron: "Great."
Friend: "As long as you ain't lying to me?"
Aaron: "I wouldn't lie to you. Everything is great. How could I not be
free when I'm innocent? It don't make no sense."

—AARON HERNANDEZ, JAILHOUSE RECORDING

When watching a trial on television, it is natural for observers to empathize with the defendant. Most of us, when we hear about a man or woman being sentenced to life in prison, imagine ourselves in their shoes.

It is a horrible thing to imagine.

For most of us, the shift into a life behind bars would be jarring and life changing. In many cases, we would literally not survive it.

But most of us are not Aaron Hernandez.

Aaron took to the prospect of a lifetime in prison like a duck takes to water. It was familiar turf. It was the kind of place where he felt at home. The sort of men Aaron met behind bars were exactly the kind of men he had been palling around with in the free world. In terms of who he would spend his time with, this latest change was not altogether that jarring.

In a way, a life sentence further allowed him to become his "true self" to a greater extent then he'd been before. Because he would never again be an NFL player, he was able to drop the pretense of having a public, honorable face that his admirers would see. There was no more need for a double life.

Aaron was sent to Souza-Baranowski Correctional Center, a maximum security prison. Every record to be found shows us how Aaron embraced the new world behind bars with great enthusiasm.

Not long after starting his sentence, Aaron participated in perhaps the ultimate prison initiation—he received a jailhouse tattoo. Using the crude makeshift tools available to prisoners, he had another inmate put the words LIFETIME LOYALTY on his neck. No doubt, this was a reference to the fact that he would be behind bars for the rest of his life. More tellingly, the ink on his neck also showed a five-point star around the words LIFETIME LOYALTY—a common image used by the Bloods gang.

Prison records also show that there were several inmates who had an eye to making a name for themselves by roughing up Aaron. Now that he was there for good, attacking him seemed more accessible to other inmates. There were several scuffles at the beginning of his time in prison, but Aaron gave as good as he got; he was never seriously injured by any of these attacks.

Though the illegal prison tattoo and the fighting caused Aaron to be disciplined, albeit temporarily, he was eventually released into the prison's general population. Once there, we can see an even clearer picture of Aaron's metamorphosis into his authentic self. This included regular drug use, and—eventually—transitioning into being centrally involved in running the largest drug ring behind the bars of Souza-Baranowski Correctional Center.

This is evidenced by none other than his own mother in a recorded jailhouse phone call, which runs in part:

> Mom: What do you think, you're in the Ritz Hotel?
> Aaron: I am! I'm living good. I'm way less stressed in jail. I'm actually enjoying it, to be honest with you.
> Mom: Well, if you think about your life, since high school, you were always the best. College the best. NFL the best. You had to live up to these expectations, now you can be Aaron finally.

But we have more than his mother's word that he could now "let Aaron be Aaron." For this part of the story, we also have world exclusive and intimate knowledge of Aaron's prison life via his connection to a man named Kyle Kennedy—also known among rank and file prisoners as "Pure"—who served time with alongside Aaron.

Kennedy was the wild-child son of a stripper and a logger. He was a career criminal and card-carrying member of the notorious Bloods gang. He was in prison for holding up a convenience store with a knife, and then escaping from a police station after he was captured. This "escape" put Kennedy on the list of prisoners classified as flight risks, and earned him a lengthy sentence when the law caught up to him.

Like Aaron, Kennedy was an athlete who had been connected to crime and gangs for all his adult life. Also like Aaron, he had struggled with his sexual identity.

When the two men connected in the surreal world of the incarcerated, it was explosive.

They became confidants, drug dealers—and something more: lovers.

In a letter from Aaron to Kennedy prior to the pair meeting, and obtained by this author and extracted here, it is clear he immediately took a liking to his fellow prisoner.

I don't want to keep you too long. I just wanted to write you and send my love while letting you know to have faith in God, and most importantly have faith in yourself at the same time. All of your dreams can and will come true if you envision them, and believe with no doubt, they will come true. Never doubt yourself and the power you have within. I hope all your dreams come true, and I know they will. You can anything you put your mind to. Never let anyone tell you otherwise. Feel free to write me back if you want. In the meantime, stay out of trouble, so all your dreams can come true.

Your friend, Aaron Hernandez

Kennedy's nickname "Pure" was a mystery to everyone, but Aaron began using it soon after the men met. As their time together increased, he would call the man nothing else.

Aaron used the opportunity of prison's seclusion to grow a close bond with Kennedy. A lawyers for Kennedy saw firsthand that their relationship defied the stereotypes of prison that so many of us hold:

> There's a belief that behind bars, these guys are just having sex, and everybody is getting raped, and this is what's going on, but that's not what happened here. This was a relationship. It became very clear to me that this wasn't somebody that had an agenda; this was somebody that had a genuine love. However you want to categorize that love is really up to you, but this is an individual who had a real deep love and a deep affection and a deep connection with Aaron Hernandez.
>
> What you see with Kyle Kennedy and Aaron Hernandez was the kind of love that I'm not sure either of these two had ever been able to give anybody else. It was a freedom of being behind bars that allowed them to actually be who they wanted to be.
>
> Aaron didn't have to worry about the NFL, Aaron didn't have to worry about a sponsor by coming out and saying he was a homosexual, and Kyle didn't have to worry about any of that. It's a completely different world, and once you're behind those walls your reality changes.

Phone call recordings made during this period support this account of the situation.

When speaking with his mother, Aaron would often say that—in a strange way—he was happier in prison than he ever had been in his outside life. Even though he could no longer determine the most basic things about his existence— like when he rose in the morning, what time he ate, when he went to bed—Aaron felt a sense of peace with where he was... and who he was with.

The lawyer also shares his firsthand knowledge that the respect and attraction between Aaron and Kennedy was powerful and immediate... even if it was not initially physical.

It was instant. I mean it was instant. The friendship. And that friend-ship went from you're cool, you're one of us, you're loyal, which is a big word for Aaron Hernandez and Kyle Kennedy. Because I don't think either of them had that much loyalty in their lives. That friendship turned into something that then went to the next level. And the next level is this is somebody I can tell my thoughts to, that's not going to judge me. This is somebody I can tell my fears to that's not gonna tell me I'm right or wrong.

And that is where the love comes in. When you realize that you have somebody you can talk to, you can tell them the things that you can't tell everybody else and you're not gonna be judged, because they understand you. They have a lot of the same things that happened to you, that have happened to them. That's where the love developed.

In speaking with Kennedy, the question that I kept asking was why? What drives a man to risk all that he has worked and bled for since he was a child to embrace this violent, tortured life that Hernandez seemed to lust after?

A drug-dealing lieutenant in the same Bloods gang that Aaron lorded over in Souza-Baranowski, Kennedy became Aaron's business partner, second in com-mand, best friend, confidant, and lover. He was the one person who truly saw behind the façade that was Aaron's double life.

The crowds, the fans, the public who stood and cheered as the Patriots super-star burst through opposing teams ... they all thought they knew Aaron—and they were wrong.

What Kennedy told me painted a portrait of the real Aaron who was somebody else entirely, and had always been someone else. The real Aaron was a kid infatu-ated with gangster film Scarface, who grew obsessed by the power that guns gave him, who craved after the feelings of invincibility he felt when taking drugs. The real Aaron was a violent, unpredictable bully tortured by his own denied sexuality.

That was the side Kyle Kennedy knew, the Aaron he fell in love with. He saw his true side—the man who wanted to be the guy that made people cross to the other side of the street when he walked by. And he, perhaps alone in the world, knew why Hernandez wanted to be that person far more than he wanted to be the guy crossing the goal line on NFL Sundays.

Kennedy spent every day of the final year of Aaron's short and brutal life by the ex-gridiron great's side. They ran the Bloods' lucrative prison drug-dealing operation together, smuggling synthetic weed and opiates into the jail to cash in on their fellow inmates' addictions. They conspired to control the prison rackets. They pummeled rivals into bloody submission. They protected each other. They loved each other.

For the first time, their story is being told—and for the first time the world will find out the truth behind who Aaron really was from the man who understood him better than anyone.

The story of Aaron as the world knows it is shocking and brutal and tragic. The real story—the whole story—as revealed here for the first time, is nothing short of unmissable, for if it was not for Kyle's revelations about Aaron that set us on a path that would uncover secret after secret—for it was not for Kyle—we would never have known about a fourth unknown murder that Aaron had confessed to.

In an exclusive interview for this book, Kennedy—the last person who saw the football star alive—describes his initial meeting with Aaron:

> When I first met Aaron Hernandez, we had just like a connection like when you just meet someone, like even when you're a kid you know, you just know, this is going to be my boy, this is going to be my friend. I came walking on that unit, I came to cell. He brought me a TV and MP3 player, a bag of food. You know, I wasn't even on the unit ten minutes and I had everything I needed. We did everything together. Like I said, that was my boy. That was my best friend.

The relationship between the two men graduated from friendship and companionship to sexual. Kennedy confirms that Aaron performed oral sex on him during one of their first encounters. After that, they would have regular sex—once or twice a week. According to Kennedy, Aaron even spoke of the pair getting married at some future date.

We used to walk into together all the time on, you know, people would go to the yard. I'd walk in his cell. He'd walk in my cell... At first, it was just we would walk in to either cook food, or smoke, get high, listen to music, just chilling. We didn't want to be around other people.

One day we were in a cell smoking, and you know, he just broke down to me, and he started telling me about his past, things that had happened to him.

You know, he had told me, originally, he had said that his, I think it was either [redacted—a family member] that was close to him and they molested him when he was a kid. This went on for several years and he didn't want to tell his mother in fear of whatever the consequence might be.

I didn't know if it was just because we had gotten high or if we were just ... you know, whatever. He was opening up to me. A few days later, he writes me a letter saying, "Look, I want to talk to you about something."

He told me, he said, "I don't know if I'm gay or I'm what," but he told me, "I'm attracted to men. I can't." He said, even with his kid's mother, Shae, he said that she... he told me he used to always have to think of a man.

He used to tell me all the time that he didn't care. He wanted everyone to know. He wanted it to be known. He wanted to come out.

We walked in the cell one day and he just told me, he was like, "Bro, just sit down, close your eyes. I'm telling you, just relax." From there, that was the first time we had a physical encounter.

Could the NFL star have found more than a sexual arrangement of convenience (since his options were limited by incarceration)? Could it in fact be that Aaron had found the *true* love of his life, here, in what were to be his final years?

Aaron's high school confidant—Dennis SanSoucie—for one, believes that incarceration may have opened up Aaron in such a way that connecting with another human became possible in a way it never had before. As Dennis puts it:

[When Aaron was incarcerated] there was definitely a page that was turned. My father is a retired correctional officer and he said it best to me. He said, "When you're locked up for the rest of your life, the last thing you're worried about is speaking about your sexuality at that time. You have other things on your mind." So I think there was a page turned within the jail, but that's different than it being brought out as national media news to everyone. It wasn't something Aaron wanted out publicly, but I'm sure in jail it wasn't something he cared about anymore either.

Kennedy seemed to fill a need for Aaron that his fiancée Shayanna and a string of male-to-male casual encounters in the past had never been able to do.

There is strong evidence that this may have truly been the most meaningful relationship of Aaron's life. As the relationship between the two men blossomed, Aaron took the time to write letters to each member of Kennedy's immediate family. The letter to Kennedy's father was especially poignant. . . and revealing.

Per a member of Kennedy's legal team:

The letter to Kyle's dad—which we have and which I've read—was really the kind of letter that you would expect somebody to send to a father, for example, if your kid's going off to college and there's an RA on the floor. That's the kind of letter that it was. "Hey, just want to let you know, your son's here, he's with me, I'm taking care of him. I know this kid's messed up in the past, but I want you to know that what I've seen of this kid is special. And I want you to know as long as I'm here, and as long as I'm breathing, this kid's gonna be safe. I'm gonna make sure I take care of this kid. Just so you know dad, I'm gonna make sure this kid stays straight. I'm gonna make sure this kid stays in line and I'm gonna make sure when this kid gets out, he's got a future. That's what I'm gonna do."

It was a touching letter. And again, when you read that letter, when I read it now, knowing the entirety of the relationship, you look at the words a little bit differently than when you saw it the first day. The first

time I read this letter, I said, oh that's cool, he's got a friend that's taking care of him. Somebody that believes in him, but when you read it
the next time, in conjunction with the letters that he wrote to my client, and in conjunction with the letters that he wrote to his brothers
and sisters, you can see there was much more going on there. It was a
real relationship.

For the most part, prison employees—from the warden on down to the guards—
were fine to allow the relationship between Aaron and Kennedy.

Officially, sex between prisoners is not allowed, but guards routinely look the
other way as long as the prisoners involved are not causing problems in other
ways. (In prisons, guards have far more difficult challenges to deal with than
prisoners having consensual sex.) The only area where Aaron and Kennedy may
have skirted the line of acceptability was when it came to drug use.

Aaron's ability to enjoy a robust sex life had not been curtailed by the prison
doors, but his ability to enjoy alcohol and drugs certainly had. Some drugs could
be smuggled behind bars, of course, but it was risky work and the amounts transported were very modest and not always as pure as those Aaron had been accustomed to. There was just no way Aaron would ever again consistently enjoy the
superhuman amounts of marijuana he'd smoked on the outside as a free man.
(He was also forced to be very discreet about the drugs he *did* use in prison.)

There were rumors among other prisoners about drug use involving Kennedy
and Aaron. Yet representatives for Kennedy are curiously silent when it comes to
this private aspect of their relationship. However, that does not mean it must
remain unknowable to us.

Did Aaron share drugs with Kennedy? According to Sheriff Hodgson, prison
or jail would not have been particularly difficult for Aaron to become involved in
drug trafficking:

In prison, there's *always* the opportunity for people to try to manipulate the system to either sell the medication that they're being given by
not swallowing it and trying to hide it in their mouth somewhere and
then sell it for canteen or somebody that's trying to access it from the

individual when the individual wasn't trying to sell it or what have you in the prison.

That could be a medication, for example. We had a pregnant female who bit the pill in half, hid part of it in a cavity in the mouth with a flap of skin, the part that the nurse was watching dissolved so presumed it was all gone, but, in fact, the person took it out after and walked away and sold it to someone else. This is what goes on. We know that Aaron was attempting at one time or another to try to access something from one of the inmates right down two cells from him, and we were always on the watch for that.

Sheriff Hodgson's expert perspective makes it clear that a life of regular drug use is possible for any prisoner who sets his or her mind to it, and since everything we know of Aaron dating back to high school indicates a deep, primordial need to use drugs, it is reasonable to conclude that he was very interested in obtaining all the drugs possible for himself and his new lover while behind bars.

Whatever their drug use, Aaron and Kennedy were able to keep it inconspicuous. We know this because, as the relationship between the two men grew into something undeniably powerful, Aaron and Kennedy petitioned to be made bunkmates, and the request was granted. This would not have been done if either of the men had had a reputation as a problem drug user.

Yet just when things seemed headed on the upswing for Aaron—as much as they could, considering a lifetime prison sentence—it was all about to come crashing down.

Did Aaron *really* think that his newfound love with Kennedy would come free of consequences?

We cannot know that.

We only know what happened next.

CHAPTER 14

"If you're not happy inside, then you'll never be happy. Just like me, like, by having money I still was miserable. Having everything in the world, I still was miserable."

—AARON HERNANDEZ, JAILHOUSE RECORDING

Life behind bars was not all Ozzie and Harriet for Aaron and Kennedy. They were soulmates and deeply in love, but it's there that any similarity to an idyllic sitcom couple ends.

While connecting and growing as a couple, Aaron and Kennedy were incarcerated in a sea of murderers. This forced them to make compromises in order to survive. In a world where someone could be attacked seemingly at any time—and for any reason—forging allegiances and alliances was key. And that was *especially* true for someone as respected and feared as Aaron.

Motivated by a need to keep his new lover safe from jailhouse violence, Aaron returned to the life of gang association that he had pursued in the streets. It may have been something he never would have otherwise sought out. But in order to ensure the safety of Kennedy—who was physically smaller—Aaron began to rekindle his associations with the gang.

But that rekindling soon resulted in a full-on bonfire.

As Kennedy himself shares in his first ever interview about Aaron to this author:

Bloods, Crips, Gangstas, Disciples, Vice Lords, all thrown together. I started my sentence off right away with a big gang fight in the chow

hall. Seven Bloods against six Crips. And that was my reputation coming upstate almost immediately. [Aaron and I] sold drugs every day.
We did drugs every day. We were always trying to find a way to make
money. The thing is that me and him, we grew up the same. You know,
we come from a good family, wealthy, always had what we needed. We
seeked the street life or the gang life. We always went looking for it.

Before long, Aaron was not merely associating with the Bloods inside the facility
where he was serving time. He was running the show.

As a source close to Kennedy from inside jail adds:

My understanding was that Aaron Hernandez ran that click of the
Bloods in that correctional facility. I mean, if I'm in jail, I'm not starting a fight with an NFL tight end, not somebody that big, ever. When
you hear Kyle talk about the fights that went on behind closed doors
there, because they were many and they were often.

   You hear things like "Aaron hit him once in the head and I thought
the guy died, he dropped so quick." I mean, he's just not a human
being that you mess with, at least I wouldn't anyways. When you're
that tough, and when you're that big and when you're that notorious. I
mean, let's be real, if everything they say about Aaron Hernandez is
true, in all likelihood he's a serial killer.

It would have been easy for Aaron—who had been part of the Bloods before—to
find that relationship again once behind bars.

   In addition to protecting Kennedy, Aaron also may have sought their protection out of sheer necessity. As one jailhouse recording of Aaron speaking with a
friend during this period illustrates, Aaron felt that his Bloods tattoos made him
literally a marked man:

I'm trying … I'm trying to get transferred out of this jail. I need to.
'Cause, cause you know how they talkin' about my tattoos and shit.

This is a Crip jail. They be talkin' about my tattoos and how Crip will get mad.

Dr. Jeff Gardere, the clinical and forensic psychologist with expertise in Aaron's case, strongly believes that Aaron's prior experience in the gang propelled him toward seeking out the Bloods organization once more.

In Aaron Hernandez's history there is an affiliation with gang membership as a young man. Therefore, it is not such a strange thought, to me, that he would end up being in a gang in prison. Now, did he do that because it was something that was familiar to him? Or the gang that he was affiliated with as a youngster had their extensions into that particular jail, so it was an easy fit?

Some might say, "You know, Aaron Hernandez—there was a very sensitive side to him." But at the end of the day, this is a kid who survived—a young man who survived. Therefore, going into jail he knew that he had to be a badass. Because he was Aaron Hernandez. He had to be the real thing. His reputation preceded him.

So we often see that people survive by having to affiliate and be part of a gang to get that protection. But Aaron was the kind of guy—just as he did on the football field—where he commanded that as being a great athlete, he also commanded the gang. He was a guy who was able to call the shots and in many ways was viewed by the prison population as the real deal.

As Aaron provided protection for Kennedy and showed he was willing to use violence to keep his lover safe, it added a primal element of connection to the mix. It may have been very intoxicating to Kennedy, and their relationship likely grew even closer.

Kennedy had seen Aaron commit violence firsthand to protect him. He had watched Aaron form criminal allegiances with powerful gangs. This intimacy is important to note because it helps make a case that the two became intimate enough for Aaron to do one thing more. Namely, he confessed to Kennedy that he had committed yet another murder—a murder that is thus far unknown and unchronicled. "I have four bodies," Aaron told Kennedy.

As Kennedy told me exclusively:

> He's told me stories of, you know, "We were out this one night. I knocked this dude out," or "We were out this night. We got into an argument with this dude. I shot this dude."
>
> Every story included a fist fight or a shooting, something very dramatic.
>
> He would always bring things all the way to the extreme. If someone wanted to fight, it's, "Alright, we're going to try to kill you."
>
> One day we were in a cell smoking, and you know, he just broke down to me, and he started telling me about his past, things that had happened to him.

A jailhouse sources describes the kind of mental state that led Aaron to make this shocking disclosure:

> Look, when you have everything on the outside, you have the money, you have the fame, you have the fans, you have the girls, or the men or whatever it is that you want, and you're committing murders. I mean, let's not forget he was convicted of a murder. While the appeal went away and technically the murder charge went away with it, he was still convicted by a jury of his peers of murder.
>
> We know that he was accused of attempted murder in Florida, not once but twice. We know that he had double murder that he was accused of in Massachusetts.
>
> We also know something that nobody else knows, that, according to Kyle Kennedy, Aaron Hernandez admitted to killing a fourth person.
>
> We also know that while in jail, Aaron Hernandez admitted to killing all of the people that he was accused of killing to Kyle Kennedy.

The double murder that he was acquitted of, the murder that he was found guilty of and the murder that nobody knows he committed.

If you look at what Kyle says and you look at the facts on the outside, I believe Kyle Kennedy.

Dr. Jeff Gardere also confirms that Aaron's behavior shows that he was emotionally closer to Kennedy during this time than he'd ever been with Jenkins. This is because Gardere has been able to review the in-person phone call recordings between Aaron and visitors obtained exclusively for this project. These recordings were made when Aaron spoke to visitors through glass using a prison phone.

These recordings show what Aaron prioritized while in prison—often using a break period of 45 minutes to spend 40 minutes with Kennedy… while giving his visiting fiancée only five minutes of his time.

The below transcript is of a representative visit between Aaron and Jenkins—which has never been shared before—and it seems innocuous at first.

But only at first.

Jenkins: I really came here for five minutes?
Aaron: I'm going to stick with . . .

Jenkins: Are you for real? I can [unintelligible] came up next week.
Aaron: No, are you crazy?

Jenkins: I told you and that I didn't want to come up in the first place, because you had another visitor.
Aaron: Yeah. What do you mean? I'd rather you come here. I was thinking—first of all, I didn't think I was talking to him.

Jenkins: Aaron, unless you tell the COs to cut you off at a certain time, they won't. So you have to tell them.

Aaron: Yeah. But I thought you could just walk in after 30 minutes.

Jenkins: No. You have to tell the CO. You have to tell the CO, "Okay, stop me at a half hour. Or [unintelligible]—"
Aaron: You can't just walk in?

Jenkins: No, I can't just walk in. You have to call. They call the front. And then the guy that I always deal with, he's like, "Oh, you only have five minutes."
Aaron: What?

Jenkins: Or ten minutes—that's what he told me. And I was looking like, "What's going on?" But I don't know. I don't know what I'm supposed to do. I told you that I didn't want to [unintelligible] a visit in the first place. I don't know. I don't know if I have to [unintelligible]—
Aaron: I'm glad I never him. Because I told the CO to [unintelligible] been 30 minutes. And then right before you walked in, he said it's been 25 minutes. So I was thinking he was probably saying how long it's been. But he wouldn't say like [unintelligible]. What am I doing? [Unintelligible].

Jenkins: [Laughs] You [unintelligible].
Aaron: [Unintelligible] crazy.

Jenkins: Yeah, [unintelligible].
Aaron: That's crazy.

Jenkins: Is that your CO?
Aaron: Yeah. That's the one I told you [unintelligible].

Jenkins: Well, Bo said he loves you.
Aaron: Yeah, tell him I love him, too.

Jenkins: He said that [unintelligible]. Okay?
Aaron: Yeah.

That's the end of their exchange. Jenkins hung up the visitors' phone and walked out of the room afterwards. Aaron returned to his cell.

However, with his expert ear, Gardere is able to bring a revealing expert analysis to what is really happening.

> Here you are in jail—and I've worked in jails for many years myself—I know that one of the first things that you need is the comfort and reassurance of your significant other, of your romantic other. To just spend five minutes with Jenkins, I thought, was just a little odd, maybe even more than that as far as being kind of strange. So spending that 45 minutes with the previous person tells me that there is some sort of a significant relationship.
>
> Here you are with what most people would be a crisis situation. You would think you would need your significant other to be there to support you; to see that person's face. I would think Jenkins would be that person that he would want to spend that significant amount of time with; the person that he would want to see first. It's kind of strange to me that he brings in Kyle and spends that time with Kyle.
>
> Then he only spends a very short amount of time with Jenkins. What's more, their conversation—there's nothing there that seems to me like it's very serious, that it's very romantic, or that it's very reassuring. It's like a lot of small talk. There's like a disconnection there.

Gardere also concludes that the recording indicates that Jenkins may have been resigned to the reality of the situation by this point in her relationship with Aaron.

> She doesn't seem that upset that she got that last few minutes; the last five minutes. He offers it as being some sort of misunderstanding:

"The correctional officer should have said something. I asked him to let me know when the 30 minutes was up," or whatever the case may be. They are having this small talk. Here is a guy who has lost his living. Here is a guy who is now considered to be, in some ways, a pariah to his team; who is behind bars for murder. I would think, "Oh, my God, thank God you're here! Thank God you still believe in me." Or Jenkins even saying, "You know, my goodness! What has happened? Are you okay?" But it's this kind of small talk. I think some other people would say, "You know what? Instead of meeting with Ryan right now—my personal assistant—what about my lawyer?"

In another exclusively obtained recording, Gardere illustrates how the relationship between Aaron and Jenkins had further deteriorated to almost being nonexistent.

Aaron: What you been up to? [Unintelligible]. [Unintelligible] doing at least?
Jenkins: [Unintelligible], that's it.

Aaron: Yeah. Well, explain it.
Jenkins: Explain what?

Aaron: You're the one that is like, "Hey, call me every day." And then, see what I'm saying, you're the one telling me to call me every day. And then you tell me I can't call you for a month.
Jenkins: I had to use the money elsewhere. Like, what's the big deal?

Aaron: What's [unintelligible] doing?
Jenkins: [Laughs] Baby stuff.

Aaron: Baby stuff?
Jenkins: [Unintelligible].

Aaron: Yeah, maybe [unintelligible].

Jenkins: [Laughs] [Unintelligible].

Aaron: [Unintelligible] baby stuff.

Jenkins: And him being [unintelligible]. Wait, so when are you going to call me?

Aaron: Call you?

Jenkins: Yeah.

Aaron: I don't know. Why?

Jenkins: [Laughs] Just tell me.

Aaron: She didn't tell you. [Unintelligible]. I did.

Jenkins: [Laughs] What?

Aaron: [Unintelligible].

Jenkins: Aaron, [unintelligible] such an argument. [Unintelligible] call me between 1:00 and 2:00 or 6:00 and 7:00?

Aaron: [Unintelligible]. One of these days I'm going to call you.

Jenkins: One of these days? [Laughs]

[Baby crying]

Aaron: What?

Jenkins: Okay. One of these days, maybe, I'll pick up.

Aaron: I just said, "Why don't you have your phone on you? I know you ain't going nowhere without your phone."

Jenkins: Aaron, it's a simple fact that I want to know when you're going to be calling me. Because

if I'm doing something in between I don't want to
have to rush to answer it. So just tell me when
are you going to call me?

Aaron: I [unintelligible] your schedule and just
know and I can possibly call.
Jenkins: When can you do that?

Aaron: I don't know.
Jenkins: You don't know? Now, you don't know?

Aaron: I—
Shayanna: [Talking over him] And the other time
you gave me specific times.

Their communication abruptly ends here.

Gardere believes exchanges like this one provide a revelatory insight into the state of Aaron's relationship to himself, his own identity, and the exterior world.

Aaron Hernandez was a big guy. When you look at someone like that, you're thinking they are older than their actual years. They are playing on a pro football team—the New England Patriots of all teams. You are thinking that this is a person who is a fully developed adult. But in many ways, Aaron was very childlike. Part of that was because of his young age. The other part of that was because he was immature. You could see that playing out in his relationship with Jenkins; the way they were talking during this jailhouse visit. The way that they were almost child-like in how they interacted. It almost seemed like there was almost an ambivalence in that relationship. "Why haven't you called me? When are you going to call me? Do I need to tell you exactly when I need to call you?"

The other part of that is that she is saying to him, "Look, life goes on. I'm a young woman. I still need to do my thing. I still need to get out there and live my life. So let me know when you are going to call."

It's not unusual for Aaron to say, "I don't need to tell you that. Whenever I call, you just need to pick up."

Another call exclusively obtained for this book is perhaps the most chilling of all.

In a call with an associate, Aaron alludes to being checked on by guards. He then reveals how commonplace suicide attempts are behind bars. In an eerie turn, he describes an inmate seeking to take his own life using similar methods to those he himself would one day employ.

Only the relevant portion is excerpted here:

> Aaron: They check me every 30 minutes. Sometimes you have to hurry and get in so they check.
>
> Friend: They do [unintelligible].
>
> Aaron: A lot of people try kill himself here. Some dude tried to use a sheet and they tried to hang themselves from the bed or something. And you heard them all running to go see the dude.

Analyzes Gardere:

> That is prophetic. Because here he is talking about the procedures; the observations of people who may be suicidal: checking on them every 30 minutes, doing it with a bedsheet.
>
> Then later on, this is what Aaron does. He uses the bedsheet. He ties it to the bars on the windows. Somehow, they missed him on that 30-minute check. Was this something that he kept in his head, knowing exactly when to do it and how to do it?
>
> Shakespeare couldn't have written this any better.
>
> You don't make this stuff up. This is real life. Because here you have this individual who couldn't escape an upbringing where he was suffering emotionally. Where he had these demons that he was dealing with. Where, perhaps, he wasn't being his true self. With all the money in the world, all the luxuries, all the breaks that one can get being a

multimillionaire—none of that could save him from what his fate appeared to be.

There is also evidence that Kennedy may have been another person to whom Aaron telegraphed the way his story was going to end. A jailhouse insider close to Kennedy reveals that in one of Aaron's most personal letters—one written to Kennedy himself—he hints at something ominous.

That source reveals:

> That brings us to one of the letters. The letter that I have that Aaron wrote of Pure. One of the letters Aaron wrote. The other one we haven't been given access to by attorney Baez—or the family—yet. But it does exist. In the letter I personally read, Aaron says in the letter, "You know, I'm thinking about hanging it up. You know." It's an innocent phrase until somebody actually does what that letter says and he literally hung it up. Kyle [Kennedy] read it, didn't think anything of it until he was told that [Hernandez] hung himself in his cell. Then he went back and he was like, "Oh my God. Did he tell me this? Did I miss the signs? Could I have helped my friend out?" There was a level of guilt because it literally said right in there, I'm thinking about "hanging it up."

It is worth pausing to review the changing factors in Aaron's mental state at this juncture.

His relationship with Pure is deepening and intensifying. It gives him something to live for, but also something to do violence for. It causes him to get back involved with the Bloods, and soon he is essentially running the Bloods click at his prison. That's added responsibility and stress.

At the same time, he is distant with Jenkins. She—and to a lesser extent, his mother—are the central remaining connection to the outside world, and that connection is fading fast. Aaron's identity becomes more and more that of a prisoner for life. What's more, at the same time, he is bringing up suicide. He is

talking about how people kill themselves in prison, and details to his closest con-
fidante that he has thought about suicide.

As one of the calls unearthed in our research shockingly reveals, Aaron began
speaking candidly and openly to his mother about his suicidal thoughts.

Mom: I know—I know for a fact that something good
is going to come out of this.
Aaron: What?

Mom: Something good's going to come out of this.
Aaron: That's how I feel. There's a light at the
end of the tunnel, because. . .

Mom: Something good's going to come out of this.
Aaron: Nah, because I know this thing happened for
a reason. There's a reason this all happened in my
life—me being innocent and going through this is
like, there's something.

Mom: It's for you to think about life again.
Aaron: It's, no. Something good is coming about
this. It's a messed-up world, like I know that, but
it's not like I'm in here stressing or all down.

Mom: No. The only bad thing is people that don't
understand how you had it all and couldn't understand how that wasn't enough. You wanted a gangster
life.
Aaron: That's not true, I didn't want a gangster
life. That's what white people think. . . that's
not true, I didn't want a gangster life. That's
what white people think.

Furthermore, in a subsequent call with his mother, Aaron signs off in most ominous fashion. It is hard to believe that his words to his mother may have a deeper context and meaning.

> **Aaron:** It's not goodbye; it's see you later. . . there's no way I'm sitting in here forever.
> **Mom:** How did we get into this?
>
> **Aaron:** I don't know but I'm innocent, so I'm going to get out eventually.

On top of all of this, he has to go on trial… again.

The final major event in Aaron's life before he went through with his suicide was the trial for the 2012 double murder in Boston. This trial came about because Alexander Bradley had made a deal with authorities. Bradley would serve only five years in jail for his role in the murders, with the understanding that he would agree to testify against Aaron.

Kennedy claims that Aaron was guilty of these murders, and had copped to them … secretly, to his jailhouse paramour. (In an interview for this book, when asked if he lied in court about his innocence, Kennedy confirmed: "He was so worried about not beating that case, you know? How am I going to beat this?" When we noted that he lied in order to beat the rap, Kennedy replied: "Of course he did. Yeah.")

Publicly, Hernandez always protested his innocence. The lie was always the same, he never murdered anyone. In prison, however, it was a completely different story.

> **Kennedy:** We used to joke around all the time. He used to tell me you gotta get your body count up, you go to do, which means... he used to tell me he had four murders. Never gave me a name, never. He would just always all the time joke around saying I got four bodies. He used to tell me he had four murders.
>
> **Author:** He had four murders?

Kennedy: That's what he used to tell me.

Author: So, he was acquitted of a double murder. Convicted of killing Odin Lloyd. Who was the fourth?

Kennedy: He never told me. He used to...

Author: Never told you?

Kennedy: Never gave me a name, never. He would just always, all the time joke around saying I got four bodies.

Author: If there's a fourth person that was killed, that may well be an unsolved crime or someone may have been inappropriately convicted of that murder. So if you have information, shouldn't you disclose it?

Kennedy: If I had information I'd tell you. Like I said I don't. I just, I remember from a conversation we had a few times and he would always bring that up joking around.

For this trial, Aaron hired a different legal team. His new layers were led by attorney Jose Baez, who was infamous for working cases involving celebrities and ripped-from-the-headlines drama.

He had recently represented Casey Anthony—dubbed "Tot Mom"—in the murder trial of her two-year-old daughter Caylee, in which she had been found not guilty. (In the legal community, Baez's star continues to rise today. Some of this is because of the success of his book *Unnecessary Roughness*, which he penned to chronicle his experience representing Aaron. He also, at one point, represented disgraced movie mogul Harvey Weinstein against rape and sexual assault charges in New York.)

Not only did Aaron have a celebrity lawyer this time, but the case against him was markedly weaker. The murders in question had taken place five years earlier, so time played a factor. Witnesses got forgetful. Evidence aged. And where Aaron's temperament had been a key question in his first trial—with the jury eventually deciding that, yes, Aaron *would* kill someone as sloppily and thoughtlessly as Lloyd had been killed—in this trial, there was even more of a leap for the jury to take.

They would have to believe that Aaron was willing to murder a complete stranger simply for the offense of spilling a drink on him in a nightclub—even though he had prior form when it came to such innocuous nightclub antics.

When the second trial got underway, this was precisely the argument that Baez led with.

Why on earth would Aaron kill someone for spilling a drink on him in a night-club? Why would he take that risk? Why would anybody?

It wasn't like Aaron was killing to protect his reputation. The offense had been minor, and almost nobody had seen in happen.

Baez directed the jury's attention to the fact that Aaron was being put on trial because of the cooperation of Bradley. Bradley, Baez said, was a man with an axe to grind. Bradley hated Aaron, and so was unlikely to be telling the truth. Baez said that this entire trial was just Bradley trying to settle a vendetta between them. In court, Baez called Bradley's allegations: "An unbelievable, fantastic tale of lies."

Whatever Bradley's motivations might have been, there was also the matter of evidence. Namely, the prosecution had much less of it this time. There was no DNA linking Aaron to the murder. There was no trail of cell phones, rental cars, and receipts. There was simply eyewitness testimony—and most of that came from Bradley himself.

Baez painted a picture for the jury of Bradley as a street hood and drug dealer who would lie whenever it was to his advantage. Baez insinuated that it was Bradley himself who had committed the murders.

Now, said Baez, Bradley wished to pin them on his old friend-turned-enemy, Aaron.

When he testified for the prosecution, Bradley was honest about having been a drug dealer and criminal; he did not try to deny the illegal things he'd done in the past. However, he did argue that he was now a changed man. He insisted that the justice system could trust him to tell the truth.

To observers of the trial, the biggest challenge for the prosecution was the fact that Bradley had not immediately gone to the police after the murders had occurred. Instead, he had waited several years to come forward. How would he and the prosecutors account for this?

As if anticipating that Bradley's long silence would be an issue, the prosecutors brought it up themselves. As Bradley took the stand, they asked him why it had taken him so long to come forward and bring Aaron's criminal actions to the police.

Bradley's explanation was as simple as it was disturbing.

He had been planning to kill Aaron himself, he said. Instead of going to the cops, Bradley had hoped to take Aaron's life personally, to punish him for what he'd done. Bradley hadn't done it simply because the opportunity had never arisen. Aaron, rightly suspecting something, always found a way to avoid being alone with Bradley.

When Bradley finally realized vigilante tactics weren't going to work, he made the decision to tell police what had happened.

However, in the eyes of investigative journalist Michelle McPhee, this was too little, too late. From her perspective, Bradley's testimony was more likely to have made the jury feel negatively against the NFL itself than against Aaron:

> Bradley's testimony was unsuccessful because no one believed this one-eyed drug dealer who admitted that he and Aaron smoked massive amounts of pot every day. That breeds a whole other question for the NFL about drug testing. What good is it? Because clearly, if Aaron is doing lines off of a stripper's rear end, and smoking weed every day with Alexander Bradley, it seems to me that should have been picked up in the NFL drug test, no?
>
> Again, so Aaron's behavior was aided and abetted, all along, by people who wanted to utilize his talents on the field. So, he was exploited, in some ways, by the people who are making a ton of money off of him. More importantly, those people facilitated the heinous acts of violence that Aaron Hernandez would commit.
>
> The real look, the real interesting part for the jury is who was involved in the cover-up? Who paid off the victims? Who paid off the

witnesses, and what allowed Aaron Hernandez to exist in this world where he's playing for the beloved New England Patriots when he's snorting lines with strippers and smoking hydroponic marijuana with gang-banging Alexander Bradley?

How is that missed by the league?

How is that missed by the Patriots organization?

When it was Baez's turn to cross-examine Bradley, he asked questions intended to get Bradley to admit to two things:

1. He was a drug dealer who'd spent most of his life up to his neck in a chaotic world of crime and violence.
2. That he hated Hernandez.

Baez was successful at getting the answers he wanted.

Bradley freely admitted that for most of his life he'd existed in a world of drug dealing that often involved violence. He made violence sound casual, like an everyday occurrence. Bradley was so relaxed on the topic that he began to sound like a guy who might do murders himself. Like a guy who took laws as suggestions rather than requirements.

Which was just what the defense wanted.

Baez also got Bradley to admit that he held a deep personal dislike for Aaron. Without bringing up the reasons—such as, oh, being shot in the face by him—Bradley confirmed that he thought Aaron was simply a bad person. He said that he felt personally wronged and betrayed by him. It was clear that Bradley hoped bad things happened to him.

By the time he left the witness stand, Bradley was seething.

Baez, on the other hand, was smiling.

Several other people took the stand during the trial. Most were eyewitnesses, but this was not necessarily the home run for the prosecution that it might sound like. Again, time had taken its toll. The witnesses who had been in the area of the shooting recalled only scraps of what had happened that night. Pressed by Baez, each of the witnesses conceded his or her memory was not perfect after five years. Of central importance was the fact that none of these witnesses had seen (or heard) anything that would pin the murder 100 percent on Aaron. Nobody had seen Aaron pulling the trigger. They'd only seen a man who *could* have been Aaron.

When it was time for closing arguments, Baez made a pitch that was more emotional than rational.

Baez said that Bradley was a liar who had been "dressed up" by the prosecution to give him an air of respectability. However, underneath he was still the same lying, drug dealing criminal he'd always been. Bradley was an immoral man filled with hate for Aaron, Baez told the court. There was no way the word of such a man ought to be used to find somebody guilty beyond a reasonable doubt.

And *without* Bradley? Well, said Baez, the prosecutors hardly had a "case" that could be proved beyond all reasonable doubt at all.

When Bradley was almost unilaterally declared an incredible witness, the prosecution turned its focus elsewhere.

Explains Baez:

> During the trial they decided that they were going to try another the-ory, and that was that they believed Aaron was gay and that they also believed that because he was in the closet that if someone bumped in to him he felt he had to overcompensate as a man.
>
> So as the judge put it, "So what you're saying, prosecutor, is that a gay man in the closet is more likely to commit murder than someone who is out?" And that was pretty much their theory. It was obvious the judge wasn't buying it. We were threatening to raise all kinds of hell over it so the prosecution didn't go there.

In response, the prosecution was forced to contend with the fact that their case really *did* rely on the jury finding Bradley trustworthy. They had no course other than to double down. They claimed that Bradley had undergone a change and was truly trustworthy. They argued that his personal dislike for Aaron did not mean Aaron hadn't committed the crime.

Still, the prosecution had no solid evidence.

No DNA or fibers.

No eyewitnesses other than Bradley himself.

Accordingly, after they had doubled down on Bradley, the prosecution spent the rest of their closing argument focusing on the young men who had been killed, and the horrible toll it had taken on their families.

Clearly, their finishing move was an attempt to tug the jury's heartstrings.

While the toll on the families might certainly have been enormous, the prosecution had not done a very good job of *proving* that Aaron had been the one behind the murder. After deliberating for five and a half days—almost exactly the length of the deliberation in Aaron's first trial—the jury found him not guilty of the murders. In fact, of the eight charges for which he was on trial, the only one the jury convicted him on was illegal possession of a firearm.

The courtroom erupted after the verdicts were read.

To the surprise of many, Aaron himself burst into tears.

Were they tears of relief, or surprise, or sadness? Nobody knew but him. Considered in the context of his confession to lover Pure, they almost certainly were tears of relief that he'd beaten the rap.

Although he was still sentenced to serve the rest of his life behind bars, for the moment, the day had been won.

Aaron returned to prison. By some accounts, he was a changed man now—at least temporarily. Prison guards and other inmates remembered him as especially cheerful in the days following the acquittal.

This only made Aaron's end all the more surprising.

He had the rest of his natural life in front of him … but he soon chose to end it all.

CHAPTER 15

Aaron: "They check me every 30 minutes."

Mom: "They do? What they walk by?"

Aaron: "They check on the room. The other day someone... because a lot of people try to kill themselves in here. So a dude tried to like, they used a sheet, and they had tried to hang themselves from the bed set."

—AARON HERNANDEZ, JAILHOUSE RECORDING

Why?

That was what everybody wanted to know.

Why had Aaron Hernandez taken his own life?

The first time that people heard about it, they wondered if they'd heard the news correctly. It was a real surprise—to fans, yes, but also to those who knew him personally. Aaron had given so few hints that something like this might occur. It just did not make sense.

Although he was behind bars, Aaron was not without hope, or without positivity in his life.

Every day, thousands of prisoners in the United States serving life sentences find a reason to live. They get up and stay active. They cling to hope in one way or another. Those who have only the sliver of hope of an appeal hang on to that sliver. Those who have no hope of being released find things in their jailhouse existence to hold on to. They find meaning where they are.

Some now believe that the second trial of Aaron may have actually been keeping him alive. Rather than adding new stress to his existence, it was the one thing making existence bearable. Before him, the pit yawned. And that pit was spending the rest of his life behind bars for the murder of Lloyd. The second trial was a distraction. Even though he was accused of new crimes and forced to defend himself, it was a welcome respite from his normal life behind bars. Being on trial for a double murder makes it hard to stop and think about the one you're already convicted of.

There is some evidence to support this. Researchers find consistently—and perhaps ironically—that the number one demographic of prisoners who commit suicide are those who has just had a death sentence commuted to life in prison. When they learn this fact, many are incredulous. Why would someone who has just been spared the electric chair or lethal injection decide to do the job themselves? At first glance, it seems to not make sense.

But consider the impact on the prisoner's day-to-day. When seeking to have a death sentence commuted to life, the prisoner is surrounded by supportive advocates and lawyers positioning them as a victim of unjust treatment. The death row prisoner is characterized as a sympathetic figure who will be forced to undergo a cruel and unusual punishment. Each day, the prisoner is updated on efforts to save him or her. The prisoner has a team working on their behalf. It is, if nothing else, a distraction from the drudgery of prison.

But when victory is won—and the sentence is reduced to life—that prisoner is suddenly abandoned by all of the lawyers and activists and anti-death penalty proponents. The prisoner is left alone to serve out the remainder of their sentence. And nobody is arguing that the new sentence is unjust. Nobody is saying the prisoner is a good person... that they didn't deserve to be executed.

Forced to sit in a cell and ponder their new reality of solitude, a very high number of these prisoners then elect to take their own lives.

So it may have been with Aaron.

Dr. Gardere is very familiar with the circumstances of Aaron's final moments. He believes it was likely that Aaron was an undiagnosed depressive. He is also the first to introduce the specter of CTE. As Gardere puts it:

> One of the things that continues to perplex us, even when we see that a person who is very severely depressed has some hope—and Aaron Hernandez actually had some hope, even in prison.

Baez actually had the two murder convictions overturned and was working on the third one with Lloyd. In theory, Aaron had everything to live for. There was the possibility that he could get out and live a [normal] life again.

To now have killed himself—people can't put it together. But I think what is missing in this picture here is that there may have been a very severe depression that wasn't treated for a long time; the CTE, which is this neurodegenerative brain disease. But a life that had been in many ways—the ups and downs were so many and so far apart—that at the time he was feeling that final depression, being in that valley, and feeling so low, that it had the power to take over him, and where he said, "There's got to be a better life for me, and it's not on this earth."

Dennis SanSoucie has also considered what may have gone into the suicide.

Dennis believes there may have been a particular sense of betrayal that hit Aaron at the end of the second trial. Though Dennis was not included in the final correspondence Aaron wrote, he estimates that Aaron wrote him nearly 100 short letters during his incarceration. In these letters, Dennis began to detect what he believes are clues that Aaron felt wronged by some of those who were closest to him.

There is one phrase that sticks out in my mind throughout all the letters, of which he probably sent me close to 100. I'll never forget one day he was upset, writing to me, and he had pretty much said: "I'm venting." His term to me was "You can [do] everything under the sun for someone, and they'll still turn their back on you." You never really feel like when you're helping someone you really get it back in return. I'm going to guess Odin Lloyd, and Bradley, and Wallace. Guys like that. He didn't say specific names, but he said, "You can do anything under the sun for someone, and they'll still turn their back on you." That was the most meaningful thing that stuck out to the things that he wrote to me.

Yet Dennis also feels that—at the end of his life—Aaron saw that the betrayal was more than a failure to be loyal or repay favors.

> I think he started to realize that the activities and the things that he liked to do, smoke, playing video games, doing this, having fun, going out, going to the clubs, he would have been in better hands with the right people. He didn't have the right people in his life to put a stop to shit.

Though he had lived his life as some kind of archetypal, apex thug, Aaron, at the end, seemingly sought to blame his friends for not having been better people, and for not having shown him a better way to live.

This seems risible, so late in the game.

Aaron had spent a lifetime seeking out precisely these sorts of people to associate with. Yet that does not mean his feelings were not real. Though contradictory, Aaron may have genuinely regretted who he'd spent time with—and may have honestly wished that they had steered his life in a better direction.

Dr. Gardere believes that forced to sit alone with his wasted lifetime of crime and vice—with no new distractions on the horizon—Aaron may have found that this new reality was more than he could bear.

> In life, we have to look at the positives and the negatives. Even though there are a lot of positives, at some point, in Aaron Hernandez's life— and we know what they are; I don't have to go through them—there were a lot of negatives.
>
> A lot of traumas that could take down any person, especially someone like Aaron, who through his life had ordeals that he was dealing with. Who knows? In his head, when he started looking at these negatives: He's in jail, he has to stand trial, his relationship with Jenkins and his daughter are perhaps not what he felt that they should have been. Because it seemed like there was some ambivalence building at that point.
>
> That some devastating secret about his health was or could have

been revealed; that maybe he was going to spend the rest of his life in jail; that he just didn't feel like he was receiving love. He didn't feel that he loved himself. That he, perhaps, had destroyed his own life.

In my mind, this is a story of a man who had it all, could have had even more, and lived a life of fame and fortune and athletic prowess that most of us can only dream of. But this was a person who, with all of his blessings, had twice as many curses; who really felt the pain of living a life of trauma.

In the end, he could no longer bear that existence and took his own life.

There is also a theory that during this period Aaron might have already been ripe for taking his own life, and that something specific pushed him over the edge.

That "something," in the minds of many, is a radio program that aired two days before his suicide. On this program, for one of the first times in a prominent public forum, the possibility of Aaron's bisexuality was openly discussed. One of the hosts of the radio program then put the idea on social media where it exploded.

However, it should be noted that there is also considerable counter evidence to the theory that this was the catalyst to Aaron's decision to end it all.

In the first place, it has not been established that news of this radio discussion would have reached Aaron in prison within two days. His access to both radio and social media was obviously limited.

Additionally, in the second place, there was—at the time—purportedly strong information about his sexuality *in the other direction.*

Michelle McPhee was one of the journalists speaking on the radio show in question. By her own reckoning, it was not the event that prompted Aaron to take his life.

During the broadcast I said they should interview his gay lover, and one of the other hosts was talking about, "We didn't know he was gay." He tweets it. It goes viral, and two days later Aaron takes his own life. It immediately became very easy to level all the blame on that talk radio show for driving Aaron to his death. I think that became the narrative. It was very ironic, [because] the *Boston Globe* led the charge, debunking that, interviewing people, saying he was never gay, that he wasn't gay, that he *definitely* wasn't gay.

McPhee also believes that the radio broadcast was not the inciting event for Aaron's suicide because he never talked about it to anyone, or wrote anything down about it—even when he was writing his final words.

Observes McPhee:

> In those suicide notes, there was no mention whatsoever about the radio show interview or about the fact that he felt outed. There was nothing about that whatsoever.

It is not only McPhee who considers the suicide notes definitive. Much has been made of the fact that the newly literate Aaron had written notes to several important people before ending his life.

Yet, as will now be exposed here, there are still important facts about Aaron's final letters that the public does not yet know.

By the time of Aaron's suicide, staff at the prison were all well aware of his relationship with Kennedy.

Kennedy himself shares what it was like to learn the heartbreaking news of his lover's passing, in our exclusive interview.

> They came to my door at about 6:30 in the morning and the correctional officer said, "You need to cuff-up. There's people here to talk to you." In my head, I'm like, "It's 6:30 in the morning. Who could be here to talk to me?"
>
> They bring me down to a room. In there, there's mental health, a captain, different correctional people. In my head, I'm thinking *did one of my family members die? What's going on here?*
>
> One mental health worker then came in with whom I've been working. She comes in and I could just tell by the look on her face that

something was wrong. She said, "I have bad news. Your friend Aaron, he committed suicide last night."

I told her, "No he didn't. That's not him." I got all types of things going through my head at the moment. I know it's not a joke, but I couldn't come to terms with it right then and there.

I was just like, "Get away from me. No. No. No.

"He did have a drug problem, smoking K2 which there had been a few incidents. So, that was the first thing that came to my head was he had to have taken something or done something that altered the way he was thinking because that wasn't him."

After the event, Kennedy was immediately placed on suicide watch.

Explains a jailhouse source:

After Aaron Hernandez was found in his cell, Kyle was in solitary at that point in time. So they had gone down and the mental health counselor had told Kyle what had happened and they put Kyle on suicide watch as well. Knowing the intimacy of their relationship, they felt like that was the best thing to do to protect Kyle.

Yet in relating the true account of the aftermath of Aaron's suicide, the source reveals an incredible bombshell:

After this information that Hernandez had committed suicide came out, a correctional officer came into see Kyle and said, "Hey, did you get the letter that was written for you? Kyle said, "No, I haven't gotten it yet." Now, consider this, it was within days. At that point in time, the state police had come in and this was an active investigation. They didn't know if it was a murder or it was a suicide at the time, so they had taken all the letters as evidence.

That's right. There were *four* suicide letters written by Aaron, not three, as lawyer

Jose Baez insisted to the press. There was one to Shayanna, one to his daughter, one to Baez himself . . . and also one to Kennedy.

One can only speculate as to why the suicide letter count went from four to three. Perhaps based on his desire to publish a book about his most famous client—in order to bolster his own reputation and legal career—Baez removed a startling truth from the final chapter of Aaron's life. Baez hid not only the fact that Aaron was bisexual, but that he had found a satisfying romance—perhaps the love of his life—while incarcerated. And that, moreover, in Aaron's final moments, his thoughts had been with his prison lover Kennedy as much as they'd been with his fiancée, daughter, and legal advocate.

Confronted for this book, Baez made clear he intends to stick to his story.

"Regarding the claims that there was a suicide letter written to Kyle Kennedy, I can tell you for 100 percent of a fact that there's no letter in existence anywhere written to Kyle Kennedy," Baez told me.

"No letter, period. Period. No suicide. No writings. Let me see if I can be as clear as can be. There's zero writings to any individual in any prison."

Yet Kennedy confirmed to me that Aaron routinely gave him letters, many of which professed his love in no uncertain terms. Confronted with this fact, Baez merely responded: "I can tell you this much. Aaron told everybody he loved them."

As the jailhouse source makes clear, Baez used all of the tools of his trade to obscure the truth of Aaron's situation.

> There were four letters at the time. One to the daughter, one to the fiancée, one to attorney Baez, and one to Kyle Kennedy. Now, if you look at what attorney Baez says, he uses words and he's cute with his words. It's easy to say there was no letter written to Kyle Kennedy because there was no letter that was written "to Kyle Kennedy." There was a letter that references Pure. Everybody in that jail knows that Kyle Kennedy is "Pure." That letter does exist and it did exist.

Yet while the jailhouse source confirmed the letter's existence, he has not personally held it in his hands and read it; he cannot speak to its contents. Because it was addressed to Pure, it is reasonable to assume—as Jose Baez could have done—that it concerned only his affection for Kennedy. Yet the possibility remains that it could contain something even more revealing… and explosive.

However, those in Kennedy's camp have little reason to believe that the fourth letter—if it has not already been destroyed—will ever see the light of day.

> Once the state police had possession of the letter, it becomes part of the evidence of an active investigation into the suicide. At some point in time in April, the family—through their attorney, not attorney Baez, but the estate attorney—petitioned the court to have those letters released to the family as their personal property.
>
> That order was executed by the judge. At that point in time, the four letters went to the family. That was the day that Kyle Kennedy knew he was never going to see the fourth letter. People close to him have called for them to release the fourth letter. I think the interesting thing is, if it wasn't sent to Kyle, if the letter didn't reference Pure and it wasn't a letter to Kyle, then why not release it?

Why not indeed?

The friend of Kennedy is quick to conjecture that the reason may lie in the inability of Aaron's family to accept the reality of his personal truths.

> If you look at the timeline . . . The letters are given to the family and then after that point in time, the fiancée goes on the *Dr. Phil* show and basically says, "No, Aaron was not a homosexual. He was not gay." She goes into this in great detail. But that's not what the letters revealed. Aaron Hernandez was a homosexual. Whether he was a bisexual, a homosexual, a heterosexual, I don't really care about any of that. It makes no difference in my life, but I could tell you, without question, that Aaron Hernandez had sexual relationships with men. His lover was Kyle Kennedy.
>
> At the end of the day, I can't imagine being in his fiancé's shoes and trying to process all of this. You have a child with somebody, and then

you find out that the person you had this family with is . . . well . . . he's not attracted to you. Instead, he's attracted to men. I don't know how anyone would process that. I don't blame her for saying whatever it is that she said—I might have done the same thing, for all I know.

But I think there's a different standard when you look at attorney Baez and if he's gonna hide through attorney-client privilege, you don't say anything. But when you start saying things, you must be truthful. Based on what I know, it doesn't appear, at least based upon the information that I've been provided, that he was truthful.

The source reveals Aaron's immediate family even continued to deny Kennedy when it came to Aaron's explicit final wishes for what should happen after he was dead.

There was a big deal made at the press conference that Aaron Hernandez had given one of his expensive watches to Kyle [Kennedy]. That happened. Kyle was sitting with Aaron Hernandez when he was on the phone with Baez and he said, "Hey, I want to gift my boy Pure this watch. Make sure that happens." According to Kyle, Baez said, "Yep, I'll take care of that. We'll handle that."

The watch never went to Kyle. The reason that Kyle wanted that letter was never, ever because we thought it was the last will and testament of Aaron Hernandez. We didn't think that letter would declare, "I bequeath to Kyle Kennedy, my watch." That wasn't the point.

What makes such actions doubly tragic is that Aaron's gift was obviously about more than money. The watch would have been tremendously meaningful to Kennedy. Per the source:

The point about the watch was to show that Kyle was there. He wanted the letter because he wanted to read the words that his best friend and, at the time, his love, had said about him. Same thing with the watch. Closure. He was looking for closure. He wasn't looking for a $50,000 watch.

The source is sure that the sentimental value of the wristwatch far transcended its value in dollars and cents. Here, among one of his last acts, Aaron was attempting to tell those around him how important they were, and how much they meant to him.

It may have been a final mercy of the universe that Aaron was spared the knowledge that his last message to Kennedy wouldn't be immediately delivered—if at all.

Yet, for those who are committed to understanding the entire truth of Aaron Hernandez, a hope still remains. We know the letter was entrusted to his family. They may have suppressed it—or worse still, destroyed it. If they have merely concealed it, then it may still see the light of day. If they have destroyed it, they very likely read it before destroying.

A glimpse at that can be found in a newly unearthed third letter, provided to this author, in which Aaron wrote to Kennedy's father with an unsolicited update on his son's life behind the walls of Souza. It read:

> I say this out of love and I know these are only words, but all I ever did in life was given my heart to those I love and want the best for them. All I do for your boy. Am I perfect? No. Who is. But we live and grow as we journey through life. The reason I felt the need to write it's because he is always like, "Shut up, leave me alone. You sound like my dad. Leave me alone," etc., etc. But he finally started to listen and make strides and I wanted to tell you that man to man. I'm not writing to get you to like me or anything. In all reality that's the last thing on my mind. I could just tell as a man seeing from the outside how much you truly love him and are there for him. He is blessed to have you, and I mean that and he knows it too.
>
> I thought you might want to hear he's been making changes and truly growing, becoming clean, and really beginning to grow up. I will never give up on him. All I know is loyalty. It's my weakness and he's got mine beyond words. He has ways to go and I'm on him with tough love and almost kiss his ass a few times, but always gave in because your son can talk his way out of anything, but his problem is he thinks

he is smarter than everyone. Until he realizes that some people see through the bullshit, lol.

I don't know how you'll take this letter, but I only follow my heart and right out of love. I don't need a response. I just wanted you to know and deserve to know your son is doing well, 100 times better, and as long as he's with me nobody with disrespect him, move on him, nor will he go without if I can help, because I will always give my last to ones I love.

He recently was lugged to the hole all over some bullshit, it wasn't his fault and that's real. Well, I'm gonna let you go and I know over time we will build a friendship because Pure's family is my family and will always be. No ifs, ands, or buts. If you want to respond, that's on you. I come before you with respect and zero motive except to let you know good news about your son, and if you ever wrote me it stays between us. My word. All we have is our word in life.

He'll cry because he hates not knowing things or when things aren't how he wants it when he wants it, lol, but for some reason he listens to me and has made huge progress. He's still gonna whine like he always does because I won't tell him why I wrote you, but if you ever want to know what he's up to you can get at me and I'll keep you in tune and be real with you. Hope all is well when you received this and you and your family are filled with love, joy, peace, and light. Have a blessed day. Tell the kids I said hi and the family. I'll be out one day and I'll definitely come through to send my love to Pure's fam. Love as love. Double.

Aaron's story was so remarkable and tragic—and it impacted so many lives—there are few whom he touched that do not want to know the full extent of what drove him to do what he did.

Perhaps, in time, we will know the entire truth.

EPILOGUE

"I just want to tell you this morning that I love you and you never have to question us. Over the past few days I realized how much I love you and how much I want you, us and mainly how I want you to know what real love, real loyalty is."

"I just wish we were cellies so I could at least kiss you on the forehead and say I love you then let you sleep while I make sure you have your coffee ready when you wake up."

"I can't even imagine them separating us. I'll feel like I'm missing all of me, fuck half of me."

—EXTRACTS FROM AARON HERNANDEZ'S JAILHOUSE LOVE LETTERS
TO KYLE KENNEDY

Millions of people have learned about the tragically strange life and death of Aaron Hernandez. Some of these were football fans. Some were merely residents of New England vaguely aware of the local player for the Patriots. Others were people who knew him personally. A few, knew him *very* personally.

For some, his story remains something they would like to forget about. To keep out of sight and out of mind. They dislike even thinking about Aaron because it is a reminder that life can be full of horrible surprises, and that even an

All-American, Super Bowl–bound athlete can contain, hidden deep within himself, the seeds of murder and deception.

Other dislike thinking of Aaron's tragic tale because of the larger implications for entities like the NFL and football in the United States. Like many calamities, there were many places along the way where a man like Aaron might have been saved from himself. It is easy to see these places.

A high school administrator or educator might have stepped in and said something like: "Aaron's not yet 18, and he has a drug problem, a discipline problem, and can hardly read or write. It would be immoral to graduate him early. It would mean we haven't done our job."

Someone at the University of Florida might also have stepped in and let Aaron feel the consequences of his actions for once. Someone could have said: "Forget the upcoming football season for just a moment. This young man learning not to hit people in bar fights is more important than another national championship."

And when he got to the NFL?

But no. By then, it may have been too late. Asking the Patriots football team to "solve" a dangerous jumble of desires like Aaron had was probably asking the downright impossible.

Each link in the chain had passed Aaron along. Each link was looking for someone else to "do the work" and make the sacrifices it would take in order to correct the young man.

The high school coaches told themselves that a good college program would "fix him," and Aaron went to arguably the best college program in the country.

But Urban Meyer and the Gators did little more than cover for his bad behavior before sending him along his way. "The NFL'll fix him" must have been a common refrain.

And so, there he was. The youngest player on the biggest stage of all. He was playing in the NFL. Not just playing, but playing as a record-setting star. But none of his vices had been corrected.

The NFL and the Patriots likely wanted to cry: "Oh *come on*! You're in the NFL now. Didn't you learn how to behave in high school? Or in college? Didn't anybody ever teach you?"

No.

They didn't want to do the work. They wanted to believe someone else would do it. Someone else would make the sacrifice, put in the man-hours it might take to reach a troubled soul like Aaron, and to do that even if it meant him missing a football game (or season). Even if it hurt that year's championship chances.

The horror of Aaron Hernandez is that he might be a kind of Frankenstein's monster that we all helped to create. We wanted to believe some other entity—either up or down the chain—*had* taken care of, or *would* take care of, the demons so evidently writhing just underneath the skin of his man. But not us. Not *now*. Not when another championship is so close. Not when our team is about to break another record.

Certainly, Aaron's troubling flaws should have been addressed.

Just not now.

Then it was too late. Aaron found himself a child in a man's body, with a $40 million contract. The drugs he had used to dull the pain of a troubled existence for so many years now used him. Now they were in control. His very inborn sexual identity had caused him to evolve a strange multiple personality disorder. Nobody wanted to crack down on the casual (and not-so-causal) homophobia in football. Nobody wanted to give a team of monsters who were bringing home championship after championship a lecture on respecting different sexual orientations. So better to let Aaron keep his bisexuality to himself.

Nobody wanted to do the work. Everyone wanted to get as much as they could from him, while giving almost nothing in return. Certainly, not the powerful intervention he so clearly needed.

As all the evidence in this book should make clear, Aaron was never going to be a Boy Scout. He was never going to be the kind of a guy the NFL made an ambassador and used in its commercials.

But he might have been able to manage his drug use, as so many do. He might have been able to drink and smoke on the weekends, or perhaps even kick the habit.

He was never going to be a priest, either. But a little guidance and help navigating his sexual appetites might have steered him to a place where some version of healthy, normal romantic relationships were going to be possible.

Finally, yes, he was probably always going to be a guy with inclinations towards violence. He checks all of those boxes. He grew up being the victim of violence at the hands of his own father, and then achieved a life of wealth, fame, and esteem by playing the most violent game in the world. Any anger management therapist looking at Aaron as a potential patient was going to tremble at the prospect and have their hands full. But that doesn't mean we were right to try nothing at all. With counseling, an intervention, maybe his violent nature would have de-escalated. Maybe some punches wouldn't have been thrown in the first place. What's more, maybe Aaron would have been able to see that cold-blooded murder should never be an option.

Aaron would not have been a perfect person. He might not have even been a good person. But with effort and care demonstrated by the institutions who benefitted so much from him—his high school, his university, and his NFL team—he might have been something less horrible than he was. He might not have been a drug-addicted, gang affiliated, gun-toting killer who found it necessary to maintain his sex life through a vast and mysterious web of lies. He may have not changed at all, but any effort could have made a difference. And even if it didn't, at least there was an attempt to help.

The question of what could have been is an open one. It is perhaps most appropriate to let those with expertise on Aaron's case the final word. From their many joint perspectives, a vision of the true man may yet emerge.

As his jailer, reading teacher, and erstwhile friend, Sheriff Thomas Hodgson got to spend more time with Aaron at the crucial junctures in his life than almost any other outsider. He relates that his own feelings about the end of the story are a mix of surprise and sadness:

> When I heard that Aaron had taken his own life, I was shocked because, number one, I always saw him as somebody that had that metal trap, that in his own mind, he was a master manipulator on the outside, but he was also a master manipulator within himself. He could always manipulate and keep things in that metal trap so that he wouldn't deal with all the realities. That way, he would survive, and he

would just transition into state time being his time waiting to go back to the Patriots or home or whatever.

That really struck me and surprised me, shocked me when he did it.

Secondly, there was a piece of me that liked him a little bit in his personality. I knew there was a piece of him as a person, as a human being, that there was down below in some part of him a place where he did have sensitivities about people and life and certainly about his dad and what he went through.

The writing of the verse of the Bible on his forehead is part of his process of committing suicide... I think it sort of speaks that the Bible was, in some way, maybe his sort of small little area within himself of salvation; that he believed that this is where he was going to be absolved of all.

That much—like the order that he spoke to his mother in prison about everything being in its place—perhaps that was the place that he felt would give him the safety net in life and in death. That there would be life thereafter for him, but it would be because he would be forgiven, and he was a son of [God].

The Aaron Hernandez story is about, in my mind, a guy who had some good human traits, who had some real sensitivity about people and life. I think there was a very sensitive part of him.

But there was also a place, experiences along his way in life that I think molded him and I think became even more difficult, leading him to the unfortunate problems that he ran into. I think it was accelerated by his father's death.

I don't know that we know the whole story yet about his family and how he may have been molded into being different by maybe some more traumatic experiences within his own personal life that he buried and were sort of dark. They would emerge at certain times, complicated by the fact that I think he was a sociopath.

It's hard to believe at 27 years old that he saw such fame so early in life. People all over, kids revered him. People all over revered him for his talents. And people would often say to me, "Wow, he had money, fame, he had everything, beautiful home here. How could he throw all that away?" Therein lies the story.

Most people who have all that would never have had that other piece of their lives be so destructive. But for him, it tells there's a deeper story.

Others seeking to wrap their own minds around the story see the many blows the young man took to the head as the final, unknowable horror.

Sportscaster Joe Kayata characterizes Aaron's CTE as a ticking time bomb that the athlete never even knew was there—although in one phone call, he seemed to acknowledge all was not well. ("You know I have no memory. You know my memory's cooked," he told his fiancée.)

That's the worst part about it. I don't think these players know. But I know certain players that I've spoken with who go get their brain tested in the offseason and are forced to do things to stay ahead of the curve. A guy who take a lot of hits, it's inevitable that you're going to get CTE and they desperately want to make sure that their brain isn't at that level yet.

Aaron was not a normal tight end. He did so much, so he got the ball a lot. So, he was either in the back field as a running back kind of H-back position. Or he was also lined up in the tight end position, or he could be at the wide receiver position, so he was kind of all over the field. So, he was a guy that you could hand the ball off to, you could do whatever. You wanted the ball in Aaron's hands, because he was a playmaker. Playmakers are the guys that get hit a lot because they have the ball a lot. He probably got a lot of hits during his career—even though it wasn't a very long career. You date back to high school, college, peewee, all that. There's a lot of hits.

This is a story of tragedy, at the end of the day.

Tragedy and wasted talent. It's a guy that had all the talent in the world—and didn't use it.

Dennis SanSoucie is also haunted by the specter of CTE in the tight end's final days:

> My first reaction when hearing about Aaron having CTE was, "This all makes more sense now." His behavior as a kid makes sense to me, I think Aaron had CTE as early as a kid, and I think that's what led to the multiple personalities. I think this is someone who struggled tremendously growing up and dealing with the way of life and how to even go about living it. The disclosure of CTE answered a lot for me. I think him having the CTE is almost, to me, a good enough excuse to put all the other stuff to the side and say, "This is such a severe thing that everything he was doing, he couldn't even control." We were always hitting each other. I remember we were doing things that kids shouldn't be doing, we were playing this game called Space Monkeys where we would choke each other out and watch each other fall on the ground and then wake back up. Then, also, Aaron had a severe concussion senior year of high school, he got knocked out of a game against Maloney, so it is definitely something that the more and more head trauma, the more and more it's gonna increase, I think, with the CTE.
>
> There's so many things that bother me about all this that it's hard for me to put into words what bothers me the most, but I do feel that there's some injustices that Aaron couldn't overcome. That if the right people were around him, a better supporting crew, that he would have.
>
> Now, I wanna personally remember Aaron as someone who's been a big impact on my life moving forward, and even though I couldn't share the good life with him, I'm gonna live my life knowing that he's always watching me and he cares and he's smiling.

According to Dr. Jeff Gardere, who has analyzed some of Aaron's final recorded words, there appears to be a multitude of factors that led to Aaron's story ending the way that it did.

Yet he also grants that the powerful impact of CTE cannot be underestimated:

When I read that Aaron Hernandez's brain was examined post-mortem and they found that he had one of the worst cases of CTE that they had ever seen—and he had it at such a young age, the extent of it at such a young age—it begins to make sense of all of the impulsive, inappropriate, acting out behaviors that we saw that just didn't seem to make sense for someone who had so many reasons to live a prosperous and peaceful life.

I think when we address the combination of things, the perfect storm if you will: a young man who had a conflicted relationship with his father, a conflicted relationship with his family, who had what appears to be impulse issues, who was involved in situations where he was plucked from obscurity and into fame and fortune perhaps too early in his life, who wasn't prepared to be a super successful professional athlete, to have played for one of the best teams at the time, to have a contract worth $40 million, and then you put the overlay of the CTE—this brain damage—where one doesn't have control over their own behavior—all of that together, to me, is the perfect play of destruction and death.

In the end, the role of the CTE may be unknowable. Was it 10 percent of what drove Aaron over the edge and forced him to take his own life? Or was it 50 percent? Maybe even 90 percent? There is almost no way to guess accurately. Aaron was not an otherwise healthy person. He was a criminally inclined ball of pathologies and self-destructive behaviors that seemed to feed off one another. Adding CTE to that was like throwing gasoline on an already-raging fire.

Jose Baez explains:

The brain sits in a liquid-like substance inside the skull and every time there's a tackle or a blow to the head, the brain rams up against the skull and it's the repeated blow that start to cause damage to the brain. What's interesting about this is everybody thinks, oh, well they wear helmets. Well, the helmets just make it worse because the players have this false sense of security. Helmets don't protect the brain, it only protects the skull and the skin above it from a contusion.

I mean 90 percent of our conversation was things we were going to do. He was ecstatic. He was extremely happy. The last letter he wrote to me which was written hours before he passed and in there you can see he's joking around and really happy. He starts writing his letters to his family which are suicide letters and I believe based on the evidence and the research that I've done that this was the CTE taking over.

They described his brain as being in the condition of a 40-plus-year-old man who had been playing in the league for about 18 years.

There were times that Aaron was sharp as a tack and then there were times that he would just simply forget and we would kind of I guess blow it off with his goofiness. I believe that the CTE comes and goes in an individual. They can be seemingly normal one moment and then at another moment they start having these tremendous headaches for which Aaron complained about all the time. Overwhelming migraine type headaches also memory loss.

The NFL purposely conducted research that they knew was flawed and if you look at what they told their players that they were completely safe. They've quite frankly misled them.

We know this game is bad for your brain but we're going to allow children to play football. Pick your poison. A cigarette for your lungs or football for your brain. I think they're both bad and I think they're both child abuse.

For some, the lack of concern for players in regard to CTE is just part and parcel of the larger lack of concern across the football ecosystem. Dereck Faulkner believes the lack of concern for Aaron started early, and extended into the NFL. In both cases, it was Aaron's own success as a player that made it so hard for the forces in power to give him the help he needed.

Explains Faulkner:

For Aaron, if he had gotten some help early on and someone had really identified it, it probably would have saved a bunch of lives and saved a bunch of broken families. But again, on the college level, a university's looking at it as we have hundreds of student athletes, and the football program has a hundred or hundred-plus student athletes as well participating. It's definitely tough to be identified. What they did do that was wrong was probably Band-Aid his activity and kind of turn a [naked] eye. That ultimately hurt.

I think the NFL definitely cares about their players.

But, at the same time, there's a lot of—a lot of guys can slip through the cracks. The NFL definitely cares about their bottom line. They care about what the product they're putting on the field, what that matters, and what that looks like.

With Aaron and different players with troubled pasts, sometimes they turn a blind eye if you're producing on the field. I think it's all about production. If you're able to produce on the field, they'll turn a blind eye. That's in all of sports, in different leagues. If you're producing and you're actually making the league or team money, they may give you a chance to kind of turn a blind eye if you're doing something wrong or if you're not doing something ethical off the field.

Others analyzing the aftermath of the situation credit the fans as well—and their need for superhuman stars on the field—with creating a situation where Hernandez's dark side was allowed to run out of control.

To investigative journalist Michelle McPhee:

I think that we're at a time in our society where people don't really want to know the truth. They don't want you to pull back the curtain. They don't want you to pop the balloon. They want to live with the legend of somebody, and Aaron Hernandez was a legend. He was part of a franchise that is beloved in my native Boston. He helped take the Patriots to a Super Bowl, and people loved him. Women were showing up in his trial, wearing [No.] 87 jerseys. He definitely was a beloved figure. But when my law enforcement sources started telling me some of the very sordid history—and some of the details that led him to murder of Lloyd—that was run-of-the-mill gangster stuff. Only it had this added aspect of a very complicated sex life.

Yet McPhee also makes clear that despite her hundreds of hours spent studying the story of Aaron Hernandez, compassion is the last thing she feels for the one-time Patriot:

> I have compassion for the victims. I watched Odin Lloyd's mother collapse in hysterical sobs and have to leave the courtroom. She was overwrought with emotion, listening to the details of how her son died. Then, you hear about Sandra Hines going to the vehicle where her son had been shot. Do you know what brain matter looks like in a vehicle? Then you realize that it belongs to your son, and thank God he's alive.
>
> These are the people that I have compassion for.
>
> I have compassion for the bouncer, who was making minimum wage at a bar in Florida, when he gets his eardrum pierced with a hard punch to the side of the head by this coward. Everything that Aaron Hernandez did was cowardly. He punched a guy in the side of the head. What did the guy do? He asked him to pay his bar bill. How dare you, and that guy now is deaf in one ear.
>
> You question him in any sort of altercation, he pulls out a gun. This has gone on forever, and we're supposed to feel compassion for Aaron Hernandez, and not feel compassion for the guy who was making eight bucks an hour, to lose his eardrum as a bouncer, or the mother who had to see her son's brains splattered all over a vehicle, or Odin Lloyd's mother, or the two Cape Verdean men who were slaughtered in Boston?
>
> There were a lot of victims of Aaron Hernandez's crimes.
>
> Not all of them were good guys. Alexander Bradley was a lowlife, but he got shot in the head by his very own buddy—and rolled out of a car—and left in a parking lot to die, just like Odin Lloyd was.
>
> To me, it is inexplicable that just because somebody was a decent NFL superstar that they get a pass on this sort of behavior, this

bloodletting that has gone on now, for the majority of Aaron Hernandez's life. All of these excuses that people have been making for him are irrelevant. Here is a guy who had a penchant for violence, and he couldn't control it, even with access to the best psychologists.

Let's be real. He could have gotten help. He had plenty of money. He could have done something to change his life. He could have been a good father. He could have been a good husband. But instead, he was a maggot—a 40-million-dollar maggot.

Retired detective Bo Dietl's final assessment of Aaron—based on everything he had learned and studied over the course of looking at the loose ends connected to the case—likewise remains grim.

He feels our knowledge of the crimes Aaron committed might only be the tip of the iceberg:

> Aaron Hernandez was a sick individual. He could have been capable of being a serial killer and I'd like to find and go backwards, like when we look at cases with serial murders. As a detective, you go backwards, and you look at the different locations geographically that they were during these years, You identify murders that were never solved and perhaps you could be on a tip of a serial murderer. I tell you what, if I found out he killed more than four people, I would not be shocked.

Even with these revelatory facts in front of us, it is still difficult to know if we will ever really "understand" the true Aaron Hernandez.

What drove him.

Why he did what he did.

But simply because something cannot be done perfectly does not mean we shouldn't attempt the project.

Aaron's suicide was never investigated by prison authorities with the type of thoroughness one would expect to answer many of the questions, and there are further unanswered questions.

The Commonwealth of Massachusetts Department of State Police produced a cursory report on the suicide—only five pages long, if you don't count the appendix and attachments. It lays out the most basic information only. Aaron was found in his cell and transported to UMass Health Alliance Hospital where he was pronounced dead.

He had decorated his cell and hanged himself with a bedsheet. Written notes were found in the cell. (Four lines in the report—presumably describing the notes—are redacted. Why? Who knows?) Little else of use is noted. Questions linger. Why on the night Hernandez died did security guard Gerard Breaux reportedly skip his 2 a.m. round? (He later told investigators he hadn't slept before his shift and was in a fog that night.)

When he did walk the hall at 3 a.m., he didn't have his keys with him. Why?

Corrections officials won't say whether Breaux was disciplined, but we have learned he still works at the facility.

Aaron had been found guilty of the murder of Lloyd, but a motive for that execution-style killing was never established and his attorney was preparing for a retrial. Was he worried something new was possibly going to come out?

Most of the speculation surrounding Aaron's motive for killing Lloyd centered around his hidden sexuality.

Could it be the case that Aaron actually murdered Lloyd because Lloyd found out that he was gay? Or did Odin uncover a secret that could not only destroy Aaron Hernandez, the NFL superstar, but rattle the NFL as an entity?

This investigation definitively establishes that in the days before Lloyd was killed, Aaron had two encounters that now seem profoundly important in terms of establishing a motive. One was with Chad the stripper. The other was with the drug dealer known only as "Q."

According to Q, Aaron had one central fear—that his use of HIV medication would come to light.

If a $40 million NFL superstar was on some kind of secret medication, this would be a bombshell revelation—the type of which would rock the highest levels of professional football.

In the course of concluding our investigation, we took our findings—and our questions—to Assistant District Attorney Jarrett J. Ferentino.

After reviewing the central questions remaining, he had much to say:

If confronted with the statements that these two witnesses have made regarding Odin seeing meds, doing my job as a prosecutor, I would have to run down the answer to the question. What meds could we be talking about? What conditions could he be treating? What meds would create a desire so compelling to silence Odin Lloyd?

I would think it's a medication that may be tied to some sort of stigma. That may be tied perhaps to something that could be extremely embarrassing or that can be career ending.

I've reviewed documentation from Aaron Hernandez's attorneys. They requested medical information from the New England Patriots. First, they requested it via a letter that the information be voluntarily provided to them. It included in that packet, a signed release from Aaron Hernandez. That information was not provided willingly by the New England Patriots, according to those records. The next step was Aaron Hernandez's attorneys sought to subpoena those records from the court system and in that documentation, they've requested the following information: One, his physical health records; two, his mental health records; and three, any drug testing or drug records. The box that was not checked on that subpoena was any HIV or STD testing or diagnostic record.

I would say there are three possible scenarios why that particular HIV/STD information would not be sought. One, Aaron Hernandez may have instructed his attorneys that in fact, that information is non-existent, that he did not have HIV or any other STD. Two, they did not want to request that information because checking that box would create the inference that that information exists and he may or may not have that disease. Or three, he was aware that there was a record and didn't want it to come out. If I believed the information contained in any of those medical records or any defendant's medical records was related to the murder itself, then I would absolutely want to know the answers to those questions.

I have seen in my career people kill for a lot less than the jeopardizing of a multimillion-dollar career.

Aaron Hernandez was a killer. He killed. As we look at the things we still do not know about him, the question remains: "To what extent?"

As we prepare to close the door on the story of Aaron Hernandez, the words of Kyle Kennedy still resound like a drum.

"He used to tell me he had four murders."

But as to the specifics?

Says Kennedy: "[Aaron Hernandez] never gave me a name, never. He would just always, all the time joke around saying 'I got four bodies.'"

If there was a fourth person who was killed by Aaron, then that person's murder has likely never been solved—or, worse, the wrong person may have been convicted of it. This makes discovering the truth of this final killing the most pressing aspect of the Hernandez case going forward.

For his part, Kyle Kennedy maintains that he has no remaining information to share about the fourth murder. No clues to give. The scant information Aaron did tell Kennedy about the fourth murder—which is not much more than "it happened"—is additionally difficult to process because Aaron so often spoke in jest.

As Kennedy puts it: "He would always bring that [fourth murder] up joking around."

The professional investigators engaged for this book believe the most probable candidate for this "fourth body" is Jordan Miller, as outlined in Chapter 10.

The team contacted Jordan Miller's aunt—Tara Davis—in the search for one final answer. Davis remembered Miller as a good and loving person, and his death was crushing to her.

As she recalled:

> Jordan was a good kid. He was family oriented. He worked. He went to school. He helped take care of his younger sister and brother. He lived with my mom, his grandmother. This was devastating to my family. It's still ... as I talk about it now, it's devastating still.
>
> I received news that Jordan had been shot from his sister. She arrived at my mom's house which is literally around the corner from Jordan. When we arrived [at the house] it was very stark. It was very surreal, and a sense of foreboding just came over us.

What struck me, initially, is this seemed personal. They came to his house. They shot him through a window. I saw the bullet holes in the walls, in the doorway. His blood stain ... it was still on the floor. I've also heard that there were three individuals near his home that night. I was told they were noted on camera running from the scene.

Three individuals. One of whom could have been Aaron Hernandez.

In addition to this compelling information, we discovered something more when we took out a picture of "Q." Tara Davis's boyfriend (who did not wish to give his name), recognized the man, and with no prior information about his name or nickname, identified him as "Q Money." The boyfriend indicated that he'd previously met with Q/Q Money—and with Miller. On top of this, the boyfriend confirmed that he knew Odin Lloyd.

The only silver lining to the Jordan Miller murder is that it appears no other person has been falsely convicted in Aaron's place. The case remains unsolved to this day. Though more than six years have passed, the authorities are still waiting for a clue—or for someone to come forward with information—that will tie it to the killer.

Tellingly, the case report of the murder contains some notable absences.

The type of vehicle that was allegedly at the scene and the type of shell casing found are both omitted. Yet we know that Aaron had the means, motive, and certainly the opportunity.

According to Detective Michelle Wood, killing Jordan Miller would have been "typical Aaron Hernandez behavior," and there are still many clues strongly pointing in his direction.

"The gun used to kill Odin Lloyd was a .45 caliber," Wood continues.

"If the ballistics used to kill Jordan Miller came from a .45, we have another possible link. However, if the ballistics do not come back to a .45 caliber handgun, it doesn't mean that Aaron Hernandez didn't have anything to do with it, because we know that Aaron Hernandez has access to multiple different type of weapons."

Wood also believes that Miller may have been killed accidentally by Aaron—and that, even for this, there is precedent.

"It's possible that it was a case of mistaken identity," explains Wood. "The 2007 Florida shooting of Sandra's son, Corey Smith, was a case of mistaken identity. It's possible the murder of Jordan Miller was also a case of mistaken identity."

Other facts in the case file also see Wood looking in Aaron's direction.

> In reviewing the case report from his murder, the only two things I cared about is the type of vehicle that was allegedly used in the murder and the shell casing—of which neither are detailed on the documents. One of the witnesses that came forward during our investigation revealed that he spoke to Aaron Hernandez at a graveyard and this person claimed to be a drug dealer. This person mentioned that Jordan Miller was murdered, and actually, the only unsolved case that I know of in that area that fits the description provided by some of the witnesses is Jordan Miller.
>
> You would have thought Hernandez would've got caught before this and perhaps he should've been caught before this if people weren't covering for him.
>
> He doesn't commit these acts as a lone offender, so what I would look for, other cases that are similar in nature, that a black SUV was used, multiple occupants were inside the vehicle, and I would expect to have similar shell casings if he did, indeed use the same weapon and that would've been a 45 caliber.
>
> There's nothing here in the Jordan Miller murder incident report that shows me anything other than typical Aaron Hernandez behavior.

Kyle Kennedy, too, is willing to admit that the murder of Jordan Miller would have been par for the course for Aaron.

When asked directly if he believed Aaron was a "cold-blooded killer" Kennedy responds in no uncertain terms:

> I have seen him like that. We would talk all day about guns and murder and robbery and that was our choice of topic. He was just

infatuated by that stuff. He was infatuated with hurting people. He just took it a little out of control. He always did everything to the extreme.

At the end of the day, it is remarkable that Aaron was only convicted of one murder.

We do not know the complete extent of his crimes, but it must be as extensive as it is stomach-churning. It is almost impossible to imagine that we know everything.

So many tangential questions remain.

How many victims are there in total?

Could there be more than four?

Where is the gun that killed Odin Lloyd?

Who hid the gun?

Who else knew what Aaron Hernandez was doing?

As more and more sources are revealed and come forward in the days ahead, we could have new moments of clear vision into this very muddy water. It is sometimes possible to guess with confidence what might have been happening inside his mind—or the extent of Aaron's horrible crimes.

We know the life Aaron was attracted to. We know the people he was attracted to. Almost every story is of someone going after something they want. Perhaps, in the end, Aaron simply wanted too much. Too many things.

His appetites and desires were as outsized as his enormous corpse the jailers found hanging in his cell hours after he killed himself.

If he had been raised in a different environment, would his story have ended in a better way? What if his father had not beaten him, or passed away when he was at such a young age? What if coaches and football programs had not covered up his bad behavior time and again, but rather let him suffer the consequences and learn from them?

Again, we will never know.

But what we do know is that the secrets surrounding this remarkable and sinister man are not through revealing themselves.

Not by a longshot.

"I know it is really difficult for people to hear this," explains Dr. Gardere.

"But even though there were many alleged victims out of this Aaron Hernandez story, there was also another victim—and that victim was Aaron Hernandez himself.

"Here is an individual who showed some great talent when he was very young, loved his father, but was in an abusive relationship with his father. But he still idolized the man. Then one of the greatest traumas in his life is his father's death. Who does he have to guide him at that point?

"Here he is in high school trying to get an education. But then the fickle finger of fate steps in. He's taken right out of high school into college where, obviously, he wasn't ready. He was given many opportunities to not have to account for his behaviors, which in many ways is not a good reinforcement for bad behavior.

"Then, all of a sudden, he is thrust into the limelight, doing well in pro football.

"But who is helping him deal with these psychological demons?

"Who is helping him deal with his feelings about sexuality that we've heard so much about?

"Who is helping him be a person who needs to be loved? He was basically on his own.

"That was the formula for disaster: going from multimillionaire, world famous pro football player, to now dead in a jail cell by himself. That is tragedy. That is a tragedy. *That is a Shakespearian play to the max.*"

THE TOLL OF HIS CRIMES

"I tried as hard as I could to live the dream life. It just didn't work out. Whoever listens to this call, fuck you."

—AARON HERNANDEZ, JAILHOUSE PHONE CALL

4 Murders

3 Attempted Murders

1 Bar Fight

The opinions and conclusions of the investigators who participated in this book about how it may have occurred represent just some of a number of possible scenarios.

The killing of Jordan Miller is a crime that, to this day, remains unsolved.

Following Aaron's suicide on April 17, 2017, a state judge vacated Aaron's murder conviction for the June 2013 murder of Odin Lloyd

However, in March 2019, Massachusetts' highest court reinstated the murder conviction in a ruling that also ended an antiquated legal rule in which convictions were thrown out when a defendant died before an appeal was heard.

Kyle Kennedy is still serving his Massachusetts state sentence. He is currently housed in Wyoming under an interstate agreement.

The NFL has already paid out more than $500 million in compensation claims by former players with CTE.

Boston Police now tell me as of August 2019, that the murder of Jordan Miller is an active and fluid investigation.

INCIDENT/INVESTIGATION REPORT

Gainesville Police Department

Case # *02-07-008464*

Status Codes	L = Lost S = Stolen R = Recovered D = Damaged Z = Seized B = Burned C = Counterfeit / Forged F = Found

	UCR	Status	Quantity	Type Measure	Suspected Type	Up to 3 types of activity
D						
R						
U						
G						
S						

Assisting Officers
ROWE, D.H. (0166)

Suspect Hate / Bias Motivated: *None (No bias)*

NARRATIVE

On 04/28/07 at approximately 0100 hours I was on uniform patrol in a marked patrol vehicle when I was dispatched to The Swamp Resturant, 1642 W. University Ave, in reference to a disturbance.

Upon arrival, I met with Michael Taphorn who stated that as he was escorting a H/M, later identified as Aaron Hernandez, out of the restaurant after a dispute with his bill when he was struck in the left side of the head by Hernandez. Taphorn stated that he was speaking with Hernandez about the dispute regarding the bill and eventually asked Hernandez to leave the establishment. Taphorn stated that he began to escort Hernandez out of the resturant and when they got just outside of the front doors, he turned to walk back into the resturant and stated that he was struck in the left side of the head by Hernandez. Hernandez then fled the area. Taphorn stated that he could not hear out of his left ear. Taphorn refused medical treatment on scene and stated that he would seek medical attention on his own first thing Monday.

I attempted to locate Hernandez however was unsuccessful. I did speak briefly with Timothy Tebow on scene. He stated that he was also out at The Swamp with Hernandez and another individual by the name of Shaun Young. Tebow stated that he witnessed the dispute between Taphorn and Hernandez. Tebow stated that he went over to try to help resolve the conflict. Tebow encouraged Hernandez to leave peacefully and tried to make arrangements to pay for the bill. The conflict between Taphorn and Hernandez continued and Hernandez struck Taphorn and then left the area.

Shortly after 0300 hours, Sgt Rowe, 166, was able to locate Hernandez and speak with him. Post Miranda, Hernadez stated that during the night, a waitress brought him two alcoholic drinks (Hernandez is only 17 yoa) that he did not order. Hernandez stated that he was not aware that the waitress brought them to him and thought that they were provided by a fan. Prior to leaving, Hernandez was presented with a bill for the drinks by Taphorn. He stated that he did not order the items. A verbal altercation ensued and Hernandez called for Tebow to come over to intervene. Hernandez stated that Taphorn was "in his face" and yelling at him. Hernandez stated that as he was leaving the resturant, Taphorn was still engaging him in a verbal altercation and he struck Taphorn in the head and then he left the area. Please see Sgt Rowe's supplemental report for further details.

On 04/29/07 I spoke to Huntley Johnson, legal counsel for Hernandez. I advised Johnson that I was conducting the investigation into the battery and that a sworn complaint would be submitted however I would have to wait for Taphorn's medical results to determine specific charges (Battery or Felony Battery).

On Monday 04/30/07 I received a message from Taphorn stated that he went to the doctor and that his eardrum had burst as a result of being punched by Hernandez and that it would take 4-6 weeks to heal. I then contacted Lt Etell of UPD and advised him of the medical outcome and that a sworn complaint would be filed for Felony Battery. Sgt Rowe was also notified.

Follow up regarding who served Hernandez the alcoholic beverages is also being conducted.

A Gainesville Police Department report shows that Tim Tebow, Aaron Hernandez, and Shaun Young were at The Swamp restaurant and bar on April 28, 2007.

Hernandez started to argue with manager Michael Taphorn about a bar bill. Hernandez, who was 17 at the time, ordered the drinks but refused to pay when he was given the bill, according to the report.

Tebow told police that Taphorn was being irrational and "getting in Hernandez's" face. Tebow said he didn't want Hernandez to get in trouble because he was a football player, and the manager knew he was a player. Tebow offered to pay the bill and leave in peace.

The argument continued as Taphorn escorted Hernandez out of the restaurant, police said. When Taphorn turned to go inside, Hernandez punched him on the left side of the head before running around the corner, leaving a black sneaker behind.

Taphorn told police that Tebow and Young ran around the corner with Hernandez.

One of the officers found Tebow and Young, but Hernandez was gone. The officer said Tebow told police he tried to break up the argument, identifying himself and Hernandez as UF players. Tebow said he asked Hernandez to leave and offered to pay the bill.

Tebow identified Hernandez for the police, the report said.

Taphorn complained to police about hearing loss and wanted to press battery charges, the report said. One of the officers told Tebow it would be in Hernandez's "best interest to contact us and give his side of the story." Tebow told the officer he would try to find Hernandez, but that he also was concerned "his name would get out to the media as being involved in the incident." The officer assured Tebow that he would not contact the media and that he was being listed in the report "as a witness only." Hours later, around 3 a.m., officers found Hernandez at the Cabana Beach South Apartments, along with Tebow and Young.

The officer said Hernandez didn't seem intoxicated and was "very polite and professional." Hernandez and Tebow told police they both had contacted then-coach Urban Meyer about the incident, and the officer said GPD would not pursue any charges against Hernandez for underage drinking, but that it would be noted in the report "so coaches could handle it internally." Two days after the incident, Taphorn told police he'd been to his doctor and found out his eardrum had burst as a result of the blow to the head and that it would take four to six weeks to heal.

When Aaron Hernandez was charged with murder in the death of Odin Lloyd, the big break in the case came from Enterprise Rent-A-Car and bubble gum.

At 2:10 a.m., prosecutors say they established evidence that Hernandez stopped

```
 CCIN37                    VEHICLE ACCIDENT REPORT                 PAGE    1
                          ENTERPRISE RENT-A-CAR
                        ENTERPRISE RENT-A-CAR
                        365 EAST WASHINGTON STREET
                        NORTH ATTLEBORO   MA 02760-2322

 Accident Report# DX4912J88    Date of Report  7/08/13    Taken by: 500FF
 Date of Accident  6/19/13     Time of Accident 08:45AM   Rental Contract# 346167

 Vehicle ID:    Unit Yr Make Model Series Color License#  St VIN#
            7HH7FG 13 CHEV SUB1  1LT4   BLACK 442427   /RI 1GNSKJE71DR286383

 Street/Intersection of Accident   DORCHESTOR
 Purpose of Trip PERSONAL                       State of Accident  MA

 Accident Description:
 CAR WAS IMPOUNDED BY POLICE FROM DORCHESTOR, MA DUE TO THE FACT THAT THIS VEHICL
 E WAS INVOLVED IN A FELONY. BRANCH HAS NOT BEEN ABLE TO SEE VEHICLE YET SO WE AR
 E NOT SURE OF ANY DAMAGE TO THE VEHICLE AT THIS TIME. THE VEHICLE IS
 STILL A PART OF AN ONGOING ACTIVE INVESTIGATION BY BOTH STATE POLICE A
 ND LOCAL NORTH ATTLEBORO, PD. BRANCH DOES NOT KNOW AT THIS TIME WHEN T
 HE VEHCILE WILL BE RELEASED BACK TO ERAC.

 Current Vehicle Location       LAKEVILLE POLICE BARRACKS
 Damages to Enterprise Vehicle  UNKNONW

                          ***  PARTIES  ***

 Lease/Renter/Employee                 Driver (if other than Renter)

 HERNANDEZ*  AARON*
     9 MESSENGER ST
 PLAINVILLE              MA  02762-2267
 Home Phone#  562-481-8106        Home Phone#  000-000-0000
 Work Phone#  562-481-8106        Work Phone#  000-000-0000
 DOB 11/06/89    SS# 999-99-0000  DOB            SS# 999-99-0000
 License#  XXXXXXXXXXXXXXXXXXXX   License#
 Employer  N.E. PATRIOTS          Employer




 Driver's Signature:_____  Date:_____
```

at a gas station and purchased several items including Bubbalicious blue cotton candy gum.

Later, prosecutors claim to have found a piece of Bubbalicious blue cotton candy gum in a dumpster that was used to clean the rental car.

They said the gum was originally discovered under a seat in the car next to a shell casing.

The shell casing, a .44 caliber, matched five casings found at the crime scene.

BostonPolice
DEPARTMENT

INCIDENT REPORT

ORIGINAL   STATUS: APPROVED

KEY SITUATIONS		COMPLAINT NO.	RPT DIST.	CAD RA	RPT RA	CLEAR. DIST.
VICTIM SHOT		130341422	E18	479	479	

UCR INCIDENT DESCRIPTION	UCR FINAL INCIDENT DESCRIPTION	STATUS		DATE OCCURRED FROM	DATE OCCURRED TO
DEATH INVESTIGATION	HOMICIDE			06/05/2013	06/05/2013

LOCATION OF INCIDENT		APT.	DISPATCH TIME	TIME OCCURRED FROM	TIME OCCURRED TO
633 CUMMINS HY			11:51 PM	11:50 PM	11:50 PM

NEIGHBORHOOD	TYPE OF BUILDING	PLACE OF ENTRY	WEATHER	LIGHTING
MATTAPAN	RESIDENTIAL HOUSE		CLEAR - NIGHT	OUTSIDE - NIGHT - LIMITED/NO STREET LIGHT

TYPE OF WEAPON-TOOL	SUSPECT MODE OF TRANSPORTATION	VICTIM'S ACTIVITY	SUSPECT RELATIONSHIP TO VICTIM
HANDGUN		AT HOME	

UNUSUAL ACTIONS AND STATEMENTS OF PERPETRATORS

1 TYPE	NAME (LAST, FIRST, MI)	S.S. NO.	BOOKING NO.	DOCKET NO.
VICTIM	KNOWN TO COMMONWEALTH		0	

ALIAS	ADDRESS	GENDER	RACE	DOB	AGE
					0

HEIGHT	WEIGHT	BUILD	HAIR	EYES

OCCUPATION	MARITAL STATUS	EMAIL ADDRESS	CONTACT #1	CONTACT #2

SPECIAL CHARACTERISTICS (INCLUDING CLOTHING)

2 TYPE	NAME (LAST, FIRST, MI)	S.S. NO.	BOOKING NO.	DOCKET NO.
REPORTER	P.O. R BOYLE			

ALIAS	ADDRESS	GENDER	RACE	DOB	AGE

HEIGHT	WEIGHT	BUILD	HAIR	EYES

OCCUPATION	MARITAL STATUS	EMAIL ADDRESS	CONTACT #1	CONTACT #2

SPECIAL CHARACTERISTICS (INCLUDING CLOTHING)

3 TYPE	NAME (LAST, FIRST, MI)	S.S. NO.	BOOKING NO.	DOCKET NO.
OFFENDER	UNKNOWN		0	

ALIAS	ADDRESS	GENDER	RACE	DOB	AGE
					0

HEIGHT	WEIGHT	BUILD	HAIR	EYES
		N/A		

OCCUPATION	MARITAL STATUS	EMAIL ADDRESS	CONTACT #1	CONTACT #2

SPECIAL CHARACTERISTICS (INCLUDING CLOTHING)

4 TYPE	NAME (LAST, FIRST, MI)	S.S. NO.	BOOKING NO.	DOCKET NO.
OFFENDER	UNKNOWN		0	

ALIAS	ADDRESS	GENDER	RACE	DOB	AGE
					0

HEIGHT	WEIGHT	BUILD	HAIR	EYES
		N/A		

OCCUPATION	MARITAL STATUS	EMAIL ADDRESS	CONTACT #1	CONTACT #2

SPECIAL CHARACTERISTICS (INCLUDING CLOTHING)

V E H I C L E S	STATUS	REG.STATE	REG.NO.	PLATE TYPE		YEAR(EXP)	MODEL
	LV SCENE	MA		N/A		0	
	VEHICLE MAKE YEAR	V.I.N.		STYLE		COLOR(TOP-BOTTOM)	
	- 0						
	OPERATOR'S NAME		LICENSE NO.	STATE	OPERATOR'S ADDRESS		
	OWNER'S NAME			OWNER ADDRESS			

NARRATIVE AND ADDITIONAL INFORMATION

On Wednesday 6-5-2013 at about 11:50pm the L202A, Officers Boyle/Hubbard, received a radio call to the above for a report of shots fired. While enroute the call was updated to include one person shot at this location.

On arrival officers observed that EMS had already arrived at the scene as well as the T528 Officer Bowden and the 1E511 Officer Coyne. Upon entering the apartment officers observed EMT's Lt John Cotter EMT's Rivas/Dinis performing CPR on a ███████ inside apartment █ of 633 Cummins Hy. The ███████ was suffering from 3 gunshot wounds to the left side of █ body. Officers were informed that the victims wounds could be life threatening.

At this time officer secured the scene and full notifications were made. The victim was transported to the Faulkner Hospital in Ambulance 3A19 were he was later pronounced.

The following Units also responded

YC09 - Superintendent Will Gross
L982 - Sgt Det John Rouvalis
L912 - Sgt Dan MacDonald
C901 - Sgt Keith Webb
L101A - Officers Coleman/Thomas
Lk01A - Officers Layden/Roberts
L411A - Officer Spilane
L412A - Officer Borbee
CK01A - Officers Goggin/Buiel
VA04 - Lt Det Darrin Greeley
V905 - Sgt Det J Wyse
V815 - Det Benton
VD209 - Officer Ward
VD186 - Officer Sullivan
ETAL

UNIT ASSIGNED	SHIFT	REPORTING OFFICER'S NAME		REPORTING OFFICER'S ID	PARTNER'S ID
L202A	1	ROBERT C BOYLE		8934	90499
SPECIAL UNITS NOTIFIED(REPORTING)					
AREA E-13					
DATE OF REPORT	TIME COMPLETED	APPROVING SUPERVISOR NAME		APPROVING SUPERVISOR ID	
06/06/2013	03:40 AM	SEAN WILBANKS		80394	

The investigation into the murder of Jordan Miller in Hyde Park in 2013 is still open, but no arrests have been made, the Suffolk District Attorney's office has said.

Miller's assailant fired nine shots into the victim's first-floor bedroom window in his home at 633 Cummings Highway the night of June 5, the Boston Globe reported.

Miller was taken to Faulkner Hospital, where he died the next day.

CRIME SCENE INVESTIGATION NOTES

EXAMINATION DATE	INCIDENT LOCATION	ANALYST
6/17/13	344 John L Dietsch Blvd N. Attleboro	ALF

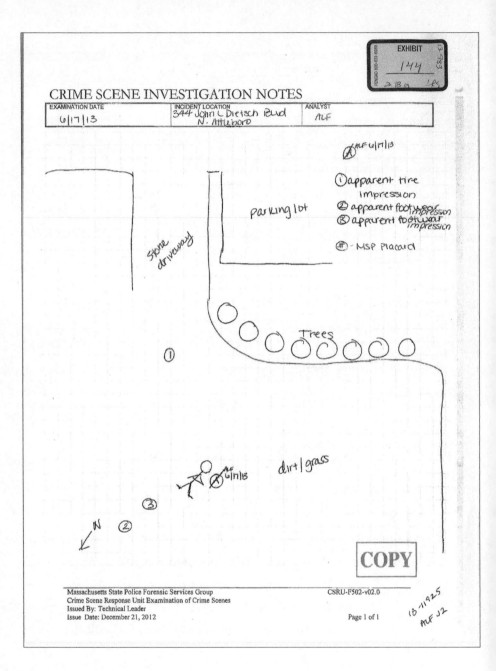

ALF 6/17/13

① apparent tire
   impression
② apparent footwear
   impression
③ apparent footwear
   impression

④ - MSP Placard

parking lot

Stone driveway

Trees

①

dirt/grass

ALF 6/17/13

③

N

②

COPY

Massachusetts State Police Forensic Services Group
Crime Scene Response Unit Examination of Crime Scenes
Issued By: Technical Leader
Issue Date: December 21, 2012

CSRU-F502-v02.0

Page 1 of 1

13-11925
ALF J2

Just like O. J. Simpson, prosecutors in the murder trial of Odin Lloyd attempted to establish footwear impressions found near the body of the victim established that Aaron Hernandez was at the crime scene.

This document is hand-written crime scene analysis from police.

On the 29th day of the trial, jurors heard hours of testimony from Massachusetts State Police lieutenant Stephen Bennett about footwear impressions. Bennett is a crime scene supervisor for the state's crime services lab unit.

Most significantly, Bennett testified that one set of footprints found at the crime scene matched a pair of size 13 Nike Air Jordan Retro 11 sneakers—the very type of sneakers allegedly worn by Hernandez the night of Lloyd's murder.

Bennett's testimony included a description of how law enforcement collected evidence at the Lloyd crime scene and the important role rain played in that collection.

After Lloyd's body was found on June 17, 2013, law enforcement became aware of substantial rain in the forecast.

Police officers then used tarps and other measures to preserve the evidence from contamination.

Bennett described how law enforcement found footwear impressions in two basic locations at the crime scene: (1) One location was a sandy silt gravel area not far from Lloyd's body; and (2) near tire tracks.

TO: New England Patriots
        One Patriot Place
        Foxboro, MA 02035

FROM: Aaron Josef Hernandez
        Bristol County House of Correction
        400 Faunce Corner Road
        Dartmouth, MA 02747

I, AARON JOSEF HERNANDEZ, hereby request that you furnish my attorneys, RANKIN & SULTAN, 151 Merrimac Street, Second Floor, Boston, MA 02114, or their representative, any and all medical records which may be requested regarding treatments/tests/diagnoses/discharge summaries/operative notes/consults rendered by or on behalf of the NEW ENGLAND PATRIOTS during my employment between 2010 and 2013, inclusive. I specifically authorize you to release to RANKIN & SULTAN information contained in my record in the categories initialed below:

_____ HIV or sexually transmitted disease   ✔ Drug or alcohol abuse

__✔__ Psychiatric/psychological information   ✔ Social worker information

I understand that some of the above information may be protected by Federal Regulation 42 CFR, Part 2, Confidentiality of Alcohol and Drug Abuse Patient Records. This information is to be released for the purpose of legal representation.

I understand that the protected health information requested herein may be subject to redisclosure by RANKIN & SULTAN.

Page 1 of 2

Aaron Hernandez requested extensive records during the course of his employment with the New England Patriots, including, but not limited to, medical records and psychological rest results.

Hernandez argued they were potentially evidentiary and relevant to the case in that they could bear upon his "circumstances and state-of-mind prior" to the murder of Odin Lloyd "as well as his physical and mental state at the time."

We now know Hernandez was bisexual, had numerous encounters with men, and may have even contracted HIV.

This document proves that Hernandez's own lawyers sought to suppress the disclosure of such medical information.

Commonwealth of Massachusetts

BRISTOL, ss

SUPERIOR COURT

EXHIBIT
89

TO: Keeper of the Records
     Enterprise Rental

(if said person may be found in your precinct) to appear before the **SUPERIOR COURT**, holden at the **FALL RIVER JUSTICE CENTER, 186 South Main Street, FALL RIVER**, within and for the County of **BRISTOL** on Thursday, the 22th day of **January 2015 at 9:00 in the forenoon**, and from day to day, thereafter, until the action hereinafter named is heard by said Court to give evidence of what you know relating to an action then and there to be heard and tried between

COMMONWEALTH v. AARON HERNANDEZ
TRIAL
Indictment No. BRCR2013-00983

AND PLEASE BRING WITH YOU: Any/all records including but not limited to ticket notes, correspondence to & from customer, toll violations & accident reports connected to the following vehicles:

1. 2013 Black Cheverolet Suburban, RI #442427, VIN: 1GNSKJE71DR286383, Rental Contract #59MW2X;
2. 2012 Nissan Altima, MA #536MX2, Rental Contract #59N60R, Enterprise Rental Accident Report #DX4912J66, Toll Violation on 6/17/2013 at 2:53AM on Massachusetts Turnpike;
3. 2013 Chrysler 300C, RI #451375, VIN 2C3CCAKG0DH665474, Enterprise Rental Accident Report #DX4912J66

COMPLIANCE with this subpoena may be made *without appearing by providing the records and a Keeper of the Records affidavit*** with the requirements listed below. Please return the requested materials and Keeper of the Records affidavit on or before January 22nd, 2015 to the attention of the Fall River Superior Court Clerk's Office,186 South Main Street, Fall River, MA 02721, in which case your appearance before the Court will be excused.

**A written affidavit is needed from the Keeper of the Records certifying that:
  (i)   The business record was made in good faith;
  (ii) It was made in the regular court of business;
  (iii) It was made before the beginning of the civil or criminal proceeding in which it is offered; and
  (iv) It was the regular course of such business to make such memorandum or record at the time of such act, transaction, occurrence, or event, or within a reasonable time thereafter.

WHEREOF FAIL NOT, as you will answer your default under the pains and penalties in the law in that behalf made and provided.

Dated at NEW BEDFORD, on this 22nd day of January in the year of our Lord two thousand fifteen.

William M. McCauley
William M. McCauley
Assistant District Attorney
(508) 997-0711

Prosecutors subpoenaed information from Enterprise Rent-A-Car in the Odin Lloyd murder because they believed it was the key to unlock Aaron Hernandez's guilt.

Keelia Smyth, who worked at Enterprise Rent-a-Car at the time, said she found a bullet casing while cleaning the rented Nissan Altima after the former NFL star had returned it.

Not knowing Lloyd had been murdered, she said she put the shell casing she found—along with some chewed blue-colored gum and a bottle of Vitamin Water—inside a trash bin.

Smyth said she didn't realize the importance of the car or its contents until she saw media reports of Lloyd's murder. That's when she called the police, who recovered the gum and shell casing.

The defense questioned the findings, saying that Hernandez's DNA may have transferred to the gum in a state police lab.

The Commonwealth of Massachusetts
Executive Office of Public Safety & Security
Department of Correction
Office of Investigative Services
50 Maple Street, Suite 3
Milford, MA 01757
Tel: (508) 422-3635
Fax: (508) 422-3652
www.mass.gov/doc

CHARLES D. BAKER
Governor

KARYN E. POLITO
Lieutenant Governor

DANIEL BENNETT
Secretary

THOMAS A. TURCO III
Commissioner

JOHN A. O'MALLEY
Chief of Staff

PAUL DIETL
BRUCE I. GELB
MICHAEL G. GRANT
CAROL A. MICI
Deputy Commissioners

PATRICK T. DEPALO, JR.
Chief

TO: Bruce Gelb, Deputy Commissioner, Prison Division

FROM: Patrick T. DePalo, Chief, Office of Investigative Services

DATE: May 1, 2017

RE: **Aaron Hernandez, W106228**

On April 19, 2017, at approximately 3:25 a.m. the Office of Investigative Services (OIS) was notified of inmate Aaron Hernandez (W106228) being found unresponsive and suspended from a ligature in Cell 57 of the G2 Housing Unit at the Souza-Baranowski Correctional Center (SBCC).

A joint investigation conducted by the Massachusetts State Police Detective Unit (MSPDU) assigned to the Worcester County District Attorney's Office and the Office of Investigative Services (OIS) concluded there was no indication of foul play. Autopsy results from the Chief Medical Examiner's Office indicates his toxicology report was negative and the cause of death was suicide. The investigation into the death of Aaron Hernandez will be closed pending the receipt of any new or additional information that would warrant a re-opening.

cc: Thomas A. Turco, Commissioner
         John A. O'Malley, Chief of Staff

When prison authorities discovered Aaron Hernandez's body April 19, one of the first things they noticed was that Hernandez left multiple references to one specific biblical passage before committing suicide.

Heranandez killed himself while serving a life sentence at the Souza-Baranowski prison in Lancaster, Massachusetts.

According to the report, Hernandez was placed in his cell at 7:59 p.m. on April 18 and wasn't seen again until an officer discovered his hanged body at 3:03 a.m. on April 19.

At first the officer wasn't able to enter Hernandez's cell because the former NFL tight end had put pieces of cardboard in the door tracks to prevent anyone from getting in.

When the officer finally entered the room, he found Hernandez, who was naked, hanging from a bed sheet that was attached to the window bars in his call.

The report also noted that Hernandez had covered the floor in shampoo to make it more slippery.

After his body was discovered, Hernandez was rushed to the hospital, but he never regained consciousness, and he was pronounced dead at 4:07 a.m.